THE STREET
IS MY PULPIT

INTERPRETATIONS OF CULTURE IN THE NEW MILLENNIUM

Norman E. Whitten Jr., General Editor

A list of books in the series appears at the end of the book.

THE STREET IS MY PULPIT

HIP HOP AND CHRISTIANITY IN KENYA

MWENDA
NTARANGWI

UNIVERSITY OF ILLINOIS PRESS

URBANA, CHICAGO, AND SPRINGFIELD

Library of Congress Cataloging-in-Publication Data
Names: Ntarangwi, Mwenda, author.
Title: The street is my pulpit : hip hop and Christianity in Kenya /
   Mwenda Ntarangwi.
Other titles: Interpretations of culture in the new millennium.
Description: Urbana : University of Illinois Press, 2016. | Series:
   Interpretations of culture in the new millennium | Includes
   bibliographical references and index.
Identifiers: LCCN 2016003055 (print) | LCCN 2016005502 (ebook)
   | ISBN 9780252040061 (hardcover : alk. paper) | ISBN
   9780252081552 (pbk. : alk. paper) | ISBN 9780252098260 ()
Subjects: LCSH: Juliani, 1984– | Christian rap (Music)—Kenya. |
   Christianity—Kenya. | Music and youth—Kenya. | Youth—
   Kenya—Social conditions—21st century. | Rap musicians—
   Kenya.
Classification: LCC ML3921.8.R36 N83 2016 (print) | LCC
   ML3921.8.R36 (ebook) | DDC 782.421649112—dc23
LC record available at http://lccn.loc.gov/2016003055

Frontispiece: Juliani in action

CONTENTS

ILLUSTRATIONS

FOREWORD

When I was growing up in Dandora, a suburb of Nairobi, Kenya, music was my identity. I never saw beyond getting noticed and performing at school outings and joining drama festivals. After high school, music gave me a place in my surroundings. For a young person to be noticed, he or she had to join a gang. To be a member of a gang, such as Kamjesh or Mungiki, back then was the in thing. Later, the more I worked on turning my talent into a skill, the more I got the attention of many people, including those at Mau Mau Camp, a group of rappers famed for speaking on what was happening politically and socially in society, who later welcomed me into the group. At that point, music became more than an identity: it was a skill I had acquired. From a skill, music became a career, especially after getting paid a couple of times for appearances and getting invites to performances in various platforms.

I knew I was good at what I did; I knew I was one of the best rappers among my peers, but I had this feeling that always disturbed me. I knew there was more to it. So in 2005 I was born again and became a Christian. I knew it was the right decision, but a lot was still not clear. Reading the manuscript for this book gave me a lot of answers, and things started making sense, especially after my interaction with Professor Ntarangwi.

My contribution to the music industry and my belief are aligned to a higher purpose. Hip hop isn't just a genre, and the expression of my faith isn't just my style and personality. *Pulpit Kwa Street*, the title of my second album, is synonymous with the great commission given to Christians in Matthew 28:19–20, "Go out and make disciples." If I am going out to make disciples, then the only thing that doesn't change is the authority I am given; the tools and packaging of the message have to be within the surrounding culture, and we must not distort the message.

My background in music is mostly from the Mau Mau Camp. My background is socially conscious music built by my conviction of faith. Normal conscious music just captures what is happening and is without a solution or way forward. Through the projects I support, I try to provide not just the message but actions to make a difference. Since 2005 when I was born again, my music has been spiritual and conscious, which was later confirmed to me when I read Isaiah 58. I like using imagery I find around me to explain the spiritual truth I present in my songs.

Juliani (Julius Owino), Nairobi, July 2014

PREFACE

This is a book about hip hop music as it is composed and performed by a Kenyan artist named Juliani (Julius Owino). Juliani is a Christian, and it is his identity as a Christian that gives weight to the analysis carried out in this volume. This book is also about ethnography, the kind of ethnography that is only possible when carrying out research on a transient entity, such as popular music. It is about the nature of collaboration that shapes all ethnographies: collaboration between the researcher and those being researched upon. It is also a book about me as the ethnographer, my own subjective identity that is deeply tied to the topic of research and the process of research. Ultimately, this is a project about a slice of life that the hip hop music of a single artist represents and that is used as a window into the workings and reconfigured frames of what it means to be Christian in contemporary Kenya, especially for the country's growing youth population. Methodologically, it is a work full of collaboration and intersections, as I rely upon Juliani's own story about his music, life, and Christian faith.

This book is a result of a long scholarly journey into popular music that began in the late 1980s. At the time, I was one of a few Kenyan high school graduates who secured a spot in the similarly few public universities that stood at the top of our elitist education system. It was also a time when we experienced a rapid spread of (mostly) US and European popular culture through music, film, and magazines that we all wanted access to for a glimpse of life overseas. But, more specifically, our hearts and imagination had been captured by the break-dancing craze that was sweeping across the popular culture universe at the time. We, therefore, sought to define our identities not only within our new intellectual context of the university but also the larger world such media availed to us. Little did I know break dancing would be a key marker of what would become my own study subject almost two decades later.

This book is an attempt to capture a genre of music born out of that break-dancing craze I participated in as a young university student in Kenya. It is also a project that brings to the fore another part of my own identity, my Christian faith, that seeks to cultivate enough critical distance to articulate its workings and expressions as embodied in the public via hip hop music. This volume is, much like many other prior scholarly works I have undertaken, a combination of subjective and objective analyses of cultural practices and expressions that I have observed and experienced. It is a book about youth participation and production of hip hop as a productive medium through which to explore multiple practices and meanings expressed within contemporary Christianity in Kenya. I see a kind of expressive glue bonding these two otherwise seemingly different genres of public life. As a form of religious expression, Christianity has an intrinsic tendency to produce a kind of moral and purposeful individualism that leads the individual to focus first on a personal relationship with God and then an individualized reward or punishment in the afterlife. Similarly, hip hop has a tendency to focus on the individual, the musician, as the storyteller, and the sound and lyrics as an embodiment of a specific kind of individualized expression. And, yet, both are geared toward a corporate audience with a goal of providing some form of influence.

Three interrelated phenomena have precipitated the arguments this book captures and help to frame this individualized expression of both Christianity and hip hop. First, scholars agree that Africa is one of the regions of the contemporary world where Christianity is growing the fastest; second, Africa has had a rapid growth and spread of hip hop music in the last few decades; and, third, youth constitute the largest percentage of Africa's population—85 percent of its population is under thirty-five years old (Ministry 2009; Youth and the African Union Commission 2012). These three factors come together in a powerful way to create an almost perfect platform from which to observe the workings of a musical genre that is creatively articulating the combined realities of everyday lived spirituality. Kenya provides an interesting case study for these three phenomena, given that it has a very large youth population, 83 percent of its total population self-identifies as Christians, and its hip hop scene is active and growing quickly in its major cities (Pew Research Center 2015a).

Juliani (given name, Julius Owino) performs songs that provide a window into how youth and Christianity intersect. This window shows his own stated identity as a Christian and a commitment to expressing that identity through hip hop. Many of his songs focus on the challenges facing Kenyan youth, not to simply mention them but to generate, organize, and establish their significance in shaping an understanding of how they intersect with what it means to be Christian and the efficacy of such an identity in navigating the complex realities of daily lives. Bringing together Christian faith and everyday reality is not always an easy articulation, given a history of Kenyan Christians seeking to separate social reality into the spiritual and secular, especially where popular music is concerned (Nyairo 2004). Indeed, this separation has led some observers within Kenya to question whether Juliani's music can be categorized as gospel. It is this "blurred" representation of Christianity by Juliani's music as well as his publicly stated identity as a born-again Christian and the specific themes found in his music that constitute the analysis carried out in this book. This volume is an exploration into Juliani's music and the meanings generated, through an ethnography that captures the tensions between hip hop as a genre forceful about individual expression and Christianity as a religious expression of raw emotions and lived realities that promotes a pietistic approach to public life.

OVERVIEW OF CHAPTERS

As an exploration into Juliani's music and the meanings generated, this book provides a story of many intersections and overlaps. Chapter 1 introduces Juliani, his work, and his relationship with my ethnography. A short episode in the studio captures the collaborative nature of this project, highlighting how much of the work is actually a process of intersections among history, identities, and music that all culminate in my connections with Juliani that are hard to ignore. I let Juliani do quite a bit of introducing his own work as I ethnographically sift through public statements made via social media, interviews on television, and my own interactions with him, in order to weave them into a coherent story about his identity. This identity is then juxtaposed with some of the recent studies of hip hop, Christianity, and youth that I see as the three interrelated threads running through this book. I also provide some examples of Juliani's relationship with people of different social categories and explain why he continues to have such a wide appeal.

Chapter 2 foregrounds the importance of understanding youth and the efforts they are making in using music to redraw Christianity's social boundaries.

I use my story in Meru, in Kenya's eastern region, where I grew up, to locate not only the motivation for the personal stories that intersect with Juliani's music but also frame the history of Christianity in Kenya. I show the tremendous changes that have occurred in the sociocultural practices within the larger Kenyan church, especially in areas of music and dance, while highlighting parts that have persisted. I discuss Juliani's role in the larger Christian and gospel-music terrain, and his ability to transcend the confines of Sunday and church messages as gospel music is placed alongside the notion of the "street" that requires a more complex, creative, and even "dirty" engagement with social reality.

A closer look at the relationship between hip hop and Christianity is explored in chapter 3, especially as the relationship shapes and is shaped by the lives of youth. The chapter explores different explanations of hip hop as a genre and then gives an overview of the emergence of hip hop in Kenya. This exploration highlights the global processes that brought about social, economic, and political changes that made it possible for youth to enter into public spaces in an unprecedented way. A combined analysis of gospel music and practice of Christianity in Kenya is then cushioned in a discussion of the role of youth and hip hop in reconfiguring gospel music.

Juliani's approach to gospel music through a socioeconomic program mobilized by a philosophy of youth empowerment is the focus of chapter 4. Using his Kama Si Sisi (If not us) program, I discuss how Juliani operationalizes his faith through social programs, placing him within the general African philosophy of Ubuntu, which focuses on community building. I provide ethnographic vignettes of the relationship between beliefs in the power of the Christian faith and those of the occult, especially when it comes to responding to economic and social problems. The chapter ends with a discussion of Juliani's own response to economic challenges and how he promotes an asset-based development of communities instead of the common needs-based approach preferred by many development agencies.

Chapter 5 provides an in-depth look into social media and Christianity, especially the opportunities and even controversies that emerge out of such a relationship. An analysis is undertaken of a specific controversial incident involving a poster posted by Nairobi's Mavuno Church to advertise a teen sex-education program. The poster is a window into the changes taking place in some practices of Christianity in Kenya as well as the push-back applied to these changes. Later in the chapter, I dive into the world of media as a source of ethnographic data, showing how my accounts of Juliani's life and music have very much benefited from already existing data, created by Juliani himself to produce an autoethnography.

The blend of lyrical creativity and socially conscious music is the focus of chapter 6, in which I share analyses of Juliani's song texts that highlight issues of sex and sexuality, socioeconomic challenges, politics, and religiosity. Even though any one of Juliani's songs captures many of these topics, some songs do so more than others, and some themes are almost always present in his music. The book concludes with a reflection of my own journey into the ethnography of youth and hip hop, along with my attempts to apply to my own research and writing suggested changes in ethnographic research within cultural anthropology. I also add reflections on Juliani's role as a Christian artist that are shared by individuals who know him well.

ACKNOWLEDGMENTS

I thank Julius Owino, aka Juliani, for his willingness to share his work and time with me, and my longtime friend Dorothy Akinyi Ooko, who introduced me to Juliani and made it possible for us to get together. Initial drafts of parts of this manuscript were presented at different forums at Calvin College and specifically supported by the Nagel Institute for the Study of World Christianity and the Calvin Institute for Christian Worship. Questions raised at these sessions were helpful in sharpening my thinking and writing this book. I thank both institutes for the platform and opportunity. A scholarly group at Calvin College, comprising Jeff Bouman, Joe Kuilema, Mark Mulder, and Lissa Schwander, read the initial draft of the book proposal and made very useful comments. I am grateful to them for questions and suggestions that helped me think about ways of writing the different chapters. Thank you, too, to Dr. William O. Obaga for sharing many resources on Kenyan Christianity and pointing me to his own work on the topic that proved very helpful. I am also especially thankful to peer reviewers engaged by the University of Illinois Press, whose thoughtful comments have helped shape this manuscript in tremendous ways. Working once again with members of staff at the University of Illinois Press has proven to be such a good experience. I am grateful to Jennifer Comeau, Marika Christofides, Kevin Cunningham, Jennifer Holzner, Danny Nasset, and Norm Whitten Jr. for providing support at various steps of getting my manuscript ready for publication. I am also grateful to Mary Lou Kowaleski for reading the entire manuscript meticulously and providing very insightful edits that without a doubt improved the quality of this book.

The bulk of the writing of this project was made possible by the emotional support I continue to receive from my family. Thank you, Gatwiri, Margaret, and Nkatha, for your love and encouragement. This is a product of the kind of work that can happen only when I am relaxed and free to devote hours upon hours to writing and travel. You all made it possible for me to do that, and I am forever grateful. All shortcomings and gaps to be found in this book are mine.

THE STREET
IS MY PULPIT

1

INTERSECTIONS, OVERLAPS, AND COLLABORATIONS

"Najaribu kusema something about paka lakini iwe na rhyme" (I am trying to say something about cats that rhymes), Juliani said as he turned to Saint P, who was putting the final touches on Juliani's song "Shuka Roho" (Spirit come down). I had accompanied Juliani to Saint P's studio at his invitation to, as he said to me over the phone earlier, *"uone vile tunafanya kazi"* (see how we work). This was May 6, 2014, when I already had done most of this book's final draft, but this was a rare opportunity for me to be in the studio with Juliani as he refined his songs. Patrick Mbaru Kazungu, commonly known as Saint P, is a musician in his own right but spends more time producing music for other artists. Prior to producing music on his own, Saint P worked with Kenya's famed group of DJs and music producers known as Homeboyz. Saint P's studio is in Nairobi South B, a middle-class residential area approximately a mile and a half from the city center, and is located on the third floor of a high-rise building that holds about twelve apartments. Juliani was getting ready to finish his new album *Exponential Potential*, which contained the song "Shuka Roho."

Juliani, Saint P, and I were in a room converted into a recording studio. I was seated in a corner, Juliani was standing close to the recording microphone, located where a closet likely would have been, and Saint P was seated at a desk to my right, mixing the vocals with music on his MacBook Pro laptop. The room was dark except for light from the adjacent room, which had a couch and a coffee table. The sections of the songs being worked on were blaring from the speakers repetitively until both Juliani and Saint P were satisfied that what they had edited was ready for the public. Wanting to record what was, for me, a special moment, I tried to take a picture of Juliani "in action" at the mike. Saint P turned to me and politely said that the click from my camera's flash had been captured in the song recording. I quietly put my camera down. Juliani, penciling something in a notebook he had brought with him, started trying out different words that would rhyme with a line in the song he already developed: "*Kuliko ngurumo za simba wa yuda*" (More than the roar of the lion of Judah). He tried using "*paka wa Mombasa*" (Mombasa cats), but it was not quite what he was looking for.

Besides replaying each verse Juliani sung and then mixing it with the music, Saint P also played some tunes on a keyboard next to his laptop. He added these sounds to the song and played each new section over and over to make sure it was just right. Meanwhile, he made sure that Juliani stayed within the number of lines available to him for the vocals. I realized that Saint P was not just producing the song; he was also collaborating in its overall composition and production. "You have two lines," Saint P told Juliani as he tried different lines for this part of the song. "Two lines?" Juliani asked. "*Wacha niandike*" (Let me write). He extended his right hand toward Saint P, who read his gesture and handed him a pen. Juliani started scribbling in his notebook.

I was not sure if Juliani would be interested in my participating in this final composition process, but seeing Saint P's contributions encouraged me. As Juliani tried out different words for this one line, I chimed in, "*Jaribu paka wa Tudor*" (Try Tudor cats). Juliani stopped, turned, and ran out of the room, slapping the wall on his way out. I was convinced that he was excited about this addition. He came back to the room, walked over to me, gave me a high five, and scribbled the words down in his notebook. I thought that Tudor (pronounced locally as "Choodah"), a residential area in Mombasa, would rhyme with Yuda. Juliani redid the verse with this new line and moved to the next verse, which ended up as:

> *Sin ilinipunguza, nikaamini vishindo za paka wa Tudor*
> *Kuliko ngurumo za simba wa Yuda, ushuhuda ya punda*

> Sin belittled me, till I believed the scare of a Tudor cat
> Instead of the roar of the lion of Judah, the testimony of a donkey.

That small exchange in a recording studio is representative of this book as a whole, providing a small but critical glimpse of the kind of collaboration and overlap that characterize this project. It symbolizes how the ethnographic work carried out in readiness for this final product is indeed a close collaboration between what Juliani has already done in crafting his own story and my ethnographic training and identity in piecing it together. This project amplifies the role one hip hop artist plays in a counterdiscourse to Christianity's conservative posture in Kenya, a posture that youth present as they seek to align the Christian message with their lived experiences. This book also represents a methodological approach that blurs any assumed distance between object and subject, between personal convictions and professional practices. This volume is a reflection of the intersections, overlaps, and collaborations that have taken place in the life and work of Juliani as an artist and my own as the ethnographer. It culminates in what scholars have come to see as ethnography of one person, an autoethnography, but in this case an autoethnography that involves me as the professional ethnographer and Juliani as the storyteller.

OVERLAPPING FLASHBACKS

The Street Is My Pulpit presents ideas and analyses that have been incubating for a while even though the data come from recent ethnographic research. The focus is Julius Owino, a Kenyan hip hop artist whose stage name is Juliani. I share here an ethnography that captures both the collaboration entailed in fieldwork and the role played by past research and experiences in shaping a book. My interest in Juliani dates back a number of years, albeit indirectly. Between 2006 and 2008, I carried out research on hip hop in East Africa, with extended work on Kenya's urban group Ukooflani Mau Mau. As I learned more about the group, its history, and its music, I was intrigued by a number of the artists aligned with the group, including Juliani, who had by then left the group and was making some headway into the popular music scene with the same kind of hard-hitting lyrics—only as a Christian artist. The results of my research on East African hip hop were published in 2009.

Two years later I had a chance to work with other scholars looking at the role of Christianity in the socioeconomic realities of contemporary Africa. That project culminated in an edited volume, published in 2011, that brought together research from Africa with an emphasis on East and West Africa. The book includes a few chapters on Kenya. I was particularly interested in understanding how Africa, where scholars were reporting rapid growth and spread of Christianity (especially Pentecostalism and Charismatic Christianity), was also famed for civil unrest, corruption, and inattention to the rule of law. I wondered what role Christianity was playing in shaping its adherents' daily socioeconomic and political practices in such an environment.

I had not made clear connections between these two projects until I started looking more deeply into Juliani's music. I went back to my notes on the work he'd done with Ukooflani Mau Mau, especially his participation in their song "Fanya Tena" (Do it again). I decided to find as much information about him as possible. I knew that Juliani had left the group and was performing as a solo artist. His single "Jesusnosis" to me represented an unusual projection of Christianity. In that song he combined street language and content with biblical stories. Listening to some of the songs on his album *Mtaa Mentality*, I was struck by the connection between my two previous research projects and Juliani's music. I noticed that Juliani's songs continued to carry the hard-hitting and socially conscious lyrics that had drawn me to the work of Ukooflani Mau Mau, but his solo music was more focused on the socioeconomic role of Christianity in Kenya.

This book also provides another thread of intersections. It allows me to foreground another phenomenon related to my research—Christian identity as an ethnographic phenomenon—what Brian Howell (2007) terms a subject position analogous to other committed subject positions outside androcentric enlightenment modernity. I want to be upfront: I am a Christian. I say so because I am convinced that one's personal religious perspective, like other forms of identity, is relevant to any process of engaging in ethnographic work. I, therefore, approach this work well aware of my own investment in the subject matter, not only because it is important in understanding a society and a people in a specific place and time, but also because my own vested interest in the subject matter influences my analysis of the material. I am careful to cultivate enough critical distance to recognize and articulate the workings and expressions of Christianity in Kenya as embodied in the public arena via hip hop music. It is, much like other scholarly works I have undertaken, a combination of subjective and objective analyses of cultural practices and expressions that I have observed and experienced.

This is a book about youth participation and production of hip hop as a creative medium through which to explore multiple practices and meanings expressed within contemporary Christianity in Kenya. I see a kind of expressive glue bonding these two seemingly different genres of public life. As a religious expression, Christianity has an intrinsic tendency to produce a kind of moral and purposeful individualism that leads the adherent to focus first on a personal relationship with God and an individualized reward or punishment in the afterlife. Similarly, hip hop has a tendency to focus on the individual, the musician or artist, as the storyteller, and then the sound and lyrics as the embodiment of a specific kind of individualized expression.

These two, however, are both geared toward a corporate audience with a goal of providing some form of influence and belonging. It is this connection and relatedness that I seek to highlight and analyze.

INTERSECTING HIP HOP YOUTH CULTURE, AND CHRISTIANITY

How can I best present the connections and intersections I see in hip hop, youth culture, and Christianity? An overview of studies in these three related fields and how my work seeks to connect them would be helpful. A number of studies of African youth, hip hop, and Christianity in the recent past have slowly started to develop certain identifiable frames and ways of thinking. Youth in Africa, for instance, have been represented as a demographic challenge (Sommers 2006), a concept (Durham 2000), or ideology (Dijk et al. 2011). Others have presented youth as projecting a certain level of ambivalence, either as makers or breakers (Honwana and de Boeck 2005), as vanguards or vandals (Abbink and van Kenssel 2005), as hooligans or heroes (Perullo 2005), or as showing promise or peril (Muhula 2007). Many policy interventions have been made on behalf of many African nations' youth. Governments have set aside monies specifically targeting youth-development initiatives. In 2006, for instance, the Kenyan government established the Youth Enterprise Development Fund "with the sole purpose of reducing unemployment among the youth" ("About Youth" 2015). In 2013 another initiative, the Uwezo Fund, was instituted to allow "women, youth, and persons with disability access [to] finances to promote business and enterprises" ("About Uwezo" 2015). These studies and programs signal the importance of youth in contemporary Africa, and the challenge of fully representing their identity persists.

The study of Christianity in Africa, especially in the recent past, has produced its own frames; the most prominent is the pairing of two specific entities, Pentecostalism and Charismatic movements, that often seek to draw on the energy or assumed advantage that youthfulness brings to their identity and sustainability (Dijk 1999). Pentecostalism in Africa has specifically been seen as an important primer to understanding Christianity's history in Africa. On the one hand, it has been regarded as the "third response" to white domination and power dynamics in the Church (Kalu 1998) and, on the other, as representing the "prosperity" side of the Church that is populated by leaders greedy for wealth and fame (Gifford 1992).

Christianity's identity and practices in Africa are much more complex than stated here, but the valuable role played by youth or youthfulness cannot be ignored. When it comes to hip hop in Africa, scholars seem to agree on the dominant role played by youth as well (Mose 2011, 2013; Osumare 2012; Saucier 2011; Weiss 2005) and the opportunity it gives them to enter into public (political) discourse (Gueye 2013; Ntarangwi 2009) and entrepreneurship (Shipley 2013). Even though all these studies written about youth, hip hop, and Christianity in Africa mostly treat them as distinct entities, this project seeks to bring hip hop and Christianity together, focusing on how a specific young Kenyan artist uses hip hop to engage and embody Christianity. To do this, however, comes with its own challenges. Trying to bring together an ethnography of youth, hip hop, and the expression and/or critique of Christianity has produced for me four challenges. First, the elusive nature of the "field" represented by hip hop; second, the challenges of hip hop's "authenticity" as cultural text, mediated through new technologies; third, the almost exclusive association of hip hop with youth; and, fourth, the assumed secular identity of both hip hop and anthropology.

Having finished this manuscript the year I turned fifty, an age far from the official categorization of youth in many contexts, I have often pondered and wondered how much longer I can focus my research on youth when I am growing further and further away from that age category. Despite research that argues for youth as representing a certain form of belonging or ideology (Dijk et al. 2011), can I truly capture the realities and aspirations of youth in my research when I am getting more removed from their lives and experiences both spatially and chronologically? What ethnographic methods are best suited for the study of this transient form of cultural expression? And how best do I represent a genre that has heavily adopted social media as its prominent platform for sharing ideas and products that are easily and quickly availed through the internet? Should musicians, producers, radio DJs, or fans at concerts be my sources of information about the meanings of songs? How would I validate their ideas about certain songs or performances when I just meet them in clubs or concerts with no likelihood of ever meeting them again? How can I carry out "real fieldwork" when I am unable, for instance, to study a music fan's life for a year or follow a musician for six months and get the "real" scoop on his or her life? And how would I bring together hip hop and Christianity through the field of anthropology?

A number of scholarly works have sought to defend the legitimacy of hip hop or rap as a good instrument for expressing Christianity (Allen 2013; Hodge 2010; Watkins 2011), but there are ongoing suspicions and even demonization of the genre often seen as the wrong tool for expressing Christian faith. In October 2006, for instance, well-known US preacher John Piper

invited Curtis "Voice" Allen to rap at his Bethlehem Baptist Church in Min-
neapolis, Minnesota. This event opened up a national debate on the Christian
nature of the music Allen rendered (New Calvinists 2014). In the same year,
Juliani's first song, "Jesusnosis," was produced as part of Ukooflani Mau Mau's
second album, *Dandora Burning*. Juliani's own identity as a Christian was
often questioned because his hair was in dreadlocks (Juliani, pers. comm.).
Today, Juliani doesn't have to do much to present his identity as a Christian,
despite continuing to wear dreadlocks, but the relationship between hip hop
and Christianity continues to be tricky. In many parts of Africa, hip hop and
Christianity are simultaneously regarded as acceptable and unacceptable,
leading anthropologist Jesse Shipley to note, in the case of Ghana, "I think
hiphop and rap and hiplife have had a kind of complicated relationship to
Christianity. You see hiphop groups in churches in some places. But again
the churches have often legislated against hiphop as morally corrupt" (2013a).
A similar tricky relationship has often been present between anthropology
and Christianity. Other than being used as a tool to enhance missiological
work or evangelism, cultural anthropology does not feature as a viable discipline for professional pursuit by many Christians.[1] If anything, studies show
a strong antagonism between Christians and anthropologists (Priest 2001).
This antagonism is mostly located in anthropology's understanding of human origins based on evolution as well as its methodological approach that
promotes relativism (Arnold 2006; Howell and Paris 2010). Many Christian
assumptions and understandings of the nature of humanity, human origins,
and truth oppose these anthropological ones. But this seems to be a recent
development given that Billy Graham, one of the most celebrated Christian
evangelists, was himself a student of anthropology at Wheaton College and
saw no such tension. Writing about Graham's relationship to anthropology,
Howell notes, "Graham, and his college professors before him, understood
anthropology to be fully amenable to Christian uses, so long as secular or
atheistic influences were expunged" (2015:60).

How then do I bring all these entities together?

Armed with the discipline's emphasis on reflexivity, its tendency to always
look at its own history and practices so as to ask deep questions about current best practices in fieldwork and writing ethnographies, as well as its keen
awareness, sometimes, of the ontological baggage that certain anthropological
categories of culture carry in different contexts, I attempt to address these
questions. Following Juliani's music and identity closely gave me an entry
point into addressing these challenges. I had with me the work of an artist
who was young, performed hip hop, and was a self-identified Christian. I

wanted to capture this oneness and complexity but in ways that honored already existing thinking about the different strands of knowledge and practices I was pursuing. A number of anthropologists have articulated their own struggles, their doubts, and all manner of fieldwork faux pas (Bruner 1991; Gottlieb and Graham 1993; Onyango-Ouma 2006). I wanted to avoid some of the struggles and doubts, given the overlap of the study subject and my own subjectivity. I have critiqued in my own writing those struggles by others, which I consider to be shortcomings in ethnographic writing.[2] One of the areas I felt strongly about was the issue of coauthorship. I wanted to draw my research participants into a partnership that would be reflected in the framing and recording of their work in my manuscript. I learned from critiques about ethnographers' tendency to exclude from the final fieldwork products (books, papers, posters, art work, or performances) those individuals who had greatly contributed to the form and content of such products (Buckley 1987; Moreno-Black and Homchampa 2008), and I was determined to avoid that pitfall and embrace more collaborations and partnerships. I was in for a surprise.

In July 2008 I asked a few hip hop artists in Nairobi to meet with me. My intent was to invite them to collaborate on my project sponsored by the Council on Development of Social Science Research in Africa (CODESRIA) under its youth and identity program. My project was on youth and identity in Kenya, especially in the ways that artists articulate their specific subject positions in times of heightened ethnic identity (Ntarangwi 2015). I was excited to finally have work that would include interlocutors and collaborators in the field. I knew the individuals I was targeting for collaboration, so I sent text messages and emails and met face-to-face with each one. The responses varied: one artist did not respond at all, another was not sure he could engage in my kind of academic discourse, and a third expressed his reservations and was particularly curious to know how such a project would affect his rights to the songs used in the book. Would he be able to sing the songs whenever and wherever he wanted, and what money would he accrue from such a venture? He was well aware of the politics and practices of authorship and was asking important questions about intellectual property rights.

Given that some authors do make some money from publications, either directly through royalties from their books or by recognition and promotion in their places of employment, this artist was expecting that the same should happen to the artists whose work is used in such publications. Unable to clearly show the direct benefits (money) that would come, I told him that such a project would expand his horizons into academic circles and that probably more people would know him and his work. I added that maybe eventually more people would buy his music, but I knew he was not convinced. We parted on the agreement that he would consider my request. He never returned any of my texts or emails. I assumed that our connection had ended, until September 2009 when I heard from him again, albeit indirectly, in an email he had written to a friend of mine who teaches at Northwestern University regarding a review of my book *East African Hip Hop*. The artist had read a review of it in a local Kenyan newspaper, the *Sunday Nation*, and was sharing his thoughts. My friend happened to be the author of the review. What was interesting to me was that even though the artist had apparently not read my book, he took issue with it. He argued that I had misspelt the term "hip hop": that instead of using "hiphop," I had separated the term into two and as such had missed its core meaning. He argued that "hip hop" is different from "hiphop" because the latter denotes how one lives his or her life. Since my book had failed to reflect this core identity about hip hop by writing it as two words, he concluded that my book and the review were "officially discredited for propagating false information about our beautiful culture."[3]

I assumed that this critique of my book and ambivalent response to my invitation to coauthorship were the end of our relationship, only to be surprised in 2012 when I stumbled upon a website highlighting the work that hip hop artists around the world were undertaking to challenge corruption in their respective communities. He was one of those artists featured on the website, and the biographical information about him claims that his music is known worldwide, as captured in *East African Hip Hop*. What had happened to change his view of my work? Had he finally read my book and seen that he was represented favorably, which would have been interpreted as endorsement for his artistry and his "worldwide" presence? I may not know what happened, but in 2014 we became Facebook friends at his request.

My hopes for collaboration were rekindled later as I sat down with Juliani in the Methodist Guest House dining hall in May 2014, having dinner and reading the first draft of this manuscript together. I was humbled to hear Juliani remark, "It is like I wrote this," as he carefully read through parts of the book. I have always wanted to make sure that the people whose lives are featured in my ethnographies see themselves fairly represented. Even when such representation may carry certain disagreements based on varied observations and interpretations, overall I intend for the text to be faithful to their lived experiences and utterances. In line with that intention of realistic representation, I have tried to capture Juliani's life and words here in a way that will articulate something he would be able to see as representing a slice of his reality. I also shared a draft of this manuscript with him because I wanted him to know what I had written about him so he could provide an informed foreword to the book. In 2013 I gave him a copy of *East African Hip Hop* and asked that he find time to read and get a sense of the work I do. On January 2, 2014, he sent out two tweets regarding the book: "@mwendantarangwi Mkurugenzi, I regret why I didn't read this kitabu (book) sooner. Learning a lot #EastAfricanHipHop #Youthcultureandglobalisation" and "A generation seeking to make sense of a world they seem to have little control over" @mwendantarangwi #EastAfricanHipHop. In February 2014, Juliani and I spent a long time talking about hip hop's power and some of the stories I had shared in this book (figure 1). Maybe that is the kind of partnership I should have gone after in my earlier work.

But who really is Juliani?

1. Juliani with the author at the second Mtaa Challenge Awards ceremony

JULIANI'S IDENTITY, INTERSECTIONS, AND COLLABORATIONS

Juliani, whose given name is Julius Owino, was born on April 22, 1984, in Dandora, Nairobi, a third-born among five brothers and a sister. Growing up in a Catholic family, he attended the Holy Cross Catholic Church in Dandora parish. For primary education, he attended Wangu Primary School, near the Dandora dumpsite. At Dandora High School, Juliani remembers having enjoyed English literature and physics, but he all along had a special liking for music. In high school his interest in rap and hip hop started. He and his deskmate Rawbarz often exchanged song texts they had composed. They tried to hone their skills amidst carrying out their school work. After finishing high school, he tried his hand at a number of petty businesses, including selling eggs in his neighborhood, but was not very successful.

Juliani provides a narrative of his journey into hip hop through a series of tweets shared on his Twitter account between May 23 and 28, 2013. He remembers that MajiMaji, of the Kenyan hip hop duo GidiGidi MajiMaji, used to open his house to him when he lived in Dandora, and they would listen to music the whole day. At the time, in the late 1990s, they were especially drawn to US hip hop artist Mobb Deep's song "Shook One," which was very popular. Members of Kalamashaka would also join them at MajiMaji's place, and Juliani would be excited to be in their presence. His mother used to sell *mandazi* (doughnut-like buns) and samosa (fried savory pastry filled with meat, potatoes, or cabbage) near MajiMaji's residence, allowing Juliani the opportunity to spend a lot of time with other local musicians, such as Bryo (Brian Kodhek) of the group Warogi Wawili (loosely translated as "two witches"). Warogi Wawili was Bryo and Mc Kah (of Ukooflani Mau Mau), and their song "Mpaka saa ngapi mtafeel low" (How long will you feel low about yourselves?) had just come out. Juliani remembers that these musicians made Dandora a "cool" place to visit and an important cultural location, such that even girls from upper-class backgrounds (Manzi wa ubarbini) used to want to spend time in Dandora. Juliani was at the time fifteen and just an outsider to the hip hop scene. Kalamashaka, GidiGidi, and MajiMaji, however, provided Juliani and other youth in Dandora an alternative image of what cool meant without being a gangsta. On meeting members of Kalamashaka, for instance, Juliani was very excited and intrigued to be in their presence:

> When I met Johnny from K'Shaka, I was truly mesmerized!! Everything about him was cool, we used to *panguza* (wipe) his shoe just to be close to him. Kama of K'Shaka was the revolutionary, the teacher who used to share philosophies and history; we used to sit and listen closely to him. Roba from K'Shaka was

in the university so we hardly saw much of him. He was the intellect, the voice of reason, more organized, more focused. It was actually Bryo who introduced me to Kama at F2 [Florida 2000 Club] when I was trying out as a hip hop artist. After getting to know him, I was accepted, and Kama said, "Kuanzia leo we ni MAU MAU camp" (From today you are part of MAU MAU camp). Right there I received a stamp of approval! (Twitter, May 27, 2013)

As a young man interested in music, Juliani's mind was open to be shaped by his social encounters, and it is important that he found good role models in his neighborhood. His deskmate Rawbarz, who went on to form the group Wenyeji, who was particularly important in Juliani's earlier years of getting into hip hop. He also took Juliani to the *Kambi* (camp), where Ukooflani Mau Mau group used to hang out.

Mau Mau Camp brought together different hip hop groups, Kalamashaka, Warogi Wawili, Wenyeji, and Kitu Sewer, to form a "family" where, as Juliani remembers, there was freestyling, sharing from the same plate, and listening to music all day. This was so alluring that he admits to having skipped school many times to just hang out with Mau Mau Camp. As the main leaders of Mau Mau Camp, Kalamashaka put together many concerts in different venues where about forty people would attend free. But it was at Florida 2000 Club where Juliani and other artists honed their skills through competition. When he started rapping at these competitions, Juliani used Mbwakali (fierce dog) as his stage name. He quickly set himself apart from his peers as an artist who had fresh verses every Sunday, whereas many other rappers repeated their rhymes. This creativity won him a number of admirers, even among fellow hip hop artists.

Juliani is arguably one of the most popular hip hop artists in Kenya today, and his name has been used to promote new farming techniques, cell-phone products, environmental issues, political change, wildlife conservation, and economic programs, among many others. His ability to traverse all these different social terrains is what makes him such an intriguing embodiment of contemporary Christianity in Kenya. Juliani's music follows the tradition of hard-hitting lyrics composed in poetic and textual innovativeness that he was introduced to by Ukooflani Mau Mau. His talent and ability to focus on critical sociocultural issues emerged early in his music career.

In 2004, for instance, when Ukooflani Mau Mau released their first full-length album, *Kilio Cha Haki* (A cry for justice), Juliani's song "Fanya Tena" (Do it again) was selected as the single to showcase the project. Further, when the group's second album, *Dandora Burning*, came out in 2006, Juliani's song

"Jesusnosis" was again selected as a single. Clearly, Juliani was being singled out for his artistic prowess by peers who were part of a group that already had many other talented musicians. That was the last project he officially undertook with Ukooflani Mau Mau because after becoming born-again in 2005, Juliani left and pursued a solo career. But it was not until 2007 that he got paid to perform publicly. He was invited to perform at the World Social Forum in Nairobi, marking the very first time the event was hosted in Africa. He remembers being paid 5,000 Kenya shillings (US$50) and feeling really good about it. It was after going solo that he started using the stage name Juliani, which he notes Johnny Vigeti of the group Kalamashaka gave him (2014a). Despite leaving Ukooflani Mau Mau, however, Juliani maintains that the group was critical in nurturing his talent and preparing a foundation from which he now operates (2011b).[4]

Upon embarking on a solo career, Juliani had other public performances, including at Daystar University, Nairobi Pentecostal Church (many of the branches), Mavuno Church, and the Nairobi Chapel. He has also performed at the Carnivore Restaurant in Nairobi and in road shows across Kenya with the support of various corporate sponsors, including Kenya's largest cell-phone company, Safaricom. Juliani also went on to record his own full albums, including *Mtaa Mentality* (Street mentality) in 2008, *Pulpit Kwa Street* (Pulpit on the street) in 2011, and *Exponential Potential* in 2014. These compilations won him numerous awards: in 2008 a Groove award for hip hop song of the year "Mtaa Mentality" and a Talent Award for male artist of the year; in 2009 two Groove awards, hip hop song of the year for "Biceps" and album of the year for *Mtaa Mentality*; in 2010 male artist of the year at the Insyder CHAT Awards; Groove Award's highly acclaimed songwriter of the year in 2010 and in 2011; in 2011 the Insyder CHAT Award for best live performer and Kisima Awards for best production, hip hop song of the year for "Bahasha ya Ocampo," best gospel artist, and artist of the year.[5] This journey to stardom was made possible not only by Juliani's artistic prowess but also by opportunities other artists provided.

During an August 2006 school mission at Moi Forces Academy, a Nairobi high school, for instance, Juliani met gospel rapper Astar (Richard Njau), who was among artists entertaining the crowd. Astar was so impressed with Juliani's artistic abilities that he introduced him to Kijiji Records. At the time Astar had just completed a recording of his debut single, "Close Your Eyes," with Kijiji Records, which was quite popular on the local music scene. In recognition of Juliani's talent, Astar invited him to feature on the remix of "Close Your Eyes." While at Kijiji Records, Juliani recorded "Pendo Kweli" with Kanjii Mbugua, who founded the production company and was an established gospel musician in his own right. From these opportunities, Juliani's star started rising slowly in the gospel music industry and in the country in general. People started paying attention to him, and he became a cultural icon, often invited to headline social causes and promote commercial products. He had a following, he could draw crowds.

In 2009 Juliani represented Kenya at the UN Climate Change Conference in Copenhagen, and in late 2011, he headed the We Have Faith Road to Durban Climate Change Caravan as the initiative's ambassador; culminating in him traveling across six African countries and through live shows promoting a message of environmental awareness. In 2013 Juliani was made Amiran Poverty Eradication ambassador in Kenya, and he traveled around the country, encouraging youth to take up farming as a lucrative way of life. In 2014 Juliani was selected as a One Ambassador for Agriculture along with Nigeria's popular musician D'Banj. The One Campaign (associated with Irish singer Bono of U2) champions agriculture through its slogan "Do Agric, It Pays," meant to motivate national political leaders to adopt better policies that will boost agricultural production to secure Africa's future. Juliani has also supported other causes, such as the World Vision Peace Tour; Vina Na Maana (a campaign against economic partnership agreements); Stand Up against Poverty (UN Millennium Campaign for millennium development goals [MDGs]); South Sudanese musician, former child soldier, and political activist Emmanuel Jal's Lose 2 Win campaign (Juliani committed to send a share of every CD sale to a school building project in South Sudan); and Hands Off Our Elephants, a campaign against poaching, initiated in 2014.

All the recognition and accolades have neither come easily nor provided Juliani a noncontested identity as a Christian. If anything, many of his songs focus on the challenges facing Kenyan youth in language not always considered as Christian. He delivers a mix of hard-hitting lyrics mediated through a play with words and often accompanied by artistic videos that make it hard for his music to be easily defined as what many Kenyans consider as gospel. Larry Madowo, host of "#theTrend" on Nation Television (NTV), exemplifies the sentiments of many Kenyans who follow Juliani's music, when in a December 2012 interview, he asked if Juliani's music was gospel. Juliani told him, "*Nenda Google*" (Go to Google), and

> I usually want to use this example every time. When Christ *alikuwa anauliza madisciple* (was asking his disciples), "Who do people say I am?" "*Madisciple wakasema*" (disciples said) "some people say you are David, *sijui wengine*

wakasema wewe ni Moses" (others said you are Moses). Then Christ asks, "W*ewe unadhani mi ni nani*" (Who do you think I am)? So at the end of the day, it depends on what you see me as. *Kama unataka kujua* (if you want to know) more about who I am and what I represent go online, search me, buy my music online, listen to my whole album, and definitely you will know who I am. ("Unmasking")[6]

Not satisfied with Juliani's answer, Madowo pushed him on his identity: "A lot of people want me to ask you this, and I am going to ask you a straight question, are you a gospel artist?" Juliani responded, "In 2005 I was born again. One of the best decisions I have ever made in my life. Everything I do *hiyo ndiyo* (that is the) foundation" ("Unmasking"). Juliani expounds on this Christian identity: "I got saved in 2005, but even before that, I was not such a bad kid. I would say I was a mama's boy 'cause every time I came from school, I would go to my mom's restaurant and start helping with chores, such as making mandazi or beans. But what I remember very well is that I was very much aware of the things around me, and they were not very pleasant. But I felt so powerless" ("Juliani Live"). Juliani has been consistent in this line of self-definition in public interviews. These responses align with his public identity, easily accessible through the World Wide Web. In defining himself, he refuses to fit into a small box of either gospel or secular artist that would otherwise enable people to manage who and what he is. Instead, he refers Madowo to social media and to his music as the loci of his identity, which in itself symbolizes something more. In a country where identity is increasingly mobilized through ethnicity, Juliani's refusal to be narrowed down to easy and neat categories of identity signals his ability to challenge received wisdom about not only musical genres but also youth identity. In a related question about identity from another television personality, Jeff Koinange, Juliani says that Kenyan youth mostly recognize two tribes—the rich and the poor (2011b). Here again, he is providing a definition of identity quite removed from ethnicity and instead locates it within socioeconomic realities. This does not mean ethnic identity is no longer important but, rather, that is it is not how he wishes to be defined.

Juliani understands the power of ethnic identity in shaping the lives of Kenyans, including the youth, who, as chapter 3 shows, are deeply embedded in ethnically based social practices. Maybe that is the reason Juliani avoids ethnicity as his locus of identity. Personally, he has tried to transcend the current ethnic polarization between, for instance, the Luo and the Kikuyu ethnic groups. This polarization was made quite prominent in 1986 following the death of Luo criminal lawyer S. M. Otieno, married to Virginia Wambui, who was Kikuyu. A prolonged court battle began to decide where he would be buried (Cohen and Atieno Odhiambo 1992). Kenya's public and political history has also had its share of animosity between the two ethnic groups, including tensions between the first president, Jomo Kenyatta, and his vice president, Oginga Odinga, in the 1960s and their sons, Uhuru Kenyatta, elected president in 2012, and Raila Odinga, prime minister from 2008 to 2012. It is quite telling that Juliani, who is himself ethnically Luo, has a fiancée who is ethnically Kikuyu, and because much of his life story is available through the internet, this personal relationship is no small matter.

What drew Juliani to gospel music was not just his personal decision to commit his life to Christianity and make these important personal choices but also a desire to make a socioeconomic difference in his community. As he says, however, he quickly realized that he did not have the power or resources to do so, which led him to wonder how his spiritual life reflected his lived experiences. He wanted to sing gospel music that was different, the kind that reflected the realities of his own life and of his immediate social environment. Juliani articulates the reason for this approach to gospel music: "Growing up as a ghetto boy, gospel music was just Sunday music, it never made sense the rest of the other 6 days" (Twitter, May 27, 2013). For him, music that dominated the gospel fraternity at the time was about Sunday things that seemed disconnected not only from the general but also individual daily realities. Juliani says that the singer in such music would often say things about God that were removed from his or her life, such as:

Tumshukuru Mungu but amelala njaa
Tumshukuru Mungu but amedhulumiwa
Tumshukuru Mungu but hana kitu

Praise God but he/she slept hungry
Praise God but he/she is oppressed
Praise God but he/she has nothing.

(2014b)

This disconnect between the song texts and the singer's social reality is what convinced Juliani to pursue a different kind of gospel music, a music that reflects his own lived experiences and identity and that makes public the inner socioeconomic struggles with which the musicians and their audiences jostled.

Juliani was particularly interested in the intersection between hip hop and Christianity, but it was not until he started rapping that he managed to find his own voice. He was also drawn to Christianity because he had witnessed his parents' personal transformations when they became Christians. Juliani knew there was something different about them. They treated not only family members with kindness but also neighbors, customers, and coworkers. They also did not complain about their socioeconomic challenges and always seemed hopeful for a better future. As a rapper, Juliani was aware of all those challenges and wondered how the two realities could be reconciled. He had won rapping competitions at Florida 2000, but he still felt unfulfilled, without anything to offer in response. He started asking himself: "How can I be tough when rapping but back at home in the evening I am crying because I am powerless and feel I cannot control anything that is going on around me? It is later that I felt powerful. The more I followed God's story I started opening up; it is like the butterfly coming out of its cocoon. Now I had reason for doing what I was doing" ("Juliani Live").

The niche that Juliani had cut at Ukooflani Mau Mau was no longer about finding socially relevant verses but more of an exploration of what it all meant for a Christian. In his first song, "Jesusnosis," produced while with Ukooflani Mau Mau, he clearly states this Christian identity:

Ongea chafu si unajua nimeokoka
Niliamini alipoingia mlemavu akatoka na wheelchair kwa mabega
Kwanini una time ya pedicure lakini uko busy kushukuru muumba wako
Unapenda stra za kuvuana bra mbona ukishado unafeel guilty.

You speak in a foul language and yet you know I am saved.
I believed when a cripple came out with a wheelchair on his shoulder.
You have time for a pedicure but too busy to praise your creator.
You like to engage in removing the bra but when you do it you feel
    guilty.

Besides providing an example of how Juliani blends Christianity with hip hop, "Jesusnosis" also presents a different type of gospel music. Instead of just praising God as some of the songs do, Juliani here blends his message of his salvation with the reality of premarital sex present among his peers; he presents the two issues not as separate but as coexisting.

During a conversation at Nairobi's Art Café along Ngong Road on January 24, 2013, Juliani explained that the lyrics in "Jesusnosis" reflect what he was feeling as a Christian at the time and that people really connected with the song because it resonated with their own feelings and experiences as well. He, however, noted that not everyone thinks that this style of music is good. He remembered meeting a person who before even saying hello to him pointed a finger at him and said she did not like that he says, "Ninadara pages za Bible" (I am flipping through the pages of the Bible) in the song "Pages za Bible." In Sheng, a local urban slang that mixes English Swahili and other Kenyan languages, the verb "kudara" means "to caress" and the form "ninadara" means "I am caressing," which may explain the negative response it elicited for the woman. She went on to ask Juliani, "How can you use that kind of language about the Bible?" Juliani told me that of all his songs produced in that period, none was as popular as "Pages za Bible," making him think there is something about it that resonates with people's sensibilities. This was confirmed later as I spent time with Juliani.

On May 6, 2014, Juliani and I stopped at a small shopping location in Nairobi's South B Estate for a cup of tea while we waited for Saint P to get home so Juliani could finish polishing a few songs on *Exponential Potential*. As Juliani pulled his car up close to the kiosk at the corner of a row of many, a gentleman walked up to the car and upon recognizing Juliani shook his hand and said that he really loved his music. Curious about this random encounter, I asked the man which of Juliani's songs he liked most, and he said, "Pages za Bible." He introduced himself as Steven and followed us to a kiosk that sold food, where Juliani bought us tea. We sat down for a long conversation about music, life in other countries, and the differences between urban and rural Kenyan life. These two views of the same song give a glimpse of not only the complex identity that Juliani embodies but also the unique relationship of hip hop and Christianity in Kenya.

It might be tempting to assume that because Juliani often challenges certain expressions of Christianity through his music, he would quickly condemn practices that seem out of sync with what is expected of Christians, especially pastors. After prolonged interactions with him, I have come to respect his ability to carefully weigh all issues before presenting his critique. Prior to meeting up with Juliani at Art Café in January 2013, for instance, I had rewatched a YouTube video that reported a 2012 scandal involving a pastor in Nairobi who had allegedly asked a woman to attend his church and tell a lie in front of his congregation—that she was ill, so he could pray for her to be "miraculously" healed. It turned out that the woman was a prostitute who also alleged that the pastor was her client.

Convinced that this was a clear example of what was wrong with aspects of Kenyan Christianity, I asked Juliani what he thought about the scandal and its reflection on the Kenyan Church today. He said that we were witnessing the reality of those who go to church as well as the preachers who serve them. KTN's investigative program *Jicho Pevu* (loosely translated as "keen eye") captured the incident in a video of the alleged ill prostitute in the

Fire Gospel Ministries Church being prayed for by Pastor Michael Njoroge. She was twenty-six-year-old Esther Mwende, who lived in Kayole, a residential location outside Nairobi. On the day she was being prayed over, she claimed that her mouth was twisted because she had spoken ill of a "man of God." When the TV crew asked about her relationship with the pastor, she claimed that she had done a lot of "business" bringing other prostitutes to the church to give false testimonies about healing miracles the pastor performed ("Utapeli").

The television story available on YouTube shows the prostitutes interviewed demonstrating exactly what they did in order to appear ill. How could Juliani not condemn such outright misuse of the social trust the congregation bestowed upon the pastor? The program showed Mwende in church being prayed for and her lying about her ailment. I gave Juliani more evidence of why this was clearly worthy of his condemnation. In a follow-up story, the *Jicho Pevu* crew tried to ask Pastor Njoroge to respond to the report they had compiled of his relations with Mwende and others. The crew confronted him in his church on a Sunday. They tried to record him responding to their questions but were denied access to the pulpit, and the pastor refused to answer any of the questions. Instead, he told the congregation in Kiswahili, "You know me. Do you think what has been said about me is true?" The congregation shouted back in unison, "No!" ("'Pastor' Curses" 2012). I was sure Juliani would see this as enough evidence that even the congregation was wrong for uncritically supporting the pastor. Juliani paused and then said:

> We cannot fault the congregation for supporting the pastor, because many of the members are in that church for a specific need. They go there to get fuel for the week. There is something they get from the church, and that which they get is so important that they are willing to set aside what may seem an obvious reason to question the credibility of the pastor. Granted, some will be upset and leave the church, but the majority will remain because they need fuel from the church each Sunday to face the week, and the pastor gives them that fuel. All the congregants have their own sins as well. They cheat and do all kinds of things, so why would they find fault in the pastor even if he was in sin? (pers. comm., January 24, 2013)

I found Juliani's response quite intriguing, because instead of going for the outright condemnation of the pastor, he seemed more interested in digging deeper into issues that may not immediately stand out when one is analyzing such an incident. This deep thinking and sober response to social realities informs not only his music and artistry but his own life as well. The content and meanings of his songs are not straightforward but complex, deep, and engaging. His life choices and interests also comprise engaging with people from all walks of life and being always willing to give the participants the benefit of doubt.

It is no wonder that when Madowo asked him about a Google zeitgeist report on Kenya's most-searched-for items in 2012, Juliani's answer was not an obvious one. Google reported Kenyans had mostly searched for "how to abort" (Google 2013). Madowo wanted to get Juliani's view on abortion in a country considered heavily Christian and where abortion is illegal. Juliani replied, "The saddest thing is that people may be aborting those individuals who would have saved Kenya. . . . Abortion should be condemned" ("Unmasking"). He also said that those who had had abortion needed to be listened to so as to learn what they were going through, instead of pointing fingers at them. Juliani ended, "We should listen more" ("Unmasking"). He does a lot of listening and observing of his social and political contexts that in turn inform his music. He wants youth to see that being a Christian does not mean that one is saved from the challenges of everyday life. He understands their predicament because he has had similar experiences and also hears and sees what is going on.

When I asked Juliani what the major issues were that youth have against Christianity in Kenya today he said, "The youth are afraid of losing their identity when they become Christians. They think that there are certain perceptions about Christianity that may not be compatible with who they are and how they see themselves" (pers. comm., January 24, 2013). Juliani's responses to Madowo's and my questions reflect a Christian youth's life that seeks to bridge the seemingly divided world of the Gospel and of everyday realities. Juliani provides a positive model that could allay fears about becoming Christians. Hip hop might just be the answer to reconciling youth identity and Christianity.

Another of Juliani's prevalent traits is the energy he brings and exudes on stage. He is known for his high jumps and swinging his hair on stage. For two to three hours nonstop, he and his band perform his popular songs and always welcome the audience to sing along. At Alliance Française Gardens, Utalii Street, Nairobi, I attended a September 5, 2014, Juliani concert. He kept inviting the audience to sing along. Many did, often finishing song lyrics for him: he sang part and then extended the microphone at the crowd to complete a word or phrase. Juliani walked across the stage to bump fists with the audience close to the stage. He paused here and there for a fan to take a picture of him. Despite the mild rain showers, everyone stayed until the end of the concert. Some went backstage to congratulate him on his performance. This free mingling with his fans has often attracted people to him. He has quite a down-to-earth demeanor that I, too, have come to admire. I had brought my camera along and took a few pictures of Juliani onstage, including a very high jump (figure 2). In a gesture of our collaboration, I sent him a copy, which he used as his Twitter cover photo for most of September and October 2014. The same picture was with others on a poster for an April 19, 2015, concert in Nairobi that was sponsored by the National Bank of Kenya, Nation TV, and Amiran, among others.

Today, Juliani leads a life far from what he had growing up in Dandora, where he faced many socioeconomic challenges. He now lives in a home in a middle-class residential area located off Ngong Road on the way to Karen in Nairobi. This is a very different life experience, and Juliani recognizes it. He sings about this transformation in "One Day," which acknowledges his middle-class lifestyle that includes friendships with chief executives, those that he considers Kenya's 10 percent. He, however, still focuses his work on the challenges of the rest of Kenyans, the 90 percent. He says in "One Day":

> *Nawakilisha agony ya 90 percent*
> *Kiatu iliruka sewage inakanyaga mahogany ya 10 percent*
> *Sihustle fare ya mat nina aina zingine za shida*
> *Nachange flat, spare part*

2. Juliani performing his signature high jump on stage at Alliance Française

I represent the agony of the 90 percent.
Shoes that jumped over sewers are stepping on mahogany floors of the
　　10 percent.
I do not hustle for bus fare, but I have other kinds of problems.
I change flat tires and spare parts.

It is clear Juliani understands that his current challenges are not the same as
those that he faced when growing up, but that does not mean he does not
have any problems. He has different kinds of problems but stays focused on
representing people in difficult socioeconomic contexts that he knows very
well from his own childhood.

On February 11, 2015, Juliani shared on his Facebook page an example
of how he not only mingles with these chief executives but also seeks ways
of representing the 90 percent: "Today was a good day! Met the National
Bank CEO for lunch spent more than 2 Hrs discussing banking sector, youth
market & synergies to work together! Just before the meeting, I bumped
into IMG Sonko & Musembi QTV at the Stanley Loby! who committed in
total 90 Bags of Cement for the renovation of the Dandora HipHop City
an Art & Business incubator in Dandora. God is Good!" (Juliani Music
2014–15). Charles Gacheru, public relations director of Inter Management
Group (IMG), a public relations company in Kenya, and Daniel Musembi,
QTV presenter, pledged to donate sixty and thirty bags of cement, respectively, toward the Dandora Hiphop City project Juliani spearheaded. About
his own support for the project, National Bank CEO Munir Sheikh Ahmed
said: "This is an amazing initiative by my good friend Juliani. When I first
heard of it I immediately wanted to be part of this life changing project. I
would like to see this space develop and nurture the youths of Dandora and
its environs through Art and National Bank is going to play its part whenever
called upon. The Kenyan entertainment/creative industry got an enormous
potential that need guidance and if channeled properly our youths who've
got massive talent can earn an honest living through their talents" (Gitau
2015). This is the Juliani to whom I devote much of the analysis in this book:
showing the complexity of his lyrics, his empathy for the challenges Kenyan
youth face, his deep thinking about social and spiritual issues, his ability to
interact successfully with all kinds of people, his use of hip hop and social
media for a counterdiscourse to the dominant Christian narrative in Kenya,
his electrifying live performance, and his big heart to help others as part of
his calling as a Christian. It is Juliani with whom I partner in this project.

2

CULTURAL PREFERENCES, CHRISTIANITY, AND THE STREET

Something about Juliani's music makes him appealing to numerous people across different socioeconomic and political terrains. His ability to easily and consistently interact with both the 90 percent and 10 percent and have them as friends with interests that go beyond the immediate economic or political transactions (such as product endorsement or popularizing a cause) also points to his personal attributes. I have often wondered why it is that unlike other musicians of his generation, Juliani has had success in maintaining a public presence in an industry in which individuals often have a short shelf life. Does he have more friends in the media that make sure he is always featured on their platforms? If so, why don't other musicians have the same kind of friends? And how does he manage to have so many friends among those he refers to as the 10 percent who seem continually interested in his work and causes?

My sense from carrying out extensive research on his work is that Juliani's focus on the welfare of others often endears people to him in ways that are contrary to the common traits of self-focus often observable of hip hop artists, which anthropologist Ian Condry captures: "In hip-hop rappers are always yelling I'm this" (2001:383). The majority of Juliani's songs focus on others and especially on social issues affecting others. A good example of this approach is found in the video version of his song "Utawala" (Leadership), in which the visuals are all dedicated to other performers. While the sound and lyrics are all Juliani's, the images and singers are Kenyans from all walks of life. This is a very rare way of presenting a song, especially through video, because the common practice in Kenyan music is to have the camera focus on the musician for much of the video.

3. Juliani connecting with fans on stage

A focus on others, in my judgment, explains Juliani's ability to build and maintain relations with multiple people and for long periods of time. He also provides an important bridge for the church and the street, using music that focuses on social issues to bring people who care about them in for a closer look at his Christian message embedded in his songs. This chapter explores the basis for what I see as the disconnect between the church and the street and how Juliani's work brings them together. What are some of the ways that Christianity in Kenya found its feet in different cultural communities? How did the culture of the missionaries who pioneered Christianity in Kenya interact with the local cultures of the communities they converted? How have these influences endured or changed over time?

* * *

I am sitting in the living room at my sister's home in Meru, in northeastern Kenya, on an early Sunday morning, January 27, 2013, watching a program called *Gospel Sunday* on Citizen Television. Citizen TV is the most watched television station in Kenya primarily because of its lineup of many local and other African programs, and also because it has the clearest signal in Meru compared to the other stations, such as Nation TV, KTN, and KBC. I stay on the channel and watch part of a church service that seems to have been running for a while. Upon close observation, I recognize the worship leader as Ruth Matete, one of the past winners of Kenya's music talent show *Tusker Project Fame*. She is the worship leader at House of Grace Church in Nairobi. On stage she is flanked by a worship team of young men and women dressed in matching black and purple clothes. Matete leads them in performing a number of songs, including three gospel songs from the United States, one from southern Africa, and one from West Africa.

Below the stage are a few other young people, mostly females, dressed in black slacks, white T-shirts, and a piece of cloth wrapped around their waists. When the two African songs are performed, the camera shifts its focus from the worship team on stage to the team below, which, along with members of the congregation, is dancing enthusiastically to the music. As each song starts, Matete, along with one male worship team member, provides some quick demonstration of the dance steps for the congregation to follow. I learn later that this *Gospel Sunday* runs from 6:00 A.M. through 1:00 P.M. every Sunday and features different church groups and services (predominantly from Nairobi). Fifteen minutes into the show, I am unable to keep my eyes open as I struggle to stay awake, fighting jet lag that had made me stay awake for most of the night.

At a little after 9:00 A.M., my slow relapse into deep sleep is interrupted by what at first sounds like shouting. I focus my attention back onto the television only to realize that the "shouting" is coming from Pastor David Murithi of the House of Grace, who has now started his sermon. The sermon is on a theme that extols the congregants to rightfully claim their blessing from God. Other than the fact that it woke me up, there is nothing particularly unusual about this message. The delivery style, however, is quite intriguing. It is rendered in the African American tradition, complete with rhetorical embellishments, musical vocalization, and body movement, a Kenyan version of the African American style of whooping. Pastor Murithi was one of the junior pastors at the Nairobi Pentecostal Church's Langata branch, where my family and I attended in early 2000s, before he left to start the House of Grace. At the time he had just returned from the United States, where he had undergone pastoral and theological training. Quite clearly, his American training provided him with more than just knowledge of biblical exegesis.

The church service ends, and the next program on *Gospel Sunday* is a music show called *Kubamba*, featuring a mix of Christian high-energy music, some of it from local Kenyan artists as well as some US artists. What connects all the songs is their fast dance beats with the local videos mostly featuring long shots of youth dancing to the music. I recognize many of the US artists' songs because I have heard them on a local radio station in Grand Rapids, Michigan, where I live. I also recognize a few of the Kenyan artists whose songs I have had access to, mostly through YouTube. Between songs, the presenters—Njugush, DJ Soxxy, and DJ Sanch—pause to have a conversation as well as speak directly to the audience on the topic of the day—forgiveness—asking viewers to participate in the conversation via social media. Many viewers tweet or post messages on Facebook that stream across the bottom of the screen during the show. Many of the messages directly focus on the discussion going on regarding forgiveness or respond to messages other viewers posted about faith. Some viewers also send independent messages about their gratitude to God's work in their own lives as others send greetings to friends and loved ones. I notice that throughout much of the program, DJ Sanch does not dance much because he is responsible for the video mixing. On occasion he cheers on the other two as they dance to the songs he is playing between conversations and sharing fan's comments. Njugush and DJ Soxxy show off their dance moves as the camera focuses on their now sweating bodies following a short session of vigorous movement.

Compared to the limited body movement characteristic of Christian (gospel) music videos played on Kenyan television in the 1980s and early 1990s, as well as the very formal demeanor taken by television program presenters of that era, these are different times. A church service that has the entire congregation dancing to Christian songs and a *Gospel Sunday* show dedicated to a mix of high-energy music where the constant theme is dancing symbolizes a different expression of Christianity. Generally, dancing to Christian music or in church was in the 1960s, 1970s, and 1980s almost always associated with breakaway congregations that formed what came to be known as African Independent Churches. For us growing up in the Methodist Church, such expressive worship was associated with those independent churches, which we collectively referred to as "*Gatombeko*," a local term used to describe them by their practice of baptism by full immersion. The word comes from the verb "*Gutombeka*," meaning to immerse in liquid, and in reference to these denominations was used variably but mostly as demeaning of their exuberant worship. When someone wanted to describe how loud some expression or sound was in our social circles in Meru, he or she used to say it was as loud as a "Gatombeko church drum." Mainline denominations, such as the Methodist, which for a long time have comprised the highest percentage of Christian populations in Kenya, have been very conservative when it comes to music and dance. Ethnomusicologist Jean Kidula observes this reality among the Avalogooli of Western Kenya: "A Pentecostal service was typically characterized by more exuberant singing than a Quaker one, [where] . . . songs were not usually accompanied by clapping of hands or any other type of instrument" (2013:51).

Mainline churches throughout Kenya, especially the more conservative ones, monitored the kind of singing and other forms of musical expression that occurred in church to make sure they conformed to what was deemed appropriate for worship and for Christians. Such conservatism was not limited to music, as I was reminded when my sister and her friend walked into the living room in matching dresses bearing a saying in Kiswahili: "*Mimi ndimi mzabibu wa kweli*" (I am the true vine). I was curious about their matching dresses, and Gladys—my sister's friend—explained that they were on their way to a local church "to witness history." The Methodist Church in Meru was installing the first female bishop, and they wanted to be part of the event because "for a long time the Methodist Church had been a male kingdom," she explained (pers. comm., January 27, 2013).

My grandparents were among the first converts to Methodism in the early 1900s soon after the first United Methodist Church missionaries from England came to Meru. As anthropologist Mark Lamont states of Meru's Christian history, some things have changed over time, but the prominence of Methodism remains. He notes the following historical trends of some denominations in Meru today: "Its mainline churches were Methodist and Catholic, established in the wake of colonial conquest, but in recent decades there has been something of a decanting effect, with many Meru, especially youth, attending the Pentecostal-Charismatic churches that have mushroomed in urban parts of the region" (2010:474). Today, Meru continues to be the one region in Kenya primarily identified with the Methodist Church and provides the denomination's national leader—the Presiding Bishop—as well as home of the Kenya Methodist University—the largest Christian university in Kenya, at least in 2015, with over twelve thousand students and six campuses.

I grew up in the Methodist Church. The Methodist Church was very much part of our lives. Our local elementary school was sponsored by the Methodist Church and was named MCK Mutuuma Primary School (MCK stands for Methodist Church in Kenya). The Christian culture that missionaries brought with them had very lasting effects on the practices of individual converts.

My grandfather was one of the notable converts in our community and tended to do things a little differently from his non-Christian peers. He, for instance, did not allow for any celebratory dancing during my uncle's wedding in the 1980s. It is notable that dancing was a practice that was one of the most important parts of wedding celebrations in Meru then and even today. He also tended to charge very little for goods that he sold at his small shop in our town center. My grandfather considered high profits a form of exploitation of customers. Finally, he was known to always insist on children going to school no matter their social background and would do whatever was within his means to facilitate that goal. All these practices stood out to me as forms of expressing his Christian identity, and I admired his ability to go against the social norm of his generation, at least in our immediate community. I, however, found his stance on celebratory dancing at my uncle's wedding a bit of a cultural put-down and wished he had taken a different stance on it. My grandfather also served in many capacities at St. Peter's Methodist Church, the local church that we attended when I was growing up. He served as a Bible reader, preacher, or Sunday schoolteacher at many Sunday morning services that I now remember as characterized by hymn singing to the accompaniment of a single drum before the delivery of a sermon that the area synod had selected. Such were the Sunday church services in which I was raised, but that was a different era with different practices. For years, my parents' generation tried to follow the social practices expected of Christians and favored by those in my grandfather's generation but with their own adjustments. In my parents' generation, I saw more and more women with shorter dresses and straightened hair that was not covered with a headscarf. The prevalent norm, however, was to follow the previous generation's notions of sociocultural etiquette for Christians.

CULTURAL CHANGES OR SILENT REVOLUTIONS?

Things have changed a lot since those childhood days in Meru even though the Methodist Church, along with many other mainline denominations, such as the Presbyterians, Lutherans, Anglicans, and Catholics, have tried to remain places of conservative Christian practices that seek to maintain hierarchies of social authority vested in older (male) members of the church. Inevitable social changes that occur in any society have, however, affected the Church in Kenya, turning it into a site for cultural negotiations between the version of Christian practice bequeathed the first local converts by Western missionaries and the one born out of erstwhile cultural practices that blended with local attempts to respond to contemporary social life. These negotiations involve, on the one hand, a Western Christian heritage that sought to produce a new "Christian culture" by mainly demonizing local cultural practices that often translated to emphasis on choral music instead of locally inspired high-energy music and dancing, and a fervent focus on the afterlife. On the other hand are local religious sensibilities that often find expression through vigorous dancing, a focus on demonic forces through prayer and "deliverance," and an attraction to Christianity as a conduit for solving socioeconomic, political, and emotional problems. Many scholars of African Christianity, such as Gifford (1998), Kalu (2007), Katongole (2010), Maimela (1991), and Meyer (1999), among others, have shown the common threads connecting African Christian adherence and expectations of immediate provisions to meet socioeconomic and political needs. It is in the balancing of these two Christian heritages that I seek to locate contemporary Kenyan church practices as a cultural continuum that also highlights the role played by Juliani in his music that goes beyond the four corners of the Church.

Other cultural changes in Kenyan Christianity have emerged as well. Following the explosive growth of Pentecostalism, especially in the 1980s, for instance, more and more women have started their own churches, including Margaret Wanjiru, Lucy Nduta, and Teresia Wairimu. Many churches now have music that reflects a more vibrant African expression. Many youth have also taken on significant leadership positions in church. As a result, churches that were earlier marked by their conservative cultural identity have gradually started to change their Christian sensibilities to reflect local sociocultural practices and assumptions in order to pay more attention to new ways of expressing Christianity. Moreover, if these churches are to compete with what popular churches in the Charismatic and Pentecostal vein are doing, especially in relation to programs for youth and styles of worship that draw large numbers of youth, they have few choices but to change.

Vibrant worship music, outright expressions of emotion, and use of contemporary musical instruments, such as guitars, drum sets, and keyboards for worship, are no longer just restricted to the popular and Gatombeko churches but have, rather, become a common fixture in mainline churches throughout Kenya, including in small rural congregations. In the 1980s when I attended St. Peter's Methodist Church, for instance, congregational participation in the part of worship dedicated to music involved hymn singing to the beat of one small drum with limited clapping and no dancing at all. There was also clear observance of divided use of space by gender with men and women sitting in separate pews and rows in the church. When I visited the same church in 2006, I found things had changed: there was an electric organ (powered by a generator) loaded with preprogrammed dance beats that the worship leader used as accompaniment to congregational singing of popular Kenyan worship songs. Men and women not only sat close to each other but they danced together in mixed-gender groups during some elements of the service. Members of the congregation also danced, swayed, and clapped their hands to the high-energy music that the youth led. A women's group, a men's group, and a youth group gave song performances. Clearly, there was much more congregational participation in the music and other parts of the worship than I had ever witnessed.

At St. Paul's Church (also a Methodist church) near Meru town, where my wife attended for many of her early years and also where our wedding ceremony took place, something similar happened in the 1980s. There used to be one Sunday service that older members planned and ran. Many youth attended the service either because they had to or because it was the church their parents attended. Clearly, many youth were displeased with the services because as soon as a new Pentecostal church, the Deliverance Church, opened up across the ridge from St. Paul's, a majority of St. Paul's youth joined it. This departure by the youth forced elders at St. Paul's Church to rethink their strategies for keeping them in the church. What was it though that either pushed the youth from St. Paul's or pulled them to Deliverance Church?

Deliverance Church had a number of things that were attractive to the youth at the time. It had vibrant worship music accompanied by drums, guitars, and other musical instruments, compared to a single piano at St. Paul's; Deliverance had opportunities for youth to take up leadership in the church, such as planning and taking part in outreach programs and all-night prayer meetings; it focused on singing praise and worship songs, instead of hymns that dominated services at St. Paul's Church; and finally, it had young professionals in the church who served as leaders and role models for the youth. Quite aware of the appeal that their music had on those located away from the church premises, the Deliverance Church strategically placed its sound system so their high-energy music could be heard from miles away. After much struggle to relinquish control of the church service to the youth, St. Paul's Church leaders agreed to institute a second service that focused more on the youth. However, it was not until the leadership of this second service was taken up by fellow youth that new members started attending. The service, now called Early Service, is managed and populated, for the most part, by youth. This approach to music and youth involvement in worship and leadership in the church is prevalent across the country.

Despite these seemingly "positive" changes that have occurred in the practice of Christianity in Kenya as exemplified by television shows and church services mentioned above, conservative Christian traditions have not completely changed. If anything, these random slices of life shared here constitute ongoing cultural negotiations that occur between youth, Pentecostalism, media, and transnational products, on the one hand, and local manifestations of Christianity, social hierarchies, and cultural meaning making on the other. Intersections of generations and cultures being witnessed here also point to how the history of Christianity in Kenya, Western missionary activity, the influx of Western cultural products into the country via mass media, and the subsequent local responses have all provided a rich platform from which to observe what anthropologist Paul Gifford (1995) calls the "public role" of Christianity in Kenya. These responses point to transnational flows of media products and the influence of US cultural practices on local pastors and television station programming, as well as persistent cultural practices, such as patriarchy, that are very much present in the Church in Kenya. Upon further scrutiny, it almost seems like two worlds are at play here—a world of youth with innovative and media-generated expressions of Christianity and a world of an older generation that retains a number of its traditional cultural practices that slowly endure various processes of social and cultural changes. It does also represent the different worlds of those in rural areas where many people are part of a more homogenous cultural group, as opposed to an urban area where people are part of a more heterogeneous cultural group shaped by different sources of images and experiences.

Caution has to be applied to this analysis, however, so as not to overemphasize these seemingly observable divisions implied in these changes and project them upon all of Kenya's Christian history. It is true that the Church of the early 1900s is not the same Church of the 2000s, but an interesting thread of continuity connects those two points in history and the period between, as well as Christians in urban and rural contexts. Both share a certain degree of affinity when it comes to the actual Christian message shared with the congregants, and many of the changes observed are more structural and physical than they are intellectual or theological. I argue that even as we observe changes in the social organization of the Church, its message has persisted, retaining traces of what it mostly was during earlier missionary times when dualism and a focus on the afterlife were prevalent. In both eras there is some hesitance on the part of the Church to commit to engaging with the tough socioeconomic issues facing their congregants each day.[1] Obviously, there are exceptions but those are few and apart.

In the 1980s and 1990s, for instance, the mainline churches in Kenya seemed to have been offering an alternative message when they provided "extraparliamentary opposition" to the Moi regime (Bratton 1994:66) and called for the repeal of Section 2A of the Kenyan Constitution that would bring about multiparty politics. Individual clergy, such as Henry Okullu, Kipsang Muge, David Gitari, Timothy Njoya, and Ndingi Mwana A'Nzeki, were the most notable champions of political change in Kenya (Gifford 1998; Mue 2011; Parsitau 2012). These churches did so at a time when many Pentecostal churches and the African Inland Church (AIC), to which President Daniel Moi belonged, did not support such opposition to the president and his regime (Gifford 1998).[2]

After the end of Moi's regime in 2002, however, mainline churches ceased to provide any notable opposition to the government and quite often openly supported it even at times when Kenyans were looking for alternative voices. A good example here is the Kenyan Church's response to the heated debate on whether to vote for a new constitution; the Church's main focus stayed on a clause allowing Muslim courts (Kadhi courts) to be retained in the new constitution (Hoekema 2010; Parsitau 2012). In this case the Church appeared to be selective about which issues to pursue, remaining quiet in the midst of postelection violence or taking sides based on ethnic identity, especially in 2007 and 2008 (Kaberia 2013; Mue 2011; Ntarangwi 2011; Parsitau 2012).[3] Unable to remain a champion for justice in these political contexts, mainline churches focused more on internal church matters while many popular churches focused on what scholars have come to term the "wealth and health" gospel that promises instant solutions to socioeconomic and political issues based on prayer and "enough" faith and personal piety.[4] Granted, many churches continue to play a key role in providing socioeconomic relief to many people who have no access to government services, such as education, health, and water, but the prevalence of prosperity gospel and a focus on personal piety dominate. The simple message of economic and physical well-being through faith continues to hold great appeal in a population where a working wage can be as little as 100 Kenyan shillings (about US$1.00) for a day's hard manual labor, whenever available.

As Ugandan theologian and cultural analyst Emmanuel Katongole argues, the dominant trend of prosperity gospel in Africa "locates itself within the dominant imagination of postcolonial politics and economics in Africa, and quite often reproduces its patterns, its modernity and its illusory promises of success and prosperity. The promise of instant prosperity that many preachers promise as part of being born again seems none too far from the shameless corruption that characterizes the politics and economics of Africa. From this point of view prosperity peddlers merely represent the religious version of the 'politics of eating'" (2010:49–50). If prosperity is not just a matter of theology but also part of the political infrastructure, then we can argue for a more intertwined understanding of the socioeconomic challenges facing many Christians in Kenya today. What does the lure of prosperity do for youth who are disproportionately faced with economic hardships and yet have access to multiple images of what such prosperous life could be? How do they take advantage of the availed medium of self-presentation in hip hop to engage with this form of Christian message? For artists like Juliani, these socioeconomic challenges are what constitute a rich bed of raw material for cultural critique expressed in both the lyrics and images of his songs.

The immediacy and rawness of hip hop as a tool for social critique and representation combine to form a potent social commentary on Christians' focus on prosperity at the expense of political engagement. What emerges is a musical genre that allows for a new reading and expression of Christianity that challenges mainstream Christianity's language and approach to lived experiences. Instead of duality, it allows for an intertwined world of the here and hereafter; instead of only encouraging young people who are facing unemployment and political marginalization to focus on "the world to come" (Gitari 1996:31), it invites them to also take responsibility for their lives by believing in their ability to change them; instead of focusing only on "spiritual matters" (Bodewes 2011:171), it invites participants to challenge existing political systems by participating as thoughtful voters in general elections and demand accountability from their politicians. Specifically, through Juliani and his songs, youth are also encouraged to engage in new farming methods, to care for the environment, and to embrace a culture of saving some of their income so as to be economically self-reliant, among other practical examples of how to be a contemporary Christian.

HIP HOP AND EXPRESSIONS OF CHRISTIANITY IN KENYA

Why have youth like Juliani been able to move Christianity in this direction? And why hip hop? I argue that Juliani's music and his publicly expressed Christianity embody three interrelated phenomena that have in turn precipitated the arguments captured in this book: first, scholars now agree that Africa is where Christianity is growing the fastest (Bediako 2000; Carpenter 2006; Jenkins 2006, 2002; Sanneh 2003, 2005); second, Africa has seen rapid growth and spread of hip hop music, especially in the last few decades;[5] and, third, youth in Africa, about 85 percent of people under thirty-five years old, constitutes the largest percentage of the population (Youth and the African

Union Commission 2012). These three frames of reference combine to pro-duce a complex set of social, economic, and political realities in the continent in general, and in Kenya specifically. Christianity is growing in Africa at a time of increased unemployment, insecurity, and limited sources of liveli-hood for many of the continent's youth. Since its entry into Africa, hip hop has been a youth phenomenon and has unsurprisingly played a critical role in helping youth engage and understand their contemporary world, in general (Ntarangwi 2009; Osumare 2012; Saucier 2011; Shipley 2013b; Weiss 2005), and, as I argue here, as framed within a Christian social canvas.

As a country, Kenya provides an interesting case study for all the three is-sues as well. According to the Kenya *Youth Fact Book*, 78 percent of Kenyans are under thirty-five years old, and those fifteen to thirty-five years old are 35 percent of the population (Njonjo 2010:xvi). Kenya is also a country in which people self-identifying as Christians account for 83 percent of the popula-tion (Kenyan Open Data 2010), and Africans between fifteen and thirty-five years of age are 80 percent of the unemployed (United Nations 2013:16). This is the population that is mostly involved in hip hop. Juliani has been in hip hop since he was in his late teens and provides a good representation of a young Christian in hip hop with its identity as a medium of protest for a disenfranchised population. Despite its entry into Kenya's musical scene only about three decades ago, hip hop grew quickly in most cities, emerging as a key medium of self-expression and protest for youth. Between September 2003 and June 2004, for instance, hip hop was played so much on FM radio that some musicians and media observers started complaining about the diminishing presence of other music styles in airplay (Odera 2004; Ondego 2004).

Juliani's identity as a Christian and hip hop artist best come together through his ability to challenge Christianity to go beyond personal salva-tion or piety and engage in the everyday "messy" life adherents experience. Instead of, for instance, focusing on Christianity as seeking to stand outside of the everyday "world of sin," he advocates for an engagement with the entirety of the world within which Christians live every day. He does so through his own identity (keeping long dreadlocks that are often associated with uncouth and rebellious youth), his performance of hip hop music (of-ten associated with secular music), and the lyrics that accompany the music (most of which neither use what would be termed "Christian" words nor focus on piety). Such a combination of music and identity amplifies Juliani's own lived experiences, some of which compel him to ask God serious questions, such as, *"Hey, Mungu wewe bwana kwani mi nitakuwa na shida everyday?"*

(Hey, God, am I going to face trouble every day?) (Twitter, May 29, 2013). His music seeks to transcend the lyrical focus of the gospel songs he listened to growing up (that only seemed fitting for Sunday) so as to make sense on the other six days of the week. He does so complete with the language and issues that make sense to many youth who are caught up in a world interspersed with a growing focus on prosperity gospel that often promises "Jesus is the answer" amidst a lived reality of unemployment, disease, political manipulation, insecurity, and hopelessness (Asamoah-Gyadu 2005; Banda 2005). Further, by performing music that engages with the world of every day of the week, Juliani provides his fellow youth a frame through which to embrace Christianity and reject a dualistic construction of Christian life into sacred and secular, or one that is conceived of as "gospel" and "secular."

As shown previously, Christianity in Kenya has a variegated history, stemming first from a Western missionary practice shrouded in ethnocentric understanding of what it means to be Christian in another culture and the subsequent practices of the early converts (Chepkwony 2005). In the process of demonizing African belief systems and emphasizing a desired break from such beliefs, Western missionary work produced a new kind of theology that emphasized life in the anticipated afterworld (heaven) and little, if any, preparation for life here on Earth (Mbiti 1969, 1980; Taylor 1963). Timothy Njoya, Kenya's well-known social justice advocate and retired Presbyterian Church of East Africa minister, faults Kenyan pastors for the way Christianity is mobilized in the society today, especially the focus on heaven and neglect of the here and now. Njoya argues that Kenyan pastors should critically engage with the socioeconomic and political issues of the day: "I was born in 1941; I started going to heaven in 1941. You cannot arrive there in a helicopter, it takes a long time and you must study this world and understand it. You must study the organization of your politics [and] your environment because the runway of going to heaven is in the things you meet day to day and there are obstacles to going there" (2010). Njoya emphasizes that Christians cannot only focus on heaven but also on the realities of the everyday faced by people here on Earth. He sees those everyday realities as the building blocks that then help Christians prepare for the afterlife. Njoya also faults the theological education that many ministers receive in Kenya: "The problem with Kenyan education especially theological education is that there is nobody who is likely to be accepted to do architecture, law or medicine who goes to our theological colleges, it is like a fall back and they only concentrate on how to go to heaven. They do not study sociology, philosophy, or political science" (2010). In the elitist education system available in Kenya, access to higher education itself and to prestigious disciplines, such as medicine, law, and architecture, is based on scoring high points in a national examination. Those that do not make the cut for these programs have to settle for other less prestigious ones. While obviously not everyone who goes to theological colleges does so as a last resort, the curriculum, as Njoya notes, emphasized in those colleges may encourage this focus on heaven. Many institutions that train pastors in Kenya are Bible schools that often focus on preparing clergy for preaching. This focus on heaven and the challenge that ministers have in connecting life lived in the now and the afterlife has real consequences for the church in Kenya today.

In February 2014, for instance, David Oginde, bishop of the Christ Is the Answer Ministries (CITAM) in Kenya, lamented the lack of well-trained pastors who can deliver the Word of God in a way that shows biblical literacy along with an ability to read the sociocultural realities of the day in order to make their preaching relevant to their congregation ("Clarity"). This shaky link between theology and lived realities means that Christianity in Kenya and its expression through music often remains restricted to the church or to Sundays with little emphasis on its relevance for the world outside those parameters. The result is that Christianity is seen either as irrelevant to people's everyday lives, because they will see what happens in church on Sunday as separate from what happens in the other days of the week (Nelson 2011), or as a mere ritual that adherents go through without much thought and reflection (Banda 2005). Such dualism and superficiality have been identified by scholars analyzing the role of Christianity in Kenya's socioeconomic terrain (see, for instance, Kasali 1998; Mue 2011; Parsitau 2012). One possibility of minimizing this irrelevance and superficiality is to provide a more holistic understanding and expression of Christianity through music. Juliani provides a good example by challenging the very idea of "gospel music" and what it stands for. When asked why he moved from secular to gospel music, Juliani says: "There is no music genre called gospel; it is just a message. I got born again in 2005, and everything made sense after that. I got direction, and I was welcomed in the gospel circles not only because I had made a name for myself as a secular Mau Mau artist but also because my music was detailed, descriptive, humorous, poetic and had depth. I brought to attention some of the things people do from Monday to Saturday. Most of the gospel music at that time was all about Sunday" (2013:58). To emphasize that there is no genre of music called "gospel" is to acknowledge the need to see the gospel as necessarily pervasive in all aspects of life and not just restricted to one corner of life. The compatibility Juliani sees between hip hop and Christianity is expressed through such songs as "Rimz and Timz" from his *Mtaa Mentality*:

> *Hamwamini Christ alikuwa DJ*
> *Aliingia Church imegeuzwa soko akaturn tables*
> *Ameremix maisha yangu mapepo nazipatia notice*

> You don't believe Christ was a DJ.
> He entered a Church that had been turned into a market and turned tables.
> He has remixed my life; I have given evil spirits a notice.

Juliani is here seeking to connect Christ's life with hip hop in a play of words but offers us an opportunity to see how musical expression can reflect actual practices. Juliani sees Christianity as fully connected to all aspects of life, and it is part of the broader world he experiences daily beyond the confines of the Church. When broadly conceived, Christianity would be not limited to any one aspect of life but lived in full "public engagement" (Mathewes 2007) and able to speak to every aspect of human existence (Boyo 2009). This is not the way much of the gospel is presented or perceived in Kenya as exemplified by the questions Juliani is asked in various interviews cited in this book. The assumption is that the world exists in dualities of sacred and secular, or gospel and secular, music. When conceived of as part of a special category of music, gospel music and, by extension, Christian faith can just be limited to Sunday or to a church context. This is the danger Juliani rightly identifies here, seeing such a dichotomy as leading to "Sunday music" that seems irrelevant for the other days of the week.

Some of the songs that Juliani composes and performs as a Christian are, therefore, opportunities for a critical analysis of the social realities of the everyday in ways that transcend the limitations that would otherwise be generated by songs only focused on themes relevant to Sundays. In one of his 2013 songs, "Voter vs. Vultures," composed to sensitize Kenyan youth on making the right choices during elections, Juliani says in part, "*Tusibleed ndio walead*" (We should not bleed so that they can lead), making reference to the violence that has become characteristic of general elections in Kenya with many youth being co-opted into violent behavior by unscrupulous politicians.[6] Although this message may be seen as targeting the actions of politicians, many Christians have themselves been implicated in political violence during or after elections and at times within the Church itself. It is a message to them, too. On September 14, 2008, for instance, Kenya's leading daily newspaper, the *Daily Nation*, reported an incident where three people were seriously hurt during a fight between two factions of a congregation at Murengeti PCEA Church in Limuru, north of Nairobi, when a new pastor was posted to the church after two church elders were excommunicated. In the news report is an image of a female congregant delivering stones in a bucket to aid in the fight.

The messiness of life that hip hop presents highlights the daily challenges Christians face as they seek to live their lives being faithful to their Christian identity and participate in the social communities that pose challenges. One of the challenges of being a Christian in Kenya, where specific denominations have adherents from specific geographic and ethnic backgrounds, is that they are also caught up in the ethnic polarization prevailing in the country. This polarization of the church has also followed ethnic lines, as noted by many commentators, including Oliver Kisaka, deputy general secretary of the National Council of Churches in Kenya (NCCK), who shows the schism and ethnicized politics that have engulfed the church in Kenya: "Kenya is generally a religious community. But how this religion works out in economics, how it works out in politics, how it works out in ethnicity, how it works out in aesthetics, how it works out in defining ethical values, how it works as a true worship, as a religion itself—those are the critical questions that we are now being called upon to engage. We have assumed we are a peaceful country. We have assumed that our religion is deep enough. The truth is that it is not deep enough" (2008). Here Kisaka echoes Juliani's challenge for Christianity to permeate every aspect of life in Kenya and is, by extension, joining many other scholars, observers, and social critics who have historically sought a full public presence of their faith. A good example here is twentieth-century Dutch statesman, theologian, and politician Abraham Kuyper, who desired to have every aspect of life be an expression of his Christian faith: "No single piece of our mental world is to be hermetically sealed off from the rest, and there is not a square inch in the whole domain of our human existence over which Christ, who is Sovereign over all, does not cry: 'Mine!'" (1998:488). The Sovereignty over all of life that Kuyper implies here is an instructive lens through which to look at the lived Christian life in Kenya and to how Juliani's hip hop music provides a platform to exemplify it. Juliani has an ability to operationalize and project in his own life the kind of Christian life that captures the complex but important intersection between piety and socioeconomic challenges that in turn makes him unique and attractive to youth, even those who may not necessarily come from a Christian background.[7]

Interestingly, this approach to Christianity seems to have captured the attention of Pope Francis, whose mission statement for his papacy, *Evangelii Gaudium* (Joy of the Gospel), was the subject of many media houses and newspapers on November 26, 2013. One of the pope's statements that caught my attention and that resonates with Juliani's idea of what his music is all about is: "I prefer a Church, which is bruised, hurting and dirty because it has been out on the streets, rather than a Church which is unhealthy from being confined and clinging to its own security" (2013:pt 49). Can we say that the Kenyan church has become too comfortable in its own security and hence unhealthy? Is Juliani's music an attempt to make the Kenyan church "dirty" by bruising it and taking it out to the streets? Does pointing out the sociocultural, political, and economic challenges of the day allow him as a Christian to expand the realm of Christianity and gospel music to include the "bruised, hurting and dirty"? In response to these questions, I juxtapose Juliani's music with the concept of the street, believing that the complexity and often unstructured identity of life on the street can help push Christianity to a different level of social engagement.

MUSIC, THE STREET, AND YOUTH LIVES

Many youth in Kenya face the same social and cultural problems that face youth in different parts of the world. To be Christian does not give them immunity. Such issues as premarital sex that are often some of those that Christian morality seeks to regulate are quite prevalent in Kenya. The Population Reference Bureau reports that 48 percent of females and 58 percent of males between twenty and twenty-four years had sex by the time they reached age eighteen (2013:12). With 83 percent of Kenyans claiming a Christian identity and the majority of Kenyans being youth, I can infer that many Christian youth are sexually active outside the bounds of marriage. Add to this reality the assertions of social science research that sex education is one of the issues that many Christians shun or oppose (Mbugua 2007). For Juliani, however, these are some of the issues that ought to be acknowledged and addressed in gospel music because they are part of the everyday. The prevalence and challenge of premarital sex are addressed in many of his songs. About his Christian commitment and the kinds of songs he composes, Juliani comments, "Gospel [music] has got to a place now where you can say you are saved and at the same time say, 'Oh that girl is so beautiful, God help me so I do not falter.' At least now we can talk about those things. In the past we did not talk about them but then we would see the repercussions. You would hear a pastor went to pray with a congregant, and it turns into another story" (Njau 2011). Juliani is not afraid to talk about sex and sexuality as he highlights the role gospel music can play in bringing them out in public. By engaging with the everyday issues of life faced by many of the youth while framing them within the larger message of Christianity, Juliani is able to provide a lens through which youth can combine lived experiences with the gospel message and see the two as intertwined rather than separate. Hip hop, like other forms of music, allows artists to engage with sensitive social subjects, and Juliani recognizes it and sees it as an indication of major changes within gospel music in Kenya. Hip hop as used by Juliani, therefore, becomes a bridge between the Church and the messiness of the world the street represents. His is an effort to bring two worlds together.

My argument is that by using hip hop as a medium that weaves these two worlds together, Juliani takes the gospel from the four corners of the church to the open streets, connecting with people's lived and imagined realities. But why is Juliani able to do this? He does this due to his ability to connect current issues and cultural symbols with popular music and deliver it in a poetic and critical way. Consider the case of his 2011 song "Friend Request":

> *Inbox imejaa invites, temptation ikiniita*
> *Comments mob nikisema condom ili-burst*
> *Wananilenga niki-update status niko church*
> *Generation wireless, undressed with no strings attached*
> *Word yako naandika kwa wall ya soul*
> *Ulituita tukafollow*
> *Niko 3G enabled, God the father, God the son, God the Holy Spirit*

> The inbox is full of invites, temptations beckoning.
> There are many comments, when I say the condom has burst.
> They avoid me when I update my status that I am in church.
> Generation wireless undressed with no strings attached.
> I have written your Word on my soul's wall.
> You called us and we followed.
> I am 3G enabled, God the Father, God the Son, God the Holy Spirit.[8]

We can see Juliani's ability to connect song lyrics to the language, symbols, and issues of the day in a way that makes him such a powerful artist. In this song he is specifically addressing the internet generation, highlighting social media and some of the language that accompanies it while making reference to God's identity and his call to him. He talks about Facebook pages in which his status is being updated, talking about a condom bursting in the same breath that he uses to talk about being in church. He talks about a generation connected wirelessly but one whose clothes are removed for sexual purposes with no commitment to lasting relationships. In the process, he plays with the ideas of wireless and connections, using words that carry more than one meaning in a way that has come to be his distinct style of lyrical form. Then he emphasizes his own Christian identity: He has written God's word on his soul's wall, and when God called, he followed. He uses a common term, 3G, for the third generation of mobile telecommunications technology, to talk about the Christian concept of the Trinity. This street or ghetto language is unlikely to find its way into many churches in Kenya. It cannot be considered the kind of language one would associate with a Christian as demonstrated in chastisement he received for his lyrics in the songs "Pages za Bible," discussed above.

Interestingly, when a church tries to engage in such street issues or uses street language, it is publicly censored, pointing to the potency of Juliani's work. This public censoring happened to Nairobi's Mavuno Church in February 2014 after it posted an invitation to a teen discussion series in church on sexuality. The invitation used an image depicting a sensual encounter between a man and woman. Immediately after the message appeared, Kenyans on Twitter took it up for discussion, with some defending the church's decision and others condemning it.[9] The main thrust of the argument is that the church had no business presenting any message in such "secular" ways. In response to the Twitter discussion, Mavuno Church tweeted, "Our intention is never to offend. Our intention though is to always be bold about what society is facing" (February 23, 2014). (The role Mavuno Church is playing and the use of social media for sharing the Christian message in Kenya today are addressed in chapter 4.) It is interesting to see the differences between the response given to a message as delivered by a church and by a hip hop artist. As far as I know, there has not been a similar public censorship of Juliani's music despite that he does highlight similar issues of sexuality in many of his songs.

What Juliani does is engage with these issues in a nonthreatening way through music. As I have argued elsewhere (2003), a kind of acceptance seems to exist of music as a medium for delivering tough social messages in ways not open to institutions, such as the church. Through hip hop, Juliani provides a forum that allows the messiness of life to be articulated alongside the hopes and aspirations of many that are simultaneously Christian and members of a world that is not neat and proper. In this way he takes the gospel to the street and allows the streets to inform his gospel. Such a unique blend of the sacred and profane allows him to enter into relationships that challenge conventional wisdom about gospel music and gospel artists. Part of Juliani's work also involves collaboration with groups or individuals who do not publicly self-identify as Christian (even if they may be Christians). In such collaborations Juliani maintains his critical edge on socioeconomic and political issues in his lyrics. In a collaborative song with the group Sarabi, "Fuata Sheria" (Follow the law), for instance, Juliani's contribution comes toward the end of the song where he raps about youth, social media, and politics, challenging Kenyans to stop complaining about corruption among leaders because Kenyans brought it upon themselves. He says that by accepting items, such as T-shirts, money, and *leso* during political campaigns, Kenyans enter into a loan arrangement with the politician who provides them (2013).[10] He sees it as a five-year loan investment advanced to the voters, who would eventually repay it once the politician enters parliament.

The title of his second album, *Pulpit Kwa Street*, released on Sunday, March 27, 2011, is a direct reflection of this approach to sociopolitical issues. It is the kind of music that takes the gospel from the church premises to the street. The album contains such songs as "Bahasha ya Ocampo" (Ocampo's envelope), in which he uses a reference to Kenya's 2007–8 postelection-violence investigations initiated by Luis Moreno Ocampo, who at the time was a prosecutor for the International Criminal Court (ICC). At the end of the investigations, names of those believed to have been involved in fueling or funding the violence were handed over to Ocampo in a sealed envelope. Kenyans were curious to know whose names were in the envelope. This came to be referred to as Ocampo's envelope. Juliani takes advantage of this investigation and says that he escaped being in Ocampo's envelope, but what he was more scared of was the finger of God pointing at him for not accomplishing what he ought to have accomplished in his life on Earth. He then talks about the misappropriation of public funds by politicians and the need to pay attention to all the ills facing the country.

Juliani's critiques are not just leveled against politicians. In "Ndani ama Nje" (In or out), he questions the sincerity of Christians who read the Bible and speak in tongues but whose words are not reflected in their actions. In "Kilami" (English), he addresses foreign tourists and development workers who take advantage of poor Kenyans, as he challenges the stereotypes they hold about Africa and Africans. He says, for instance, that he sees lions on National Geographic, meaning that Kenya is not teeming with wildlife everywhere as some stereotypes of the country might suggest. Other songs with different themes all point to the sophisticated nature of the themes contained in his music. The various themes about everyday issues facing Christians and others alike make his music attractive to people of all walks of life. In an interview with Jeff Koinange, who was host of *The Bench* on K24 television in Kenya, Juliani talks about the power of hip hop as a tool for Christian witness. When Koinange asks him about the role of hip hop in society, Juliani says: "Hip hop is the best avenue to preach or to push a message. In a pulpit you may have a congregation of three hundred or more than ten thousand, but with hip hop you change a culture, you change generations. So it is not about a certain congregation. It is about changing generations" (2011a). When Juliani says he is influencing a generation, he is including the effects his music has on those specific social and geographic spaces that may be missed by church messages if they are confined to a congregation and only delivered on the pulpit. His audience expands beyond the physical space of the church to reach those whose lives are mostly connected to the internet through Facebook, Twitter, Google Hangout, Instagram, and other social-media sites that youth have access to in Kenya. It also includes those listening to his music on radio, on their personal handheld devices, or at live concerts. Juliani also frequently shares snippets of sermon notes or Bible verses through his Twitter account in ways that extend his "pulpit" beyond the physical church. Quite often, those notes are crafted in the same catchy or witty style found in his lyrics. With an estimated twenty-six million internet users and four-and-a-half million Facebook users (as of 2014) as well as the third most active users of Twitter in Africa, Kenya provides a large audience for Juliani's music and message (Mwende 2015; Strydom 2015; Karanja 2012). Many youth in Kenya now live in this media-saturated context, and their identities are no longer only defined by where they live physically but by what they see and imagine to be their lives. Part of why Juliani's music connects with youth is because of this ability to take the Christian message beyond the "safe" spaces of the church and from its sanctified language to murky social media spaces, the streets, and the realities of everyday that include talking about God, prostitutes, saints, and condoms, as is the case in "Friend Request."

I find the metaphor of "street" appropriate for the analyses I undertake in this book, as it provides a platform through which to engage the multiple meanings and symbolisms that the street embodies. In such an engagement, I seek to bring out some of the ways hip hop and the street come together to produce a kind of Christian message that is much more complex than "safe"

Christianity dominated by a certain kind of "clean" language and confined to the church. I see streets and similar urban spaces as locations of collective memory, drawing a distinction between overt commemoration of public memory and the accumulation of group memories in the setting of the agendas and identities of the street. The street in this sense becomes a kind of "public square" for expressing, testing, and living out a Christian faith; it is a place where all ideas are welcomed and debated; it is a space in which no one controls the flow of ideas or their meanings. It is a place where each participant has to literally and figuratively fight to be heard. For Juliani's music to be directed to a wider audience that is implied in the concept of street, it has to fit all those categories of meaning and sociality that are embodied by these urban spaces.

In many urban areas in Kenya but especially in Nairobi, the street has some element of a "people's place" attached to it. Youth struggles over livelihood as played out in running battles between street hawkers and Nairobi city guards, for instance, or the use of the street for mass demonstrations that challenge election results all act as reminders of the street not only as a space for the contestation of ideas or ideologies but also as a public space that requires specific negotiations for successful utilization. Public preaching occurs on many urban streets as well, and because there is no specific captive audience ready for such a message, street preachers have to try the most creative and endearing ways to capture the attention of passersby or onlookers. Some of these preachers select their preaching times to coincide with the lunch hour in the city (usually between 1:00 and 2:00 P.M.) when they hope to get an audience. This is a time when people lie around public parks or sit on public benches along main streets or bus stops, waiting for time to go by (since they cannot afford to buy lunch) or waiting for offices to reopen so they can continue seeking employment.

The street is also primarily associated with an urban setting because for the most part there are no streets in rural areas. In Kenya the word "street" may be represented by the Kiswahili word *mtaa*, which denotes a residential area in an urban setting but whose notable characteristic points to diminished economic resources. Consequently, when someone, for instance, says, "*Mimi ni kijana wa mtaa*" (I am a street youth), one is denoting a young person from the "hood" or ghetto. It is a kind of sociocultural identity that signals economic survival or street smartness or both. Hardly any people would refer to upmarket residential areas in Nairobi, such as Karen or Muthaiga, for instance, as mtaa because not only do different residential locations take on different names and identities but they also reflect social class. Dandora, located in the eastern part of Nairobi and often recognized as the birthplace of Kenyan hip hop, is a mtaa or hood even though such was not always its identity. It was established in 1977 to cater to a high-income social bracket in Nairobi, but over time, especially with pressure for more residential space from the rapidly expanding urban population, it became much more congested with multiple additions of rooms and houses to the already existing ones that turned it into the high-density residential area it is today.

Nairobi city's largest dumpsite is also located in Dandora, posing many health challenges for its residents. Hip hop artists Ukooflani Mau Mau, Kalamashaka, and GidiGidi (of the GidiGidi MajiMaji duo) all hail from Dandora. In this sense, Dandora is Juliani's mtaa or street, on which he focuses his music. And even though he no longer lives in Dandora, Juliani often credits Dandora for his inspiration to compose the kind of songs he does today. He has memories of the real dangers of living there and shares one such story: "After completing high school we had to move from Dandora, my brother escaped with a bullet wound to his leg, some of his friends never made it" (Twitter 2013, May 25 and 27).

It is these social experiences, along with the content and delivery of his music, that allow Juliani to contribute to some kind of transformation of the street, investing time and energy toward youth living in areas similar to where he grew up. Furthermore, by pointing to the street as his location of his message, he is also providing a metaphor for the public spaces that are often areas of social and cultural contestation, of public discourse, of jostling for survival, and of constructing negotiated ways of existing together. As a scholar leaning toward symbolic and interpretive anthropology, the street provides for me a heuristic tool to use in analyzing Juliani's music because of its ability to go beyond the expected boundaries of what constitutes gospel music, as well as its appeal to a larger audience located outside the confines of a church and brought together by the symbolic power of music. Chapter 3 explores ways in which the intersection between hip hop and Christianity bring about a recasting of what is assumed to be the norm within Christianity. I provide examples of how contemporary hip hop and Christianity in Kenya interact through a focus on youth, both in their historical roots and in current practices.

3

HIP HOP'S RECASTING OF CHRISTIANITY AND GOSPEL MUSIC IN KENYA

PRACTICES AND BOUNDARIES

As a music genre that allows artists like Juliani to bring Christianity to the street, hip hop has a history that traverses different definitions and narratives of origin. Many scholars, however, converge at the point of seeing it as a genre that allows youth to make certain inroads into public discourse. Caroline Mose, for example, sees hip hop as a medium through which ghetto narratives of protest, pleasure, and the imaginations shaped by urban realities converge (2011, 2013); Raymond Codrington sees it as an "enduring and flexible mode of creative expression" because of its "ability to adapt and use available resources, tastes, and vision" (2007:138–40); Msia K. Clark places emphasis on hip hop artists' role as lyricists who variably embody their lived experiences (of hard life) through their music (2012). These studies connect well with my emphasis here on the way Juliani's hip hop extends Christianity into the street primarily because of its content and mode of delivery. Over the last two decades, hip hop has established itself as the music genre of choice for youth in many African nations. A major reason for this youth dominance of hip hop is its ability to act as a canvas onto which youth can paint or (re) present their aspired and lived experiences or both. It is a mouthpiece for a demographic often not listened to in its own communities. Juliani himself understands this role of hip hop, defining his own music in the following way: "My style of music is more contemporary, I talk about things I see, things that I see other people go through, but it's more hip hop with a taste of gospel. Gospel to me is not a genre; it is a message, is a message of hope, a message of

Good News. The hip hop or reggae that you use, it is just a medium, a vehicle that you use. For me gospel is the good news, something that touches the heart and gives people a better option" (Makers 2014). By seeing his music not only as hip hop but also as a medium or vehicle that carries his message or content, Juliani highlights hip hop's identity as a narrative of protest, its flexibility and imagination, as well as its ability to combine sound, content, and delivery, as the scholars above articulate. But for purposes of this project, I point out how specifically I am defining this genre, being aware that there are different approaches to it. When I talk about hip hop in this book, I refer to a type of music associated with youth that uses rhyme and rhythm to talk or sing over a syncopated instrumentation or melody. It is a music that is often put together using different musical instruments or tunes and relies heavily on visual and audio media for delivery. This, I believe, captures what Juliani's music is about, especially because of its style of delivery and ability to capture the social realities of the artist and his or her audience members in lyrics expressed in visual and audio creativity.

Despite its growing appeal, however, hip hop in Kenya has remained an urban phenomenon only taking root in cities, such as Mombasa, Nairobi, and Nakuru, where it not only has become a forum through which to appropriate certain notions of modernity but also an avenue through which to reflect upon and represent slices of youth experiences and aspirations of urban life. Further, even though hip hop is generally associated with rapping or mc-ing, dj-ing, break dancing (b-boy, b-gal), and graffiti art, it is the rapping or mc-ing aspect of it that is much more developed and popular in Kenya. Something about the urban space provides certain conditions that have led to the expansion and thriving that hip hop has continued to enjoy in Kenya. The urban space has a level of social anonymity that allows its occupants an opportunity to create a new kind of morality that is slightly different from that which exists in culturally homogenous groups often found in rural areas. The urban space also avails to youth a larger platform for public presentation because most national media houses are based there. Finally, urban spaces avail to youth amplified images of what a better life could be like due to the preponderant display of economic success.

As it is currently performed and developed, hip hop in Kenya owes its growth and expansion to some of these urban characteristics that have in part been fueled by a neoliberal market-based globalization. Primarily a project of the United States and its Western allies through the International Monetary Fund and World Bank, neoliberal economic reforms require a country's economic and political processes or changes or both to be directly linked to international structures that move social services from citizen entitlements to market commodities to be purchased. In Kenya these changes occurred in the 1980s and 1990s under the infamous structural adjustment programs (SAPs) that led to privatization of state services and instituted consumer payments for access to health care, education, water, and use of major roads (through tolls that were later converted into fuel tax), among other services in what was to be referred to as "cost sharing." These changes also required the government to eliminate economic protections for local producers and instead open up local markets to goods from any source in the world and allow for expanded political participation through multiparty elections (see, for instance, Edelman and Haugerud 2005; Haugerud 1997; Honwana 2012; Ntarangwi 2009). This expanded political platform in Kenya primarily resulted from the repeal of Section 2A of the Kenyan Constitution, allowing multiple political parties to be registered. All these changes have manifested themselves in the shape and content of hip hop as well as its avenues of production.

The removal of state monopoly over television and radio availed an important platform for creation of hip hop in Kenya, especially with the entry of multiple FM radio stations, television stations, daily newspapers, and magazines. The first privately owned television station in Kenya—Kenya Television Network (KTN)—which politician and businessman Jared Kangwana started in March 1990, can directly be linked to the growth of hip hop in Kenya (Kenya 2015).

Radio and TV personality Jimmy Gathu took advantage of this expanded availability of broadcast media and started promoting hip hop music through radio and television. His television show on KTN aired every weekday, and he used to popularize rap and hip hop music in Kenya with programs such as *Kass Kass, Rastrut, Jam-a-Delic, Rhythmix,* and *Rap 'Em.*

Kama (Kamau Ngigi), original member of Kalamashaka (later part of Ukooflani Mau Mau), says he started performing hip hop as a solo artist in 1993 and had been watching Gathu's show. In that year Kama entered in some music competitions in Nairobi's Florida 2000 club (the same competitions of which Juliani became part) and later teamed up with Roba and Johnny in 1995 to form a group called 3D Crew. In 1996 the three joined the Star Search competition in Nairobi, changed their name to Kalamashaka, and started rapping in Sheng (an urban slang spoken mostly by youth that tends to combine words from English and Swahili). Kama was inspired by hip hop as a culture through (US) magazines and mixtapes that he got from a friend. He also cites Gathu's show *Rap 'Em* as an inspiration, especially two artists who inspired him most—Snoop Dogg and the Notorious B.I.G. (also Biggie or Biggie Smalls) (Kamau Ngigi, pers. comm., July 5, 2013). A musician in his own right, Gathu was part of a group that performed a public service announcement song "Stay Alive," which implored public service vehicle drivers, especially of *matatus* (commuter omnibuses common in Kenya), to drive cautiously (Gathu 1991). The song, produced in 1991, combines some rap and popular music similar to the early US hip hop songs of the 1980s, especially "The Message" by Grand Master Flash and the Furious Five, released in 1982. The video depicts a scene in a matatu nicknamed "Fair Ride" that was operated on the number 32 route between Dandora and the city center.

There is an enduring connection among matatus, Dandora, Kenyan hip hop, and US rap music. Dandora continues to be a place of inspiration for hip hop music, and matatus are important purveyors of hip hop music through art on their interiors and exteriors as well as the choice of musical entertainment for passengers on board (be it audio or video). In gearing up for his April 19, 2015, public performance of *Exponential Potential* in Nairobi, Juliani advertised the concert by posting some of his song lyrics on matatus and asked fans to tweet images of those postings along with the hashtag #JulianiNa3Concert for a chance to win tickets to the show. This relationship of matatus, hip hop, and external music taste continues to play an important role in the Kenyan music scene. And there are historical trends to it.

As artists encounter and interact with sounds and traditions from different locations, they soon find something local and unique that comes to define their kind of hip hop. Ethnomusicologist Jean Kidula attests to this about Kenyan rap: "Rap acquired distinctive Kenyan features from at least four dimensions: the artists who composed and produced it originated in Kenya, whether or not they lived in the country; the lyrics, language, and issues voiced concerns that were politically or culturally rooted in happenings in Kenya; the musical forms, types, and styles appropriated had cultural roots or underpinnings in Kenya; and the music sampled was from Kenyan culture or had been composed by a Kenyan popular icon" (2012:174). This blended nature of hip hop allows for differentiation with other forms of music, but it is in the contexts within which it is produced and performed that we can find specific references to social issues of the day. When focusing on Christian themes or when performed by Christian artists like Juliani or both, hip hop provides a good platform to contrast it with other forms of popular music. Following Kidula's argument, I add that what hip hop has done to what was initially conceived of as US rap by giving it distinctive Kenyan features has

helped in the process of making Christianity Kenyan as well. As shown below, Christianity in Kenya has struggled with its own identity, not fully able
to embrace "distinctive Kenyan features," especially as expressed through
gospel music.

Everyday experiences and practices shape a lot of people's responses to
and understanding of their lives, and song texts and the meanings they create and avail to audience members are both a result and a trigger of those
experiences. As a religious tradition, Christianity is received and interpreted
through the cultural eyes of the practitioners. However, there has been a running disconnect between Christianity and its attendant message received in
many parts of Kenya. One of the results of this disconnect is a whole genre
of gospel music that has been recorded and performed in which the focus
has mostly been on one aspect of the life of Christians.

GOSPEL MUSIC IN KENYA

Much of that gospel music produced in the 1970s and 1980s had a discernible
focus on salvation and limited focus on living life here on Earth after being
"born again." I was in the university in the mid-1980s, and, for instance, the
kind of music one listened to was an important test for who was a "true"
Christian even if such music had no clearly offensive or negative message.
Other cultural practices that were deemed African or traditional, such as
dancing (as in the case of my grandfather), were also discouraged because
they represented what was considered the "work of the devil." This explains
why much of the music in church that we participated in was mostly choral
and had little percussion accompaniment except for some moderate clapping.[1]
The social expectation that Christians did not dance in church or to church
music changed in the 1990s as many more youth had access to music-making
recording facilities, as well as distribution channels for various types of music,
whether through cassettes or CDs. It was also a time when gospel music in
Kenya was rapidly expanding to a point that led local music commentator
John Kariuki to see it as a genre that was "in vogue" (1990). As more young
people participated in the performance and production of gospel music, the
modes of consumption also changed. There was more dancing to music in
church and more percussive accompaniment of gospel songs during services.
But for the most part the content and message of the songs remained the
same, often encouraging listeners to get "saved" and providing Bible verses
or stories as the gist of their context.

Examples of such music from the 1980s into the 1990s abound. One such example is a popular song, "Adamu na Eva" (Adam and Eve) by Mary Atieno, with whom I shared the same undergraduate university in the mid-1980s. The song synthesizes the biblical story found in the book of Genesis in which Adam and Eve commit a secret sin by eating the forbidden fruit after being tricked by the serpent. In popular Christian discourse and creation myth, this very act points to the "original sin" that consequently meant all of humanity became sinners, and the way out was to seek God's intervention through Jesus Christ. The singer goes on to point out to the listeners the fragility of depending on such things as church and religion, education and wealth, drunkenness and beauty, which cannot save believers, but that only Jesus has the power to save. In a delivery style that focused more on the life after death than in the immediate world of the living, Atieno asks her kin where they will be on the last day, inviting them to "come to Jesus so they can see God on the final day."

What Atieno is presenting is an important message for Christians, but like many other songs within the genre, that seems to be the end of the message. There is no reference to what these Christians targeted will do during the period between choosing to "come to Jesus" and when they "see God in the afterlife." Other popular songs by Atieno, such as "Sodoma na Gomora" (Sodom and Gomorrah), "Hakuna Mungu Mwingine" (There is no other God), "Twafurahia Arusi" (We celebrate the wedding), and "Sauli Mbona Wanitesa" (Saul, why do you persecute me), among others, follow the same style of content as "Adamu na Eva." Esther Wahome, a popular gospel musician of the 2000s, follows the same trajectory in her hit song "Kuna Dawa" (There is a cure), in which she says there is a cure that heals both body and soul and that it is to accept Jesus Christ. It is only by watching the song's video that one might see what the ailment might be that Jesus cures. Esther is shown in the company of traditional Maasai people in their homestead, among patients lying in hospital beds (along with Esther wearing a health care provider's dress and stethoscope), among street children going through garbage searching for valuables, and on a city street addressing a large crowd (Princecam Media 2012). From the images in the video, the suggestion is that Jesus is the cure for physical illness, poverty, and traditional ways of life.

Some popular gospel musicians of the 1980s, such as Faustin Munishi, were considered to have been able to combine their music with "social, cultural, political, historical, and contemporary contexts" (Kidula 2000:417). Many of their song texts, however, ended up focusing on separating the everyday life from the life of being "saved." Munishi's song "Injili na Siasa" (The gospel and politics), for instance, tells Christians to stay away from politics because the gospel and politics are like water and oil, they do not mix. A similar song, "Maisha ya Mwanadamu" (Human life), was performed by a husband-and-wife team, the Kassangas. In the song, the Kassangas state that the life of a human being is similar to that of a flower; it glitters when it blossoms but quickly wilts and dies away. They explain this idea by saying that one might see a woman who adorns herself well in white outfits, but when she dies, her life just ends there. In another song, "Mjaribu Yesu/Yesu Ni Dawa ya Pekee" (Try Jesus/Jesus is the only medicine/answer), they introduce a story of someone who has gone through a lot of hard times in a way that comes close to articulating the everyday challenges that Christians encounter. The Kassangas, however, use the song to say that any person overwhelmed by life due to debt and multiple problems and who even considers suicide should try Jesus because "Jesus is the only medicine (answer)."[2] Kidula explains the underlying reasons for this kind of song content, that when Japheth Kassanga crafts his lyrics, he avoids social commentary "because he comes from a school of thought that seeks to use direct biblical quotations and stories as examples of his message" (2000:424). For many Christian musicians of this period and even later, gospel music was focused on using direct biblical quotations and stories. Atieno explains her own song lyrics as focused on telling her audience members "the importance of accepting Christ as their personal savior if they hope to prosper" (Nyanga 2010). These are the songs Juliani grew up listening to and that convinced him that they were only about Sunday and not the other six days of the week.

I argue that gospel music that is predominantly "Sunday music" and unable to be distinctly relevant to or articulate the everyday experiences of Kenyan Christians like Juliani exemplifies the disconnect between the message of getting "saved" or "accepting Jesus Christ" and the everyday lives of those converts that many scholars have pointed out (Gifford 1998, 2004, 2009; Kasali 1998; Mue 2011; Parsitau 2012, among others). Such a "disconnect" between the "message" and the "action" of Christianity can, by extension, perpetuate a sense of the Church's irrelevance to African Christians as South African scholar and theologian Simon Maimela notes: "African Christians believe that the church is not interested in their daily misfortunes, illness, practical problems of evil and witchcraft, bad luck, poverty, barrenness, and in short, all their concrete social problems" (1991:9).These daily issues are important spiritual and theological matters for Kenyan Christians and quite often entice people to Christianity in which they seek answers. I argue in this book that the practice of a disconnect between the message of Christianity and the lived experiences and expressions of Christians in Kenya makes Juliani's hip hop all the more important in "Kenyanizing" Christianity. By addressing through his music the socioeconomic, political, and spiritual challenges facing (primarily) youth, Juliani is bridging this disconnect between the message and practice of Christianity. He is tying the "daily misfortunes" and "practical problems" facing Kenyans to the message of Christianity. This disconnect is not a recent phenomenon but, rather, an expression of a tradition that has its roots in local encounters with Christianity as articulated by Western missionaries.

CHRISTIANITY IN KENYA

Many Christian missionaries to Kenya tended to dichotomize spiritual matters and their daily lived experiences while demonizing local religious sensibilities (Mbiti 1969; P'Bitek 2013[1966]; Taylor 1963). Moreover, the push to get converts by emphasizing the promise of a better life after death or the agony that would befall those who did not believe produced many adherents who primarily chose Christianity because of fear of "hell" (Nduto 2014; Nthamburi 1991). This phenomenon is not unique to Kenya but, rather, spread out in many parts of the world, including the United States, where Christianity took root earlier than it did in Kenya. During the height of racial tensions and crimes against African Americans by the Ku Klux Klan in the US south, for instance, the church faced similar challenges of disconnect pointed out above regarding Kenya. In a book that captures his life growing up in Laurel, Mississippi, in the 1960s, Charles Marsh, a professor of religious studies at University of Virginia and son of Reverend Robert Marsh, pastor of the First Baptist Church in Laurel, shares an example of this disconnect. He says that his father's sermons never featured the realities of terror and rituals of white supremacy that pervaded their main street because his father was more concerned about the "pilgrim's journey to paradise" than how they lived their everyday lives (2001:44).

In their well-received book *When Helping Hurts*, Steve Corbett and Brian Fikkert see this reality Charles Marsh reported as a case of limiting Christianity to piety and not extending it to the whole of life: "Reverend Marsh had reduced Christianity to a personal piety that was devoid of a social concern emanating from a kingdom perspective. He believed Christianity consisted in keeping one's soul pure by avoiding alcohol, drugs, and sexual impurity, and by helping others to keep their souls pure too. There was little 'now' of the kingdom for Reverend Marsh, apart from saving souls" (2009:37). How to bridge this divide continues to be a challenge for Christians in the United States today (Hunter 2010) as well as those in Kenya (Mue 2011).

Kenya is considered a predominantly Christian society. Of the 83 percent of its population claiming Christian affiliation, 45 percent are Protestant and 33 percent Catholic (Kenya National Bureau of Statistics 2015). The fastest-growing form of Christian expression, be it within mainline denominations or independent denominations, is the Charismatic one mostly identified with Pentecostalism that places a lot of emphasis on miracles, high-energy church services, aggressive witnessing through crusades, and one-on-one evangelizing. Christianity was first introduced in Kenya by Western missionaries in the 1860s and has grown ever since, even though it was slow in the initial years due to the assumed connections it had with the colonial administration that had provided protection for missionaries seeking to move into the interior of the country.

As a way of avoiding competition for converts during the colonial period, missionaries representing specific denominations were allowed to go into specific geographic locations that were predominantly inhabited by single ethnic groups. This arrangement in turn led to the ethnic identity that many denominations have embodied in Kenya to date. It is no coincidence that the Methodist Church is strongest among the Meru, the Anglican Church among the Kikuyu and Embu, the African Inland Church among the Kamba and Nandi, and so on. Such correlation between ethnic identity and denominations has often negatively shaped politics when churches are seen to support or castigate political leadership in the country. Because politics in Kenya have also taken on a predominantly ethnic identity, individual politicians who attend church services in their natal homes tend to be in the company of people who are predominantly from a single ethnic group. This precarious arrangement between Christianity and ethnic identity, on the one hand, and ethnic identity and politics, on the other, played itself out in the period immediately following the 2007 general elections. The Kenyan Church found itself unable to respond to an ethnically divided country because, as Njonjo Mue notes, the church had followed the same "volatile and polarized politics of ethnicity" (2011:178). Despite these challenges and complexities, however, Christianity continues to grow in Kenya. In 1900 Christians constituted 0.2 percent of the population, and a hundred years later they were 83 percent. This growth occurred despite earlier predictions that with the fall of colonialism, Christianity would fall as well. Christianity continued to grow after independence, and so did its effects on local practices.

The coming of missionaries and the kind of gospel they bequeathed the local communities had some lasting effects on how Christianity was to be embodied and practiced within the diverse Kenyan society. This I state while also being quite aware of the different accents of Christianity that are prevalent in Kenyan today. Overall, however, I argue that from the very beginning, Christianity produced three major effects on the life of its adherents. First, due to prevailing notions of culture and the composition of the gospel as it emerged in the Western lands from which the missionaries came, there was a strong push for local converts to abandon their cultural practices and embody a new "Christian" way of life. When missionaries came to Kenya from Europe or North America, the prevailing cultural understanding of otherness was based on the assumption that social progress and its principles were similar to those observed in nature. As a result, Western cultures were seen as representing the highest point of human progress (social evolution) and African at the bottom. These assumptions about society heavily influenced missionaries' perceptions of local cultures as well as the process of introducing Christianity in the country. The local converts themselves often accepted this approach to Christianity. Let me share an example.

When I was growing up in Meru, I was well aware that being a Christian meant that I could not practice much of what was considered local cultural traditions, such as dancing, or traditional rites of passage, such as circumcision. Moreover, any expressions of joy and excitement on the part of a Christian were regarded with suspicion and often frowned upon. Many of us local Christians projected (at least in public) a very subdued and often sad demeanor; not given to laughter or associating with non-Christians. Moreover, because some of the cultural practices that we were not supposed to participate in as Christians were connected to much of life in the community, such as sex education, histories of the community, and ceremonies to mark age sets, it was hard to find connections between the kinds of socialization expected of us as Christians and the other facets of life outside the church that we encountered and navigated on a daily basis. The Meru celebrate many social milestones with song and dance, and to exclude dancing from the daily social life was to omit an important practice from our community life. The outcome was Christian converts who were either separated from their community life or lived two distinct lives. They mostly ended up with the latter.

Kenyan religious-studies scholar Adam Chepkwony argues that such a "double life" is a result of adherents to Christianity finding out that their traditional belief system "responded to their needs better than the new faith"

(2005:1). Such a double life was our experience—constantly being pulled toward living two distinct lives and belonging to two worlds. On the one hand, our worldview and cultural orientation remained African (Meru) while, on the other, we were being introduced to a Christian worldview shaped by Western cultural sensibilities. It is only as a professional anthropologist that I was able to confirm that I did not have to give up important parts of my own cultural heritage in order to practice my faith as a Christian. Anthropology allowed me to understand the power and place of culture in expressing and understanding faith and how each person's cultural orientation shapes one's expression and understanding of Christian faith. When I shared with Juliani this analysis of the influences missionaries had on our lives as converts, he noted that there were many aspects of African culture that would have provided a very strong foundation for Christianity: "Africans have a high regard for blood sacrifice. Whenever there is wrong in the community, the solution is mobilized through sacrifice. All that missionaries would have done was to show that Christ was the ultimate sacrifice and that there needed no more sacrifices" (pers. comm., February 8, 2014). That was not the understanding many earlier (and even current) converts to Christianity in Kenya affirmed.

The second effect missionaries had over our lives as Christians was the dichotomization of our worlds into two major fragments—the life here on Earth and the life we were anticipating in heaven. The emphasis was on our life in heaven with little, if any, real theology of dealing with the everyday. One might symbolically derive this dichotomy from the continued focus on the Cross as the quintessential icon for Christianity that emphasizes eternal life. The alternative, in my thinking, should be a focus on the birth of Jesus as well so as to symbolize incarnation and the act of God being part of the everyday realities of followers of faith. But the emphasis on the Cross and the resulting dichotomy endures and may well explain the content of many of the gospel songs listed earlier that emphasize the expected good life in heaven and not much about life in the here and now. Growing up in a Christian community similar to others in many parts of Africa provided a sense of intense spiritual emphasis that would resonate with what made Kenyan philosopher John Mbiti argue that Africans are "notoriously religious" (1969). We learned that every aspect of our life was the direct result of God's intervention and that we had to commit everything to God in prayer. What we lacked in this belief, however, was a theology that would help us respond and adjust to contemporary public life, to be responsive and relevant to current issues and practices that confronted our ever-changing world. To be Christian was to be different, to abandon local culture and focus on our "home" in heaven. As our world turned to technical and scientific knowledge in response to emerging challenges of life, however, a theology focusing only on heaven was insufficient, and our Church leaders and Christian academics were not able to provide us with a corresponding theology to match our lived challenges. Chepkwony offers a telling explanation for this reality: "As Africans embraced the Christian faith, it was not long before they discovered that faith and science were perceived as two distinct entities even by the missionaries and the colonialists themselves" (2005:2). Western missionaries were themselves coming out of societies that had established clear boundaries between faith and reason or science following the growth of the Enlightenment movement.

The third effect missionaries had on our lives was the interaction or lack thereof between Church-sponsored schooling and the underlying African worldviews. Many of the initial formal-education institutions in Kenya were sponsored by different denominations. In my own region in eastern Kenya, the dominant denomination, as mentioned, was Methodist. When it came time to attend high school or secondary school, we mostly went to boarding schools, which were located far away from our local communities. What I remember clearly from my experience is that the content of courses we took in these schools was very much removed from the everyday lives we lived, be it at school or in our home communities. As a result, there was no immediate connection between what we learned through our school curriculum and our lived experiences. Moreover, there was no effort on the part of the government or even the denominations sponsoring our schools to include a curriculum that emerged from or affirmed our lived experiences. As a result, our heroes, role models, and leaders were individuals located in other cultures and in other lands that in turn exacerbated our sense of alienation and confusion. Similar to the content provided through our formal education, the gospel did not quite align with much of what we knew or were experiencing culturally, an experience that has led Juliani to aver that today the gospel is much more "real" than it was in the past because "it has the heart of God" and not representing "heads in the clouds" (Njoya 2010).

Scholars have emphasized the importance of culturally relevant interpretation of Christianity in establishing local ownership of the gospel (Jones 1925; Sanneh 1989, 2008; Walls 1996). I argue that the element of being "real" that Juliani's hip hop music embodies today through expression of matters relevant to the other six days of the week is an attempt to make the gospel relevant to the many youth who follow and embrace his artistic work.

The overall outcome of these three effects that missionary work had on our culture and belief system was the growth of a kind of Christianity that was what has been termed "a mile wide and an inch deep" (Kasali 1998; Light 2010). Formal education and Christianity were quite removed from our erstwhile traditions, and as a result, life seemed to come in dualities, sacred and secular, holy and profane, worldly and heavenly spheres.[3] Given their own cultural orientation, the missionaries' world was conceived of as belonging to at least two spheres, the natural (understood and shaped by science and reason) and the supernatural (understood through faith in God). For many of us socialized in an African sociocultural system, however, there was no such separation, believing that the entire existence was connected to the supernatural, or as Mbiti notes: "Religion permeates into all the departments of life so fully that it is not easy or possible always to isolate it. A study of these religious systems is, therefore, ultimately a study of the peoples themselves in all the complexities of traditional and modern life" (1969:1). Instead of realizing this intense religiosity among Africans, however, Western missionaries saw Kenyans as living a dark life that needed the "light" of Christianity. In the process of this encounter, Western cultural practices became the cultural frame through which Christianity was introduced, a European cultural framework that promoted the values and practices from which it had emerged, some of which the Europeans felt were slowly being lost in their own societies that were industrializing too fast. As historian Barbara Cooper notes of missionaries in the Sahel, which translates well into the Kenyan context: "Missions often strove to transform African Christians to match a certain nostalgic vision of an idealized European civilization: converts were encouraged to wear western clothing, to speak western languages, to build and maintain western-style houses, to adhere to the mores often honored more in the breach than the observance in the sending countries" (2006:5).

Such a focus on the outer manifestations of Christianity that dress and language exemplified endured beyond the encounters with Western missionaries as local Christian converts strove to physically distinguish themselves from their non-Christian counterparts through dress. The *Balokole* (converts) were determined to set themselves apart from the rest of the society and embraced this emphasis on physical distance as a mark of Christian conversion. Today, clothes are still some of the notable identity markers of being Christian, decades after the initial missionaries left. Many Christian universities in Kenya, for instance, use a dress code as one of their most visible markers of their Christian identity.[4] Hip hop culture contrasts with this dress culture and has contributed to some of the tensions that may exist between Christian hip hop artists, such as Juliani, and churches or Christian universities.

Juliani has often shared with me his earlier experiences performing in churches or at Daystar University, where he had to strike a balance between his hip hop "look" and what these institutions considered acceptable Christian personal grooming. When he performed at Daystar University in the early years of his career, for instance, he often wore a hat over his dreaded hair. Juliani also talks about the push back he received from churches regarding his style of music and personal grooming. In an interview with Nation TV's Lolan Kalu on the program *Msanii na Sanaa* (Art and artist), Juliani confirms this push-back, saying that there were times he experienced resistance from churches, but nowadays they have accepted him because the churches realize he has a lot of influence over youth ("Msanii" 2009). He also says that today's gospel music is attractive to young people because it is "real" and "relevant" to their lives as Christians, unlike in cases where it is associated with "people in suits going to church with a funny walking style" (2011a).

I am in no way suggesting that Christians ought to disregard the kind of identity they publicly express or perform through dress or other physical manifestations of their identity. Instead, placing too much emphasis on outward manifestations of one's Christian faith may overlook lived expressions of the faith. Indeed, external emphasis of Christian identity can often obscure the internally motivated, pragmatic calculations that adherents make to mobilize their faith in accessing specific answers to lived socioeconomic and political challenges. Theologian Collium Banda argues, "Many Africans embrace Christianity as a key solution to life's problems and as a bulwark to life's threats. They embrace Christianity in search of liberty from their life's constraints" (2005:2). Others may simply embrace Christianity along with the external markers of identity as a way of securing tangible material benefits, such as clothes, food, and school books. Anthropologist Amy Stambach provides an example of such practice from Northern Tanzania, where youth in a New Testament Union camp "were not so much concerned with what religion, per se, could do for the African family, or for creating peace in the wider society, as they were about picking and choosing visual markers to help shape a collective sense of an upwardly-mobile social identity" (2000:175). Similarly, when Christianity was introduced among the Kamba of Kenya, converts were drawn more to the material benefits of Christianity, such as access to formal schools, blankets in the cold season, and jobs in the colonial administration, than in the core message of the faith (Nduto 2014). Again, because of a desire to have many converts, many missionaries and even evangelists tend to share the message of Christianity as a promise of deliverance from material challenges. When Christianity fails to provide these expected answers, however, "local" responses are pursued. Instances of incurable diseases and drought and other natural calamities, as well as personal challenges, such as barrenness, all lead to cultural anxieties that call for known solutions.

When a twenty-first-century notion of development, framed in the discourse of modernity that would assure its recipients of technological advancements (modern transportation and communication), democracy, nuclear families, capitalism, urbanization, and a secular worldview shaped by enlightenment, collide with an African reality dominated by growing poverty, inequality, disease, and degradation, most Africans resort to the occult (Meyer 1999; Comaroff and Comaroff 1993; Niehous, Mohlala, and Shokaneo 2001; Ntarangwi 2011). These two worlds of Christianity and the lived socioeconomic challenges addressed by turning to local solutions, including the occult, have led many African Christians to continue embodying the double identities. Chepkwony points out, and Edward Fasholé-Luke highlights: "Western Missionaries stressed aspects of discontinuity between Christianity and African cultures and traditional religion to such an extent that they excluded the aspects of continuity between Christianity and African cultures and traditional religion. They condemned without proper evaluation African religious beliefs and practices, and substituted Western cultural and religious practices. This had the effect of making it impossible for a person to be a Christian and remain genuinely and authentically an African" (1978:357). It is through "domesticating" the gospel and making it "real" or applicable to everyday lives that Christians in Kenya can embrace the values and beliefs expressed in their faith while remaining connected to their cultural realities. Unfortunately, many churches in Kenya (and elsewhere in Africa) have not always been able to bring the two identities together effectively. Every society understands and embraces Christianity through its own cultural frame (Walls 1996), even in the United States, where there is a desire to keep faith in the private arena (Hauerwas 2013). What emerges from these expressions of Christianity is a clear indication of the value of looking at hip hop and Christian faith, especially because of hip hop's ability to be localized or as I term it "Kenyanized." But does being young and having access to new media, such as hip hop, make a substantial difference in how one engages with and practices Christianity? Let me explore a response by focusing on hip hop and how youth "perform" Christianity.

HIP HOP, YOUTH, AND PERFORMING CHRISTIANITY

Africa is considered a young continent because of the overwhelming number of young people who constitute its overall population. In Kenya 75 percent of the population is under thirty years (official definition of youth is those between fifteen to thirty years) (Ministry 2007:9). Among youth in Kenya, literacy rates are at 80 percent, which corresponds with their access to more education than previous age cohorts, even though the majority of youth constitute the unemployed. Because of their exposure to more opportunities for education and the wider world, youth also tend to have higher aspirations for their lives but lack corresponding material resources to fulfill those aspirations. One only needs look no further than music, radio, television, and the internet that youth in Kenya often utilize to define themselves and their aspirations for a better life. These media platforms allow youth to express their aspirations and experiences in multiple ways. Juliani's music fits well in this category, capturing both the aspirations and realities of his generation.

As argued previously as well as in other areas of my own writing on youth and globalization, the global economic processes that pushed neoliberal philosophies into all African economies turned out to be both a blessing and a curse for the youth (2009, 2010). Globalization has simultaneously allowed youth an opportunity to enter into public political discourse and to find new avenues for livelihood while constraining their ability to thrive. The loss of government control over airwaves, which ushered in new FM radio stations, opportunities for music recording not controlled by a single monopoly, and the expanded market for products that youth endorse, has changed the public face and identity of Kenyan youth. New media has also expanded youth public space by expanding their networks to connect with peers in multiple locations far away from local centers while also providing strategies and motivation to undertake local initiatives for self-improvement. Twitter, for instance, has been one avenue through which youth in Kenya share internship, fellowship, and job opportunities as well as information on government operations, investment opportunities, and private-sector appointments. Indeed, for many Kenyans, Twitter has become the alternative source of news and information sharing, especially in cases where the government is reluctant to share such information.

Despite these glimmers of hope social media avail, however, youth in Kenya, as with young people around Africa and elsewhere, continue to grapple with the reality of an ever-widening gap between the rich and poor (Cole

2004; Dewey and Brison 2012; Hansen 2005; Honwana 2012; Jeffrey 2010; Weiss 2005, 2009). Youth also regularly experience the disconnect between their productive potential and the opportunities available for a decent livelihood, especially in the formal sector. Born in the 1980s and 1990s, when Kenya was experiencing the height of dictatorship and falling economic prospects but more expanded access to education (which is supposed to provide better economic opportunities), Juliani's generation has grown up keenly aware of the tension between education opportunities and lack of formal employment. On top of that has been the increased influx of foreign consumer goods following the collapse of the one-party political arrangement in the country under Daniel Arap Moi beginning in the mid- to late 1990s.

Theories of hip hop's production, consumption, and performance globally correspond with these political and economic changes. A closer look at how youth use hip hop provides a window into how a disenfranchised demographic enters into the public space and reconfigures and often redefines it in ways that allow for new claims that voice lived and imagined realities for general members of society both as individuals and as Christians. Although music and Christianity have been regarded as incarnational processes that narrate themselves in lived experiences that document social reality (Kidula 2013), I argue that hip hop provides Christianity a contested arena for self-expression and indigenization because of its emergence from a socioeconomic context of depressed economies and livelihoods neoliberalism fuels (Hodge 2010; Ntarangwi 2009; Rose 1994; Sharma 2010), as well as through multidirectional processes, multiracial identities, and multicultural interactions (Osumare 2012). The large number of youth involved with hip hop in Kenya, specifically, is a result of a prolonged demographic phase that scholars refer to as "waithood," a period within which such factors as a government's inability to provide employment or meaningful opportunities for self-employment, effects of structural adjustment programs, poor governance, and limited skills training to match available opportunities lead to a prolonged phase of waiting between childhood and adulthood (Honwana 2012).

In response to waithood, youth have engaged in practices of getting by, such as street hawking, dumpster diving, border crossing, prostitution, petty and organized crime, and begging, among many others (Honwana 2012; May 1996). Moreover, other factors contribute to the growing participation of youth in hip hop. The relative spatial politics of identity that the urban setting provides for youth produces certain identities of self not common in their rural communities. As historians have observed, when African youth migrate to cities they often find that "their immersion in a new world of urban tastes, sounds, and stimuli, and new encounters with diverse peoples and conditions [lead] to relative anonymity and often a process of personal reinvention and the embrace of new identities" (Burgess and Burton 2010:1). When these new youth identities find avenues of expression that new and social media mobilize, they become constructed and patterned on a different social logic. Even the expression of their Christian identity is subjected to these multicultural and multiethnic urban realities that produce powerful political and ideological fronts that cast youth into the public space in an unprecedented way. Youth have been known to use hip hop to change political directions of communities or entire nations, redefine racial and cultural identities (Condry 2007; Sharma 2010), and reinvigorate otherwise neglected or even disabused traditional cultural practices (Samper 2004).[5] As such, Christianity cannot remain the same once infused with this youth agency and creativity.

Hip hop's unique identity as a musical genre lies in its performance and use of globally mediated images and products. The specific dress, body movements, and the gaze and relationships with the camera, as well as the use and handling of the microphone, all come together to create a globally identifiable physical identity of the artist. This performed identity allows us to recognize local brands of music as hip hop even when sung in local or national languages within a blend of local and regional rhythms. Many of the hip hop artists' performance mannerisms seem to be replicated on stages across the world and, as argued in this book, can all be tied to African American rap and hip hop styles of delivery. As such, without audio and visual media that allow for such performative styles to cross geographical, cultural, racial, and artistic boundaries, hip hop would not have such a recognizable global presence or identity.

Anthropologists, such as Louisa Scheim (1999) and Jonathan Xavier Inda and Renato Rosaldo (2007), have shown the power of performance in negotiating and contesting global processes and the power that media affords youth to create social networks and space that embody "culture as it is performed" (Bell 2008:135).[6] It is in its performance that hip hop fully attains its identity, and, by extension, it is in its "performance" or ability to be articulated practically in the lives of its practitioners that Christianity becomes identifiable as a way of life. Indeed, when Juliani performs hip hop, he actualizes a kind of Christianity that informs and is informed by the socioeconomic and political realities of interest to a wider public, providing some kind of public theology.

By using the concept of public theology here, I am pointing to a level of analysis of Kenya's Christianity in relation to hip hop music that captures the ways that Christian faith as mobilized through various discourses, messages, aspirations, and values are directed to all areas of life and how they allow for people to engage with each other in public spaces, in the "streets." This kind of Christianity, while not excluding private notions of faith that are related to personal piety or intimate relations with family members, seeks to focus more on the welfare of the masses or, as Clint Le Bruyns notes, a kind of theology that "is in contact and conversation with concrete realms of public life—political, economic, civil society and public opinion. . . . It is a way of understanding and practising theology which must contribute in constructive, dialogical, enriching and transforming ways to 'the public good'" (2012:3). Public theology is not able to distance itself from the very social context within which it exists, and just like Juliani's hip hop, it is informed by the experiences and aspirations of those who produce and consume it. The tools that hip hop avails to youth to reconceptualize what it means to be Christian in this public sphere range from creating cultural categories of meaning associated with church and the "world" to spiritual discourse of realities of lived materiality and aspirations of eternity. Instead of creating dichotomies of a Christian world and secular one, a here-and-now life and one to come, or a gospel artist and secular one, hip hop traverses both worlds in an attempt to not only connect but also to complicate them. Hip hop brings these facets together in the same way public theology, religious faith, and public life come together. Hip hop provides Christians an avenue through which to imagine and even articulate a different kind of gospel music.

A NEW KIND OF GOSPEL MUSIC?

In a summary of their book on hip hop and the church, Effrem Smith and Phil Jackson note: "Hip-hop culture is shaping the next generation. Ignoring it will not reduce its influence; it will only separate us from the youth moving to its rhythm. How will they hear Christ's message of truth and hope if we don't speak their language? And how can we speak their language if we don't understand and embrace their culture? Hear the beat. Join the beat. Become the beat that brings truth and hope to a hungry, hurting generation" (2005:34). Clearly, the church cannot ignore hip hop's extended reach into much of youth culture. Even though these sentiments are made in the context of the US music scene, the same can be said of Kenya's music scene. The authors point to a need for a conversation and even connection between the two entities of church and hip hop. But to be interested in hip hop as a conduit to access youth for Christ's message seems transactional. Rather than use hip hop as a conduit to bring youth to church, I suggest getting the church to align itself with the culture of youth that is expressed through hip hop, because hip hop is an expression of a kind of lived reality that ought to be represented in the Christian message. Hip hop artists are themselves living out their Christian lives through the genre and providing public faces of Christianity to those who consume the music. In this sense hip hop stops being a medium to deliver the message of Christianity and becomes the message of Christianity.

Christianity is messy, believers have the same life challenges others face, some pastors fail while others triumph over daily challenges, Christians kill, lie, and bribe, and this is the reality captured in expressive cultural forms, including hip hop. Today, hip hop has changed the way one might think of gospel music and the message of the gospel, especially in Kenya. Why is this the case? As noted above, Kenya, like many other African nations, is a country whose population is dominated by youth. Moreover, living in a context where youth contributions to public discourse have been limited, it is not surprising that when hip hop provides an opportunity to enter into this public space, many youth embrace it. Youth embraces it, however, along with its channels of articulating raw emotions, stifled aspirations, expected triumphs, and transformative messages of hope. Hip hop speaks the language of youth, for a number of reasons.

Kenyan youth today, on the one hand, have access to media that provide images of worlds away from their own, but there are no corresponding opportunities to replicate those worlds locally in ways that advance youth materially and culturally. On the other hand, they are often used as conduits for selfish political or economic interests of others as seen in youth being mobilized to go out on the streets and engage in violent protests when one politician loses an election, as was the case in Kenya's general elections of 1992, 1997, and 2007. Youth sometimes do enter into these activities willingly out of frustration and lack of other options or as an attempt to bring about change in their societies (Henderson 2003). Joblessness, high costs of living in most urban areas, and lure of crime as a conduit into wealth are some of the realities youth deal with daily in Kenya. Yet, despite these realities, youth like Juliani and a few other musicians made choices that were very different and that have led to some opportunities they have had to date. Juliani lived in a context where many other youth were involved in activities that were not positive, but he steered away from such activities and only appropriated those experiences and observations as fodder for his music.

Overall, many of the youth participating in gospel music through hip hop in Kenya today were raised within the Christian context discussed earlier, characterized by the kind of dualism that tends to focus on life in heaven with no clear articulation of how to live the life of the here and now. Juliani sees gospel music as expressed by hip hop as transcending this dualism. When asked why people appreciate gospel music more today than in the past, he said, "No, this time gospel has heart, it has the heart of God. That's why people appreciate it. It also expresses the reality of our feelings that allow us to say, 'Hey, I have issues, and I need help.' It's not about heads up in heaven [in the clouds]" (2011a). My own experience as an undergraduate student or even a high school student mirrors what Juliani expresses here. I remember members of what was called CU (Christian Union) in school, who always looked unhappy and who walked in what I considered a funny style while clamping the Bible under their arm as they attended after-school meetings. They would rarely interact with other students and always seemed to find fault in all that we did outside of class. I used to wonder why they seemed gloomy, and yet in their message, they would always say, "Come to Jesus, and your problems will be solved." Why were they not happy? They, like me, had been socialized into accepting that to be Christian was to physically remove oneself from one's immediate sociocultural environment. But even in my youth, I sensed a contradiction between the message of Christianity and the everyday practices fellow Christians displayed, and I wanted to know why Jesus didn't solve the problems my counterparts faced in the Christian Union and make them happy. Why was the Jesus they were preaching to us not making them happy? How could they possibly reach out to other students, especially the nonbelievers if their public displays of faith were uninviting?

As a Christian and musician, Juliani sees the potential that hip hop has in spreading the gospel in a slightly different way from what I assumed were the approaches of my CU counterparts or even from the common practice of preaching:

> It is not about a certain congregation, you change a generation because [take for instance] people stay up all night with their feet in basins of cold water trying to stay awake as they cram for an exam, but the words in music are easier to catch That is how powerful music is. (2011a)

It is not only about using hip hop but also making sure that its message resonates with the target audience. Juliani has been able to do this well, making him earn the title of Street Poet.

In the past it was very unusual for a Christian artist to engage the kinds of issues Juliani expresses through his music. As shown in my discussion, messages in gospel songs from the 1980s and 1990s were mostly about personal salvation and relationship with Christ and little about confronting everyday realities of life. Creating music that provides multiple views of the realities that Christians go through every day along with initiatives to bring like-minded youth in different urban neighborhoods in Nairobi to identify issues or challenges in their neighborhoods and together come up with local solutions, Juliani is bridging the often separated worlds of the afterlife and the here and now. For Juliani the projects he supports and initiatives he funds are exemplifications of Christian living—taking up one's assets and applying them to better his or her current circumstances as well as the rest of society. He comments: "Personally I have seen growth and because I believe in myself and I have sunk myself in God's word, have the right people around me. I have realized, hey, it is possible, Kenya is possible. Kenya being successful is possible, living off your music is possible, you see, living corruption free is possible, and even all these potholes all over is possible for them to not be there" (2011a). This personal transformation means a focus on both individual and collective action and a recasting of what Christianity means for a hip hop artist. When asked what gospel music means, Juliani talked about the values and actions of the musician rather than the genre itself. He said that being a gospel artist means:

> When you go *kwa* show, you show up on time;
> *haulewilewi; haushinashikani na warembo huko*;
> you don't do those things.

> When you go to a show, you show up on time;
> you don't get drunk; you don't flirt with girls there;
> you don't do those things. (2014b)

Christianity for him is about the message as much as it is about praxis. Besides the values he espouses as a gospel artist, Juliani has been able to make what is going on around him part of his gospel message. He takes advantage of opportunities to display his faith with others all the time. When asked why he, for instance, collaborated with a secular artist named Jua Cali, Juliani explained that it was a way to demonstrate his Christian faith without proselytizing. He shared the process of how Jua Cali called him and told him he wanted to sing a song to thank God for all he had been blessed with in his life. Juliani explains, "He came to me and said, 'I just want to thank God.' Who does that? And I have been given that privilege to do that song with him and spend time with him. I don't need to preach to him but how I do things, how I handle my things is enough to preach" (2014b). His choice of words, his willingness to dig deeper into social situations, and his ability to mix and match words within one sentence or song brings out his unique abilities as an artist. That a supposedly secular artist would call him to collaborate on a song meant to give thanks to God does point to Juliani being recognized as an important Christian artist by his peers. Jua Cali is a very successful musician, and collaboration with Juliani would definitely bring attention to both musicians' work (Ntarangwi 2009).

Juliani also connects with his audience, and his down-to-earth demeanor endears him more to his fans. He responds to questions about his songs and comments on his social-media platforms. He makes himself available to his fans for short conversations and for photo opportunities as he sells his music. He then collects all the images and collectively uses them as a form of thank-you to all his supporters. He did that with images he had taken himself or received from fans who had bought *Exponential Potential*. He put together a slide show thanking all of them for supporting him. This connection with his fans was also demonstrated during his tour from Nairobi to Mombasa by road on his way to launch his second album, *Pulpit Kwa Street*, in Mombasa, sponsored by Google+.[7] In the video, Juliani is shown visiting with a fan at her house in Nairobi. The fan says that she connects with his music very well and faults people who think that girls do not "get" hip hop. She sings part of his song "Bahasha ya Ocampo." Juliani joins her, and they sing together. Juliani later talks to a young man who says his goal is to engage culture and hip hop because Juliani preaches to him more than what he gets from a pulpit. This "preaching" must be connected to what Juliani sees as his role as a Christian by using his lifestyle as his medium through which to demonstrate his faith. When they get to Mombasa, Juliani finds time to visit a rehabilitation center, where he meets some of his fellow musicians that got carried away and engaged in drug use. Now devastated by those wrong choices, they talk about the cruelty of the addictions and the social and personal ramifications that ensue. Through this and many other opportunities to get close to people, Juliani is able to bring his "gospel" in a language and medium that many youth understand and embody. His own life is an example of the content of his lyrics, including the value of doing good for others, challenging assumptions about one's abilities, and letting others ascertain anyone's level of Christian commitment through observed behavior. The next chapter focuses on Juliani's philosophy and program that aim at improving youth lives as generated by youth themselves, especially his Kama Si Sisi Program expressed through his Mtaa Challenge project.

4

KAMA SI SISI NANI?
JULIANI'S GOSPEL
OF SELF-EMPOWERMENT

The matatu I was traveling in from Meru had just started negotiating the heavy traffic that was building up around Ronald Ngala Street in Nairobi when my phone rang. It was Juliani responding to an email message I had sent him earlier in the week, asking if we could get together. I was eager to meet with him to get responses to a few questions I had before my eventual trip to Michigan to finish this book. "Hello, *vipi* (what's up), Juliani?" I said. The young man seated to my right in the matatu turned to look at me. I assumed he turned because I had mentioned Juliani's name. Juliani has become a well-known artist in Kenya and would not be surprised that this young man knew him or his music. I ignored his look and carried on my conversation with Juliani. I told him that I heard his song play on the matatu I was on, and he laughed, saying, "*Wacha*" (Stop). My email to Juliani was also an attempt to find more details of a concert he was supposed to attend. I had read a short message online that Juliani would be at the Arboretum Gardens in Nairobi, performing along with other musicians on this same day, but it later turned out to be untrue. For him to call on the same day I was hoping to see him at a live performance was such a relief. It saved me the trouble of going to a concert at which he was not performing. He told me that he was going to be at the GoDown Arts Centre on Dunga Road in Nairobi's Industrial Area for Mtaa Challenge Awards.

I recognized GoDown Arts Centre from news I had read in the past about performances hosted there, including a concert by Juliani. On his thirtieth birthday, April 22, 2014, for instance, Juliani hosted a listening party for his third album, *Exponential Potential*. I, however, had never visited the GoDown

Arts Centre. The facility was once a parking garage that had been converted into a center for performing arts, and Juliani has an office on the premises. The center, which holds a cafeteria, a hall for all types of events, offices for art- and music-related groups and individuals, and smaller spaces for meetings, as well as a large space for parking, plays an important role in providing office and meeting space (mostly) for artists with limited resources. The Mtaa Challenge Awards ceremony was scheduled to start at 3:00 P.M., but Juliani told me he would be there from 1:00 P.M.. He said that if I had time, I could go and see "what we do." I was delighted because I had been looking for an opportunity to see Juliani "in action."

As a program, the Mtaa Challenge is currently limited to Nairobi, with plans to take it around the country in the future. It involves a group of young people from different residential areas (locally referred to as *mtaa*, pl. m*itaa*) in Nairobi coming together, working with trainers and coaches to brainstorm ideas, surveying their neighborhoods, and identifying possible projects to undertake. These project ideas are arrived at through a process involving communal discussions and prioritization. To make them more meaningful, the projects are organized as competitions with the best three projects awarded 100,000, 75,000, and 50,000 Kenyan shillings for first-, second-, and third-place winners, respectively. In October 2015 the US dollar was exchanging for 100.00 Kenyan shillings, which puts the first-place winner's award at $1,000.00. With the minimum wage for the lowest-paid worker (gardener or house help) in Nairobi, for instance, pegged at 9,780.95 Kenyan shillings a month (about US$97.81) for 2015, the first-place-winner prize money represents almost a year of wages. Other prizes to be won throughout the competition include cell phones and tablets (donated for the 2014 program by Orange Kenya[1]) (figure 4).

The Mtaa Challenge project had been running for eight weeks, and this was the day when winners would be announced, and prizes awarded. It was such a privilege for me to be part of the program.

I alighted from the matatu once it reached the end of the trip at the famous Tea Room on Accra Road. I boarded a number 46 matatu headed for Kawangware (west of Nairobi's central business district), which would get me close to the Methodist Guesthouse, where I was staying for the week. Route numbers for Matatus and buses in Nairobi mark their operating circuit and are what the Mtaa Challenge program has used as key points for identifying youth groups for their competitions. The team that won the 2013 Mtaa Challenge competition was UMOKAS, representing Matatu route numbers 19C and 35/60, which go to Umoja and Kariobangi South.

4. Juliani and Achi arranging prizes Orange Kenya donated for Mtaa Challenge winners

I had left my bags at a relative's house in Buruburu (a middle-income residential area east of Nairobi's central business district), where I spent the night upon my arrival from the United States, before going to Meru to see family and friends. With my bags in Buruburu, I did not have access to a copy of the first chapters of the Juliani book that I wanted to share with him. I checked into the guesthouse and dropped off my bag, but before turning around to go see Juliani, I picked up my camera, a notebook, and a pen. All my other "fieldwork tools" were stored in my bags, but these were adequate.

I walked to the corner of Oloitoktok Road and Ole Odume Road and boarded a matatu bound for the city center. I was eager to get to GoDown Arts Centre with enough time to talk with Juliani before the official Mtaa Challenge Awards ceremony started. In my haste to get ready, I forgot to have lunch, so I stopped at a pastry shop to buy a can of soda and two muffins and then walked toward the matatu parking lot, where I thought I would find transportation to Industrial Area and get to GoDown Art Centre. As I walked through the streets, I stopped at the local Maasai Market (open-air market that mostly features handcrafted items for purchase as gifts or souvenirs) that was going on outside the Nairobi Supreme Court parking lot. I knew I did not have much time to browse through the many items on display but stopped to look at some earrings. Our youngest daughter had requested earrings, and I wanted to see what was available. Sellers and brokers eager to make a sale immediately accosted me, but my experience in the market allowed me to ignore them and, instead, walk around on my own and try to locate good earrings. I did not find the exact style that our daughter had asked for, but there were some with designs that I had not seen in my previous visits. I purchased a few pairs with a plan to return to the market the following Saturday and look for more, especially the specific ones she wanted.

I decided to take a taxi to GoDown Arts Centre so that I could get there in time and also because I was not exactly sure where it was located in Industrial Area. I negotiated the cost of the taxi ride and got into the car. In the taxi I had an interesting conversation with the driver about governance, the infrastructure, and the threat of terrorism. These topics seemed to come up frequently in conversations that I was part of in the first few days of being back in Nairobi. The taxi driver mentioned that he had seen a slight increase in the number of people opting to take a taxi instead of a matatu. I asked him why he thought this was happening, and he referred to the reports of grenades being thrown at or in matatus in Nairobi and the fear that those incidents had caused many commuters. He added that he, too, was concerned about the insecurity in Nairobi and worried he might take up a customer who would turn out to be a suicide bomber. Such fear is no longer farfetched, given the few incidents of attacks in public spaces in Nairobi in the form of people with guns or grenades. In May 2014, for instance, Nairobi's Gikomba Market (an open-air market that features new and used items, including clothes) was hit by two improvised explosive devices that killed ten people. This and other related incidents in Kenya have been linked to a militant group from neighboring Somalia called Al-Shabaab (BBC 2014). The driver was well aware of the need to "hustle" for money by getting as many customers as possible but concerned about his own safety, given this increase in random acts of violence. This conversation gave me food for thought as I considered all the challenges facing many categories of Kenyans, not just the youth.

MTAA CHALLENGE AWARDS CEREMONY

We got to GoDown Arts Centre at around 2:19 P.M.; I paid the taxi driver and approached the security guard posted at the entrance and asked where

I could find Juliani. He told me to go all the way to the end of the walkway and take a left. I walked past a cafeteria on the left and stepped into a large space that had offices on the right and a high wall on the left. The wall was covered with graffiti art, a few portraits of famous people, including Dr. Martin Luther King Jr. and Miriam Makeba, and some posters advertising a locally popular make of a vehicle (Figure 5). At the end of the walkway, I veered left into a large hall to find Juliani and three other men setting up the space that was to be the stage. At the far left corner of the hall were four other young males seated behind two computers and a few other machines, working on setting up the connections that would be beamed on the four large flat screens arranged next to each other close to the stage. The screens were sandwiched between two large banners of Orange Kenya.

Some Mtaa Challenge team members had already arrived and were seated, chatting in small groups. I was quite surprised to find Juliani setting up the stage, including moving a big board that provided the base for the platform. It is quite unusual for the person sponsoring a function to be involved in setting up the space for a ceremony. I quickly found that not only does Juliani get his hands "dirty" but he also wants his work to be perfect. He wanted the banners, the platform, and the chairs arranged in a way that they were all aligned with each other. I observed him take a few steps away from the

5. Portrait of Dr. Martin Luther King Jr. on a wall at GoDown Arts Centre

setup, look at how well they were aligned, and then come back and move a chair here and a banner there to make sure they were exact. I had found the same desire for perfection in Juliani when I spent time with him in Saint P's studio as he polished up on his first single "Morio and Juliet" from *Exponential Potential*.

Juliani spotted me in the hall and said hello. We chatted a little, and then I joined in the task of setting up the platform not only because I usually don't like to just stand and watch people work but also to emulate Juliani's example. I had never been to any of the Mtaa Challenge meetings and knew no one else other than Juliani, but those present quite openly accepted me. We greeted each other in what I can refer to as "the Mtaa greeting," which involves a handshake with each of the participant's hand raised to an arm wrestling position, thumbs locked into a grip and with the same hand pulling the other person so that the shoulders bump followed by a pat on each other's back with the free hand. Within no time I found myself interacting with the young men and women in the hall with the familiarity of people who have been buddies for years. I liked the kind of camaraderie I observed in that hall; it made me wonder if it had anything to do with Juliani's own personality and how he interacts with them or if it was the way today's youth interact. My hunch was the former.

About a hundred green plastic chairs were in the hall, and more people were trickling in and finding a place to sit. Some brand-new cell phones (still in their packing boxes) were placed close to the entrance on a table covered with an orange cloth, signifying that the phones were from the Orange Kenya phone company. I came to learn later that Orange Money (part of Orange Kenya) had partly sponsored the event and had a few of its employees in the audience. As I walked to the table to take a closer look at the phones, I met a woman who introduced herself as Achi (for Achieng). She told me that Juliani was her boss and that for eight weeks she had had been working closely with the Mtaa Challenge teams that would be receiving prizes at the ceremony. Achi mentioned that she was pleased to see the final product of that journey and asked if I could assist in taking pictures. It was good that I had grabbed my camera on my way to the GoDown Arts Centre. Achi said that once I was done taking the pictures, I should share them with her via email so as to be posted later on the project's website. I felt honored to be included in the Mtaa Challenge Awards ceremony in yet another special way. Achi explained to me some of the strategic photos she needed taken and from what location she wanted me to take pictures of all team members. One of the main locations was close to the Mtaa Challenge and Orange Money banners outside the hall at a place she called the VIP spot.

People kept trickling in past 3:00 P.M., the time of starting the program, and Juliani and I joked about the tendency for Kenyans to go to events late. I found time during my role as photographer to walk around and see what else was there. As I was walking toward the main gate to take pictures of the premises for my own work, I met Juliani carrying a bottle of water, and he asked if I needed one. I said yes so we walked back together to the cafeteria, and he purchased a bottle of cold water for me. Walking back to the hall, Juliani mentioned that I would be asked to present one of the awards and said, "*Kama mgeni mheshimiwa*" (As an honored guest). I was reminded of how down to earth and flexible Juliani is and why he seems to connect with people of different backgrounds. He makes use of whatever resources he finds around him. I was there, he needed different people to help present awards, and he requested my participation. I said I would gladly do it.

For the rest of the time before the program started, I kept taking pictures of all the groups that had participated in the Mtaa Challenge program. Achi kept calling the different teams to take up positions near the Orange Kenya banners, and I was on hand to take their pictures. Some of them wanted their own individual photos, which I gladly took and told them to ask Achi for their individual or group copies, while others gathered in different combinations in their groups for more pictures. I planned on sending all the pictures to Juliani via email as soon as I had internet access back at the Methodist Guesthouse. Juliani told me that some guests, including the Swedish ambassador to Kenya and some representatives from some commercial banks, had been invited to the event but were not able to make it. Orange Kenya representatives, however, were in attendance, including Sandra Hua Yao, head of Orange Kenya, who wore an orange dress to the ceremony. I assumed the Orange Kenya team was there because they had sponsored parts of the Mtaa Challenge program as well as because of the partnership they had created with Juliani to sell his third album through their country-wide network of shops.

The event ended up starting some minutes past 4:00 P.M., with Juliani serving as the MC. He started off by going over the written program, mentioning all the activities that were supposed to have taken place from 3:00 P.M., and clarifying that given the late start, he would move through things quickly. He said he would have to cut short some of the events in the ceremony to make up for the time that was lost. I was asked to go up to the podium and give the first award for the Most Happening Mtaa. On stage Juliani introduced me as Mwenda, a friend he had known for a year, adding that even though I looked like a local guy, I was actually a professor and a published author. He went on to say that I would speak to the participants in *Kiswahili sanifu* (standard Swahili), which basically meant speaking the school or university Kiswahili to a crowd that I assumed had mostly grown up speaking Sheng. I hardly use Kiswahili sanifu in my regular conversations myself unless I am addressing a formal meeting or talking with a person whose social status and language ability call for such use.

Juliani provided me with the name of the winning team, which I announced, and the group members shot up from their chairs amid cheers and walked to the platform. These awards were in recognition of some of the stages each team took during the eight-week period of the competition. The three cash prizes were to be given later in the ceremony. I greeted the team members one by one with the Mtaa greeting. We took a few pictures together, and then I stepped off the platform to resume my photography as other people were called upon to give out the rest of the awards. Magneta, a team from Kayole, won the first prize for a proposed library project that was meant to enhance student reading in one of the local mitaa. Street 45 won second place, and Kibera won third.

The ceremony went on till about 7:00 P.M.. The sun had already gone down, and the hall was getting dark. In winding up the program, Juliani made a personal commitment to all the teams that had participated in the second Mtaa Challenge competition whether or not they had won one of the three cash prizes. He promised to assist them in realizing their dreams as long as they stayed focused on their proposed projects. He said that when the second phase of Mtaa Challenge started, many people thought that money was to be given out for simply participating. However, they soon found out this was a different kind of a program, not "the usual NGO style of dishing out money and no results to show for the projects supported," Juliani said. A number of those who had signed up dropped off when they realized hard work needed to be applied to participate and in order to stand a chance to win. Those participants, Juliani said, "*walichujwa* (were weeded out), and the "serious ones" remained.

Mtaa Challenge projects fall under the umbrella of Juliani's Kama Si Sisi program initiated as a way of working with youth in Kenya to make a difference in their own lives as well as the lives of others. The first installment of the Mtaa Challenge project attracted a thousand entries from youth living in many parts of Nairobi similar to where Juliani grew up. The first-place group, Umokas, representing Umoja and Kariobangi South, were going to put their prize money toward a greenhouse community project. The Umokas group was so organized and dedicated that they were able to convince their local member of parliament to allocate them land to locate their greenhouse (Juliani, pers. comm., November 26, 2013).

November 2013 marked the start of the second Mtaa Challenge project that Juliani advertised through Facebook and Twitter. These two social-media avenues are important outlets for Juliani, who by October 2, 2015, had 150,000 followers on Twitter and 132,950 on Facebook. This second phase of Mtaa Challenge attracted four thousand participants (compared to fifteen hundred in the previous year), clearly signaling the growing popularity of the project.

Seeking to provide an alternative to the usual narrative of development that often looks outward for help, Juliani wanted projects under the Kama Si Sisi program to be based on local resources that were being applied to solve local problems. To capture the aims and objectives of this program, a Facebook page dedicated to Kama Si Sisi was developed, where interested individuals and groups can find more information and updates on the competition. Juliani regularly highlights these projects and programs on his own Facebook page and Twitter account. From the beginning, Kama Si Sisi was "a one of a kind attitude change campaign [that] . . . empowers and enlightens young people to be responsible and accountable to themselves and their community, to work toward the positive improvement of their surroundings—politically, economically, socially and spiritually" (Kama Si Sisi 2014). In this campaign involving, among other issues, wise investment, governance and leadership, freedom of information, and self-advancement, its philosophy is based on a collectivist social responsibility captured in the phrase "taking care of yourself by taking care of others" (Kama Si Sisi 2014). A brochure distributed at the Mtaa Challenge Awards ceremony that I attended clearly explains the philosophy of the program. Its slogan is "Better, safer Nairobi: Solutions from grassroots." The About section explains: "The Mtaa Challenge is a grassroots campaign to build an active and engaged new generation of youth in Nairobi and across Kenya. Mtaa Challenge is an initiative of Kama Si Sisi to encourage local solutions to local challenges through a neighbourhood to neighbourhood competition" (Mtaa Challenge [2014]). The program has three objectives— political, economic, and social. Politically, Mtaa Challenge seeks to develop "a network of an informed, organized youth that will interact and keep their local leadership accountable for the betterment of the community and also a platform to encourage emergence of young leaders. Establish an organized youth in the grassroots to be agents of change as a voice to the vulnerable in their various communities" (Mtaa Challenge [2014]).

For many of the youth targeted by this program, these plans for action are not new. What may be different is that the project provides them an opportunity, a platform, and resources to actualize the plans. Moreover, the program not only calls upon the youth to make a difference but also provides training for them to be successful. Information available on the step-by-step activities undertaken by groups in the first two Mtaa Challenge competitions shows that participants underwent specific training and preparations (Kama Si Sisi 2014). The teams started with some meetings, brainstormed ideas, and established meeting venues and times. They were then given questions to use to gather more information about their mtaa, including the history of the mtaa, the occupations of most residents, special identities of the mtaa that an outsider might not know, and the assets and challenges that exist in the mtaa (Kama Si Sisi 2014).

I often wondered why Juliani chose such a program to encourage youth to engage and improve their local communities. As I interacted with him more, listened to his music, and read about his personal life and identity, however, I found that it comes out of his Christian identity. At different points in his career, he has stated that his "Christian mandate" is to focus on the vulnerable, and he cites Isaiah 58 as the foundation for all he does as a Christian. In his November 18, 2013, tweet, for instance, he said that he had a treasure, a secret to an amazing life, and wanted to share it. It was Isaiah 58:7: "Is it not to share your bread with the hungry and bring the homeless poor into your house; when you see the naked, to cover him, and not to hide yourself from your own flesh?" (Holy Bible New International Version 2011).

In his album *Exponential Potential*, Juliani starts with a two-and-a-half–minute, spoken introduction, "Isaiah 58, today's version" and ends with "and that's the word of the Lord, of course Juliani version." In the content of this piece, Juliani mixes a few lines from Isaiah 58 with his own lines that provide Kenyan renditions of the original text: "Tell my people what is wrong with their lives," which corresponds with the second part of Isaiah 58:1, "Declare to my people their rebellion and the descendants of Jacob their sins." Juliani follows this with his own words, "*Mnaregulate mpango wa kando wakawa wives*" (You regulate the law so mistresses become wives), which is a direct reference to a marriage bill passed in the Kenyan parliament on March 20, 2014, to officially allow polygamy.

Prior to this bill, polygamy was only officially recognized among Kenyan Muslims, who have a special clause in the Kenyan Constitution that allows

Muslim courts (Kadhi courts) to make decisions on adherents' personal matters, such as marriage and divorce. The legalization of polygamy only makes formal a practice that has been prevalent in many communities in Kenya through traditional cultural practices. Even among those not espousing a traditional cultural practice, there have been many incidents of married men having mistresses, which in turn resulted in the phrase *Mpango wa Kando*, which directly translates to "a side plan," in reference to a mistress. In the discussions and comments leading up to the official passing of the bill, Samuel Chepkong'a, chairman, Justice and Legal Affairs Committee, is reported to have said, "Any time a man comes home with a woman, that would be assumed to be a second or third wife" (Ngirachu 2014). This is the practice Juliani is making reference to here, but he focuses on other social challenges that Kenyan Christians ought to address: "Share your food with the hungry," which corresponds with Isaiah 58:7, "is it not to share food with the hungry"; Juliani adds, "*Si kupandisha kioo wakiapproach gari*" (And not to roll up your car window when they approach) ("Intro" *Exponential Potential* 2014). This commitment to Isaiah 58, even though articulated in his third album, has been foregrounded in his public statements and interviews made prior to the official release of the album.

In an April 2011 interview for K24 TV's *Capital Talk*, host Jeff Koinange asks Juliani about his own economic status. Juliani mentions that it is true his life has changed and he has a car and house, but if his family and community are not at that same point economically, then he is nowhere. He gives the example of wealthy people who often overlook the fact that their security guard is poor, sees all the wealth, and could one day run away with the property. Juliani adds something about his plans to go around the country to work with other musicians, help them focus on social issues, and then record an album together. Koinange says, "You like helping people along the way, don't you, Juliani. You are lifting people as you go." Juliani responds, "I am taking care of myself. That is the best way of taking care of myself. If I help others, my CD will be bought, you see. But it's not about handouts. It's about being in a place of influence, like I could go into this office and make things happen" (2011c). Juliani had been focused on the philosophy of life entailed in Isaiah 58 even before he publicly made it his guiding principle and that of the Mtaa Challenge program.

Economically, Mtaa Challenge focuses on developing entrepreneurial skills that help youth generate business ideas then supported with seed money to build them. This objective is already mobilized through the Mtaa Challenge competition that gives prize money to the winning teams. Participating teams are not only encouraged to find local solutions for local challenges but also to package their ideas as income-generating activities. The final objective for Mtaa Challenge is to engage youth socially through programs grounded in their communities that seek to bring cohesion and accountability across ethnic, gender, and religious identities. By pursuing this transformative life for youth whose success is also tied to the success of others, Juliani is embodying a philosophy that has often been termed *Ubuntu*, which denotes a collective orientation toward the flourishing of others along with self. Ubuntu emphasizes the connectedness of one's own humanity to that of others (Eze 2010; Louw 2001; Ramose 1999; Shutte 1993; Tutu 2000). This Ubuntu philosophy of community development that I see in Juliani's work corresponds with and even challenges Christianity.

JULIANI'S UBUNTU: FROM INDIVIDUAL TO COMMUNAL SUCCESS

African Christianity has continued to flourish within this African philosophy of Ubuntu that emphasizes communally oriented social success. But because contemporary Christianity entered into Africa through Western missionaries, it has tended to thrive in a context of duality as the philosophy of Ubuntu competes with individualism brought in by Western civilization as well as the various manifestations of contemporary modernity. Consequently, African Christianity is, on the one hand, experienced through existing African cultural frames that very much focus on the good of community and, on the other, through political and economic structures fashioned by years of interactions between external and internal practices that pull communities away from the collective orientation often present in many African societies (Forster 2006). Not surprisingly, contemporary Christianity's philosophy has to struggle to reconcile these two competing realities of the individual and the communal. When confronted with the socioeconomic challenges of the everyday, this contemporary Christianity tends to mirror modern-day development discourse informed by Western neoliberalism that lays the emphasis of transformation on the individual rather than on the community. As I have argued elsewhere, "success in many socioeconomic projects framed in the language of development often places emphasis on the individual as does Christianity, which emphasizes salvation and prosperity through the individual" (2011:15). In a context of limited resources, it is very tempting for many Kenyan Christians to pursue the individualist route toward prosperity. As a Christian and hip hop artist, Juliani, however, is trying to move away from the lure of such individualized success by focusing on bringing along others on his own journey of success so as to "take care of" himself by taking care of others. Theologically, Juliani is providing an African cultural backdrop to contemporary Christianity in Kenya, embedding important principles of belonging that simultaneously challenge individualized modernity and embrace modern tools for advancing it. He is providing his own version of Ubuntu that suggests that one can be Christian and still commit to communal values of Ubuntu. The idea of simultaneously being Christian and African has long been the subject of many scholars (Mbiti 1980; Mugambi 1996; Sindima 1994) but has rarely been addressed by Kenyan gospel musicians. There are a number of reasons for why this subject is rarely addressed in local gospel music. One particular reason is the difficulty of pursuing the topic given the ongoing socioeconomic development framework in Kenya as well as Christianity's doctrine that focuses on the individual. This approach to socioeconomic development is not unique to Kenya; it is part of what we may consider methodological individualism that informs contemporary thoughts regarding individual behavior and motivation.

Since the publication in 1909 of Joseph Schumeter's article on the topic in the *Quarterly Journal of Economics* (G. M. Hodgson 2007), methodological individualism has long been the operating frame for many development projects that often seek to use techniques of microeconomics to measure individually focused behavior change in programs, such as HIV infections, voting patterns, and education attainments, among others. When it comes to Christianity, there is a similar emphasis on the individual—personal salvation and individual prosperity—with converts encouraged to primarily think of themselves instrumentally as individuals because each will account for his or her individual deeds or sins on "judgment day." Many contemporary preachers, especially those of the Charismatic guild in Kenya, emphasize this individual identity, often promising prosperity for the Christian with no articulated inclusion of the community. Emphasis on the needs of the individual saturates the messages of televangelists and street preachers, as well as preachers in many Kenyan churches. Quite often, such topics as getting a promotion at work, winning a green card to live in the United States, solving marital problems, being healthy, and recapturing one's virility are some of the main subjects of prayer and are promised by many of these preachers.

These types of prayers are not just limited to Kenyan Christians but have been prominent in cities like Accra, Ghana, where believers' attention is set on economic prosperity. Anthropologist Paul Gifford notes that this kind of Christianity is appealing because it finds continuity in traditional Ghanaian religious practices that place emphasis on material success and the transformation of personal destinies (2004). People pray for those things that are in their day-to-day realities and that often correspond with the many other problem-solving strategies available to them locally. This practicality or seeking of immediate solutions to social, economic, and political problems is prominent in other sectors of life in Kenya.

One need not go very far to find examples of such prayers of prosperity. I found myself in the midst of it when, in search of a new branch of Mavuno Church, I boarded a matatu on May 4, 2014, headed for the Mlolongo residential area off the Nairobi-Mombasa Road close to Athi River. The Mavuno Church had created quite a stir on local social media in February 2014 when it advertised a series of teen programs, using a number of provocative images, including a skimpily dressed female, and captions. I wanted to experience a Sunday service at the church to get a glimpse of its identity. Mavuno had relocated to Mlolongo from its initial location close to Bellevue on Mombasa Road. As I sat in the matatu waiting for it to fill up to go to Mlolongo, I saw a gentleman dressed in a light-brown suit walk around the vehicle and say something to the driver before boarding. I assumed he was saying hello to the driver and that the two knew each other. It was only after the matatu started moving that I realized the gentleman was a preacher. He moved to the front of the vehicle and introduced himself as Apostle Paul, greeted the passengers, and then started preaching. When he had earlier gone around to talk to the driver, he must have been asking for his permission to preach because as soon as Apostle Paul started talking, the driver turned off the music that had been playing.

I have in the past boarded matatus in Nairobi that often post signs warning against preaching or hawking, practices that are common at bus stops or even inside public service vehicles in many cities in Kenya. With high rates of unemployment, any chance to sell products or service is quickly utilized, and public service vehicles provide a potential customer base. It is difficult, however, to know whom to allow access to this captive audience of customers in a matatu or bus. Many of these vehicles prohibit any hawking. This might have been the reason that Apostle Paul sought the permission of the driver. I realized that the preaching provided for me a fieldwork moment. I pulled out my notebook and started jotting down key words that I thought would capture this ethnographic episode, with the plan to expand upon the notes once I settled in my room later. Apostle Paul preached from the book of Isaiah focusing on 65:23: "They will not labor in vain, nor will they bear children doomed to misfortune; for they will be a people blessed by the LORD, they and their descendants with them" (NIV). He kept repeat-

ing the same lines about prosperity and the promises that God had in store
for the people. After about three minutes, he asked the commuters to join
him in prayer before giving another short message from the same passage.
He prayed about three other times. I was so tempted to turn around and see
how many passengers had joined him in the prayer or who had closed their
eyes, but I thought it would be rude and decided against the idea. When he
preached, his voice started low and ended high, which I assumed was geared
toward producing certain emotional effects on the listeners. In all his prayers,
however, Apostle Paul repeated the same lines that focused on one's business
prospering, getting a visa to go abroad, getting the green card to go to the
United States, receiving healing from various ailments, saving broken marriages, and getting promoted at work.

After about fifteen minutes in the matatu, Apostle Paul took an offering
and alighted at a bus stop along Mombasa Road. It seemed like he had had
many similar preaching sessions in a moving vehicle before because he struck
me as quite comfortable and composed throughout the exercise. Just like the
televangelists and street preachers, Apostle Paul's prayers were addressing
specific areas of life common among many urban Kenyans who deal daily
with economic and political uncertainties. Undoubtedly, those prayers calm
anxieties by providing participants the possibility of changed circumstances
and a hope for the future (Gifford 2004) while also addressing key areas of
life that people really worry about. The focus on an immediately relevant
area of need also points to the belief in the efficacy of prayer.

Later, as I walked back to the Methodist Guesthouse from the city center,
I was drawn to numerous posters advertising services offered by traditional
healers. The posters were glued to lampposts and perimeter fences along
Valley Road in Nairobi. Two of the healers (the posters provided their names
as Sheikh Ismail and Dr. Wazanga) claimed to assist with businesses, love,
marital problems, finding work, and restoring virility. On each poster were
cell-phone numbers for interested clients to reach these healers. It got me
wondering how Christians in Nairobi and Kenya, generally, navigate this
world of the everyday where, for instance, the focus of a preacher (Apostle
Paul) and that of traditional healers (Sheikh Ismail and Dr. Wazanga) often converge. Were these two sets of individuals just representing the lived
realities of the people they interacted with daily, or were they reflecting a
conflation of the sacred and profane in this society?

If we take Mbiti's (1969) claims that Africans are notoriously religious
and that all spheres of life are interconnected, then it need not be surprising that both a Christian pastor and a "traditional" healer focus on the

same socioeconomic topics as their elements of prayer or healing or both. Both target an audience that not only lives in the same social and spiritual world but also sees the solutions as available to all irrespective of personal convictions or beliefs. Christianity's claims that Jesus is the (only) answer clearly compete with these alternative socioeconomic "remedies" offered by the likes of Sheikh Ismael and Dr. Wazanga. This competing reality raises the question of whether churches or prayers are one among many other market options available to Kenyan Christians seeking prosperity and spiritual assistance in everyday affairs. Anthropologist Martin Lindhardt notes similar relations in neighboring Tanzania between faith gospel (a type of gospel also known as Gospel of Prosperity) and occult economies, especially in open-air revival meetings, when the preachers "take great pains to present the power (nguvu) of Jesus as an alternative to medicines provides by healers" (2009:46). I am attracted to Lindhardt's consideration of medicines that healers provide as "alternatives" because he places them on the same plane as prayers, seeing them as options available to the people who are wrestling with their daily life's challenges. Being Christian in this case does not completely erase one's belief or reliance on traditional approaches to engaging with one's challenges. If anything, it is inevitable that practicing one's faith, not just Christianity, is mediated through one's sociocultural orientation. For these Kenyan Christians, as for their counterparts in Tanzania, Christian practices and beliefs are mobilized through local or African beliefs. Even pastors can embody both of these realities.

At a seminar on science and faith the International Association for the Promotion of Christian Higher Education (IAPCHE) hosted in Nairobi on May 10, 2014, Reverend Steven Nduto confirmed this simultaneous belief in Christianity and African traditions. Nduto, chaplain at Daystar University, shared part of his analysis from his study on Kamba pastors in eastern Kenya, who confirmed the belief in the power of the occult alongside that of Jesus. Nduto argued that many adherents to the Christian faith simultaneously held onto Christian and traditional African beliefs regarding death (2014). The reasons for these practices are many and complex, but one has to do with the anxiety caused by economic and social problems where these Christians live. Anything or anyone who promises hope and options for getting through these anxieties is taken seriously. Those offering these options, be they preachers or healers, can also be predatory as seen in the growth of wealth-and-health gospel around the world. Granted, it does take willing participants to make this predatory practice successful. Moreover, lack of economic options in a country with high levels of unemployment creates patronage and a culture of dependence. Whoever seems to provide some promise of a way out of these socioeconomic challenges is listened to keenly.

Young people are especially vulnerable to these practices of patronage and can be easily misused. However, not all the challenges facing youth or those in poor economic circumstances are always caused by external agents. Many of the challenges can also be attributed to one's actions or inaction. Sometimes those involved are unwilling to forgo quick returns. Other times they lack requisite practices that would help change their economic challenges. In a June 2014 newspaper article that I found out about following a tweet from Juliani, Moses Njenga argues that a bad work ethic is to blame for high youth unemployment in Kenya. He specifically ties the "sloth" and "deceit" he sees in many youth not just to the individual actors but to the socialization they have received: "Many young people grow up in churches which talk about favour, blessings, and 'possessing' the wealth of the wicked without putting as much emphasis on hard work and discipline. The young man who will not have heard from his local preacher will have heard a slightly different narrative from his politician; the reason you are not gainfully employed is because you voted in the wrong person" (2014). On June 25, 2014, Juliani commented on Twitter, "Moses Njenga *amelenga ndipo*" (Moses Njenga has hit the target). While youth are negatively affected by many forces outside of their powers, they, too, are responsible for some of their own predicament, as Njenga argues. Such practices are in no way unique to Kenya. In a 2012 International Labour Organization (ILO) report on youth employment in Africa, there are entries on poor work ethic among youth. In one case of Zambia, the report states, "In Zambia, even once youth are offered work, they may refuse to engage in certain technical or vocational businesses because they do not see value in them. Such attitudes have led many employers to mistrust young people and refuse to hire them" (2012:8).

It is one thing to see youth as victims of external forces, but these examples complicate the issue a little more, adding an alternative view that youth are also partly responsible for the challenges they face. Juliani's songs and interviews tend to point to this specific challenge of youth and their work ethic. In his song "One Day" from *Exponential Potential*, Juliani talks about those youth who do not make much effort to work hard but instead spend their time in nonproductive activities and then are surprised that they are not successful:

Mi si pessimist but sioni ukimake it
Unashinda manaija movies, soaps
Halafu unaact surprised hauko Kwa list ya forbes

I am not a pessimist, but you won't make it.
All you do is watch Nigerian movies, soaps.
Then you act surprised you are not on Forbes list.

Nigerian movies have a large following in Kenya and have had some cultural influences for many who view them. Comedians, musicians, and even pastors, for instance, often use Nigerian English accents in their own presentations. Comedians MC Jesse and Eric Omondi, who appear on the *Churchill Show* in Nairobi, have often carved their jokes around Nigerian men or women, complete with their accents. "Igwe," a gospel song by Alphy, Jacky B, and Imani Odero, is performed in a Nigerian popular melody and has the musicians using Nigerian Pidgin English.[2] Kenya's Citizen Television during its show *Afrosinema* runs many Nigerian movies from 9:00 to 11:50 A.M., Monday through Friday (Citizen TV). Juliani is making reference to these movies and soaps that are very popular in Kenya and other African countries.

Placing emphasis on the need for youth to be reflexive, look deep inside themselves, and ask about their habits and practices toward work, toward new projects, and toward developing their skills and talents, Juliani is striking a balance between agency and determinism or fatalism. Believing that it takes more than someone having talent and being available in order to succeed, Juliani emphasizes that many youth need to take time to hone their craft, be it in music or any other form, and to continually seek solutions from the local context rather than waiting for someone from the outside to provide assistance. But he does not stop there; he provides an example of his own financial challenges, which in most cases might lead into self-absorption and a neglect or disinvestment in others. As his star was rising, especially in 2011, when he produced his second album, Juliani received many endorsements accompanied with high financial gains. Soon, however, the money stopped coming in, but he continued to pursue the programs that today make him part of a larger network of young people working toward realizing their dreams. In the same song, "One Day," he shares the realities of those ups and downs that he had:

> Ten million 2011 zero ka gurudumu za trailer
> No million 2012 zero ka gurudumu za pick up
> Difference, people before profit all ideas, all tours, all initiatives
> I contribute beyond the booth 21 gun salute
> Machozi nilifreeze kwa fridge nikahang kwa shingo kama bling
> Victory through misery

Ten million in 2011 zeroes like trailer tires,
No millions in 2012 zeroes like pickup truck tires,
Difference, people before profit all ideas, all tours, all initiatives,
I contribute beyond the booth 21-gun salute.
I froze my tears in the fridge and hang them on my neck like bling
　　bling.
Victory through misery.

In a video that provides some explanations about this song, which appeared a few weeks before the May 2014 album release, Juliani says that he talked a lot about himself in the song and the experiences he has gone through since 2004. He says that many people may not know that in 2011 he made good money through endorsements, but in 2012 he did not have the same deals and did not make money. Despite this "drought," however, he financed the projects he had already initiated besides buying himself a Mercedes Benz so as *kujituliza roho* (to comfort my heart) (2014a). He did all these projects despite there being no new money because as he says in the song, he decided to put "people before profit." The ideas, tours, and initiatives that he mounted include a Music Summit that took him around the country, where he worked with new musicians and assisted them in composing and recording songs, featured on his YouTube channel. Later, he helped publicize this new music through the Kama Si Sisi program, university campus tours, and other opportunities through which he sought to motivate youth to believe in their own abilities to make a difference in their lives and the lives of others.

Believing that Kenyan youth have what it takes to be successful, Juliani continues to share his resources with youth as captured in his Kama Si Sisi campaign that states, "*Kutabadilishwa na Nani Ka Si Sisi?*" (Who will change things if not us?). I consider this approach used in Kama Si Sisi as a motivation for self-advancement, a focus on resources already available in one's immediate context, without reducing it to the popular psychology of self-help that dominates many books available on bookstore shelves in Nairobi. I say this without denying the need to provide youth with a framework for introspection, to search deeply into their attitudes, assumptions, and practices, and to establish how they negatively or positively shape their lives. Kama Si Sisi seeks to strike a balance, providing a gospel of self-empowerment without losing the reality of the role of the communal/external. For youth to succeed, Juliani argues, they have to be informed about their challenges and possible solutions, be creative and organized in responding to the challenges, and then come together as a team in order to provide relevant solutions (2014b).

Many youth are already putting this philosophy to action. They are engaged in changing their lives and are providing leadership in their communities every day. This involvement of youth in shaping their lives as well as lives of their communities has, however, not been fully acknowledged as often captured in the phrase "leaders of tomorrow." Through his programs with other youth, Juliani is challenging this futuristic view of youth participation in developing their communities.

VIONGOZI WA KESHO:
YOUTH CHANGING THE NARRATIVE OF PLACE

It has almost become a given that youth in Kenya are considered leaders in waiting. The common phrase used when public pronouncements are made about youth is "*viongozi wa kesho*" (tomorrow's leaders). With increased numbers of youth in public spaces, along with interest and abilities in new media and technology, however, this perception is changing to "*viongozi wa leo*" (today's leaders) (Ban 2014). UN Secretary General Ban Ki-Moon, in a speech in New York to youth, confirmed this: "People usually say young people are leaders of tomorrow but I have a different view. I know that young people are also leaders of today, already" (2014). The prominent role played by youth as today's leaders is already visible in Kenya's neighbor Tanzania, where, as ethnomusicologist Alex Perullo notes, youth have influential positions in their communities: "In the music economy, youth are prominent in radio and television, working as announcers, deejays, technicians, managers and, in a few cases, owners" (2011:32). The same scenario is observable in Kenya, where youth dominate many FM radio stations, television stations, and newspapers.

With increased use of technology as well as the emergence of social media as a major part of everyday communication, especially in urban areas, Kenyan youth have found important sources of livelihood and social engagement. Juliani's slogan of "Kama Si Sisi ni Nani?" confirms that youth have a big part to play in all aspects of life in Kenya today. They do not have to wait until tomorrow to show leadership, they are leading today. In his song "Kama Si Sisi" from *Mtaa Mentality*, Juliani says:

> *Zitaendeshwa na nani ka si sisi?*
> *Zitanunuliwa na nani ka si sisi?*
> *Kutabadilishwa na nani ka si sisi?*
> *Simaanishi mwingine ni wewe na wewe na mi*

Who'll drive them if not us?
Who'll buy them if not us?
Who'll change things if not us?
I mean none other than you and I.

Juliani is playing a key role in shaping the future of his community and the belief that youth in Kenya possess what it takes to make an immediate differ-ence in their own lives as well as the lives of others runs through much of his music. Mtaa Challenge programs have already started to provide a different narrative not only about youth agency but also place. Youth are providing new ways of describing such places as Kibera, often considered "the largest slum in Africa" (Yates 2011). Writing about its history as a settlement for Sudanese soldiers, Timothy Parsons starts his essay by stating that Kibera "is a place of over-crowded, substandard housing with unreliable water, poor sanitation and minimal social services" (1997:87). This narrative is the most dominant one re-garding Kibera, drawing US celebrities and European tourists alike who them-selves reemphasize the prevalent narrative.[3] The focus in these descriptions is what Kibera lacks and what is wrong with its infrastructure and facilities, rather than its potential, assets, and resources. In the first Mtaa Challenge competition, however, some youth from Kibera, calling their team Chocolate City, provided a different narrative in their entry video for the 2013 Mtaa Challenge competi-tions. In the video narrative, they give background information about Kibera and why they feel qualified to compete for the prizes in the competition. They begin their video by describing Kibera: "This is my mtaa. We have the largest population per square kilometer in Africa: this is our greatest asset. It provides a large market for business by encouraging competition and innovation. It is also a ready source for labor. Kibrans are the most creative and entrepreneur-ial. Several youth are engaged in income-generating projects, ranging from agriculture, construction and art" (Juliani Music 2013a). On reading this nar-rative, one may immediately notice that while the same language may have been used in describing the population density in the space known as Kibera, these young people go beyond it and project a different kind of meaning to that demographic. Rather than see their large population as a problem, they see it as something positive, as a readily available source of labor and market. Such a narrative aligns well with the dominant philosophy running through Juliani's work, which instead of seeing youth and their diverse circumstances as a "social problem" considers them as assets and agents of their own success.

Seeing communities and individuals through an assets-based instead of a needs-based or problems framework is now a well-developed philosophy guiding programs and some policies in such service-oriented disciplines as nursing, social work, and international development. A whole approach known as "strengths approach" emerged based on such a framework (Saleebey 2005). Other terms or phrases used to capture a similar approach include a "capabilities approach" (Sen 1985) and "resource-based approach" (Wernerfelt 1984). Making a shift from a needs-based or problems-based approach to communities, especially youth, also moves the narrative away from one of "leaders-in-waiting" to one I would call "leaders-in-action." Youth like Juliani are already making a difference in their communities.

Jody Kretzmann and John McKnight from Northwestern University in the United States are credited with providing the impetus for another approach, the asset-based community development (ABCD) approach that counters the predominant needs-based community-development approach that still dominates much of development work in countries like Kenya. Many times a needs-based approach emphasizes what communities are lacking and is often an approach mobilized by outsiders who are quick to field needs-assessment surveys or questionnaires from which they highlight problems and then propose interventions. Unfortunately, most of those interventions are external to the community and tend to require outsiders to be implemented because the local people's existing knowledge or skills or both are overlooked. An alternative approach, reflected in the Chocolate City video, is to start by asking what strengths and assets the community has and how they can be mobilized to respond to whatever identified challenges exist. Convinced that all communities have had successes in their own lives, Kretzmann and Knight (1993) note that the first place to start is to mobilize communities to tell their stories of success and then find a committed group to carry forward strategies for engaging those successes into new projects. I argue that Mtaa Challenge programs engage this approach in making youth the center of the positive changes they seek to bring about in their own mtaa. The programs rightly assume that youth possess critical knowledge and other resources necessary to positively influence their lives. This approach explains Juliani's philosophy presented as a question—Kama Si Sisi Nani (If not us who)?

Even Christians have specifically been implored to see the importance of this asset-based approach to their lives as well as in the communities they work with or in which they live. Steve Corbett and Brian Fikkert argue that Christian volunteers and development workers should not "do things for people that they can do for themselves" (2009:115). Their book starts with a contrast between the vast wealth many North Americans possess and the scarcity of resources among the majority of the world's population. The authors even cite the challenge posed by Bible passages, such as the one found in 1 John 3:17 that tells Christians they would be lacking in God's love if they do not show pity on those in need (2009:14).

Material assistance emanating from the reality of disparities in material possessions between North American Christians and their counterparts in many countries in Africa have, for instance, led to solutions that are inadequate for the long term. With over four thousand nongovernmental organizations (NGOs) in Kenya, many deriving full or partial funding from external sources, there are many opportunities for entrenching this needs-based approach (Amutabi 2006). Many Christian organizations support projects, such as orphanages, water-well drilling, fighting HIV and AIDS, and providing elementary education, just to name a few. It is not unusual for many North American youth to spend part or all of their summertime volunteering in these projects in Kenya through short-term missions. Such volunteer work is often not aligned with or informed by local realities, capacities, or priorities. David Livermore captures this disconnect between short-term mission volunteers and local projects when he encourages short-term mission groups to go to these locations with their "eyes wide open" by engaging what he calls "cultural intelligence" (2006). It is in this vein of seeking better-informed community service that Corbett and Fikkert urge Christians working with communities in resource-poor contexts to "identify and mobilize the capabilities, skills, and resources of the individual or community. See poor people and communities as full of possibilities, given to them by God. . . . Only bring in outside resources when local resources are insufficient to solve pressing needs" (2009:128).

Moving from a needs-based to an asset-based approach when enhancing a community or individual, as I argue here, has been promoted and supported by Juliani through Kama Si Sisi projects. Not all youth, however, project such a philosophy when confronting the challenges facing their neighborhoods. In a 2013 story on youth in Nairobi's Baba Dogo slum, reporter Ryan Delaney in a story for *Innovation Trail* highlights a project by youth that use GPS technology to locate trash accumulating in the slum and then plotting it on a digital map. The youth wanted to find a way of using handheld devices to scout their community to locate trash because no local government operations assist in hauling trash away. In commenting on the trash problem in the community, Justice Muhando, one of the youth involved in the project, commented, "What I think we should do is show it to the responsible authorities. They're the one that should follow up because the person on the ground is just a resident; they can't do much" (Delaney 2013). Muhando captures here a sense of helplessness that Juliani is encouraging youth in Kenya to change as he promotes a philosophy of seeing themselves as agents of their own socioeconomic progress, rather than always waiting for external assistance. They are not "just residents" who "can't do much," but, as Juliani emphasizes through his songs and programs, they are individuals with "exponential potential." Juliani has used this phrase in a song in *Pulpit Kwa Street* and in the title of his third album released in 2014. With "exponential potential," Juliani wishes to capture the prosperous and good life Christians have today and ahead of them, similar to that in the story of human life before Adam and Eve committed the "original sin." This prosperous life, however, does not come automatically just because one is a Christian. Instead, one has to work at it and all the time seek to be self-reliant. For youth to be successful, Juliani expects them to shift their thinking from what they lack to what they possess. When a participant at a March 20, 2014, Google+ Hangout asked Juliani how someone with good ideas could contact him for advice, Juliani said that young people "should stop looking for funding" and instead "look deep inside" of themselves for solutions and connect with like-minded individuals (Juliani 2014a).

It is tempting to consider individuals asking for assistance as lazy and always waiting for others to give them opportunities while they themselves wait on the side doing nothing. I argue that there are structural explanations for such a practice, even though it is limited to a few. Kenya, like many other societies in Africa, operates a socioeconomic system primarily dominated by patronage (Arriola 2009; Haugerud 1997). Given the limited resources available to a large portion of the population, any economic opportunities available through the state are seen as avenues for advancing self and kin or one's ethnic community. Political leadership has consistently been a contested and often dangerous undertaking because of the access that politicians and senior government officials have to national resources that are subsequently distributed through clientele and ethnically driven structures (Mueller 2008). Max Weber's impersonal and impartial goal-oriented bureaucracy or public service has not yet developed in much of Kenya's public sector. If anything, it is quite unclear whether there exists the expected separation between private (personal) and public spheres in socioeconomic and political practices promoted by Weber's concept of bureaucracy. For the most part, personalized relationships and ethnic favoritism pervade Kenya's public service.

Many Kenyan youth know no other structures to follow to be successful apart from those discussed here. Juliani recognizes this reality even as he chastises youth for not working to use their potential and expand their resourcefulness. Understanding that Kenyan youth are deeply embedded into the ethnically based patronage structures they live in, Juliani says that youth know no other avenues for success other than through tribalism. When asked how he would educate Kenyan youth against tribalism, he offers this observation: "You cannot educate them because they learned it from their parents and saw that is how things work. If that is the only thing they saw working, why should they think otherwise? They saw things work through tribal lines, so why expect them to think otherwise?" (Juliani 2014a). As a young nation-state, Kenya continues to struggle with the pervasiveness of tribalism that seems to shape most political groups, especially when it comes to general elections. Ethnic identity, and the ways such an identity pervades in almost all public and even private affairs of Kenyans, leads Juliani to almost see them as so inevitable that only God can assess a person by his or her merit and not his or her "tribe." In "MH370" from *Exponential Potential*, Juliani says:

> *Nilituma application letter ukiangalia grammar sitapita*
> *Uzuri unaangalia deeper than kabila, than my past*

> I sent an application letter if you considered grammar I will fail,
> but you look deeper than tribe, than my past.

Juliani is suggesting here that when he sends an application letter (probably for a job), he does not expect to get any favor because people, unlike God, look at one's tribe and one's past. Such a sentiment does not necessary make Juliani fatalistic. He is cognizant that one can make things happen, that individuals have agency, and that one does not always have to expect that only God will make things happen. However, Juliani does also understand that one can be sitting on opportunities without exploiting them. Sometimes the youth themselves are not taking the effort to change their circumstances as he shows in "Kama Si Sisi":

> *Ni ka wanapiga picha ya ID hawasmile, ni kubaya ai*
> *Wanacheza bano na macadamia nuts halafu wanalia njaa, ignorance*

> It's like they are taking ID photos they do not smile, things are bad.
> They play with macadamia nuts and then complain of hunger, that is
>   ignorance.

Bano, in the second line, a Sheng word for "marbles," is a game children and youth in Kenya play with marbles or other round material, including macadamia nuts. Two or more players take turns trying to flick their marbles into a hole; the player with the most bano in the hole wins the game ("Games" 2013).[4] Because they are round, smooth, and weighted, macadamia nuts, a good source of income for farmers, are often used whenever marbles are unavailable. This is why Juliani says that while youth complain about lack of resources, they are ignorant because they are playing with macadamia nuts instead of translating them into money. He goes on to say in "Kama Si Sisi" that he has been advised by many on how to live his life:

> *Nywele yako si refu ya ponytail "Suka matuta tu," waliniambia*
> *Nikawajibu, sisettle for less man nadunk kwa rims ya success*
> *Nipite hata bila height ya Scottie Pippen*
> *Nina mentality ya Rosa Parks kwa bus kwa kiti sitoki*

> Your hair isn't long for a ponytail "Braid it instead," they told me.
> I told them I don't settle for less I am dunking in the rims of success
> Even without Scottie Pippen's height.
> I have Rosa Parks's mentality I am not getting off the bus seat.

As youth play with wealth as symbolized by macadamia nuts, Juliani is interested in struggling and making it against all odds. He has a way of working with words and referents that give his songs deep and multiple meanings. Because this song was produced in 2009 when his dreadlocks had not grown long enough to be held in a ponytail, these songs texts are about him as much as they are about others. He, however, goes beyond talking about himself and goes on to turn that observation into an opportunity to talk about his approach to life. He talks about refusing to listen to negative comments and instead moving into "bigger" things similar to dunking in the basketball rim of success despite not having the height of famed Chicago Bulls basketball player Scottie Pippen. Juliani is about 5 feet, 5 inches tall, so he could not easily dunk a basketball, which explains his statement about Pippen's height. But he is determined and stubborn in whatever he puts his mind to, similar to African American civil rights activist Rosa Parks, who refused to move to the back of the bus as instructed by the bus driver and as was the law of the day in her time. Such is the attitude youth can adopt in order to rightfully claim their place as today's leaders. They do not have to blame their circumstances for other challenges but, rather, use them to change their lived experiences. In the same way that a short Juliani can "successfully" play at the same level as a tall basketball player, youth in Kenya can focus on what they can do rather than what they lack. I now turn to the world of social media and how it shapes Christian identities in Kenya with an exploration into how even urban churches, such as Mavuno in Nairobi, are tapping into such media to engage youth on matters of faith and lived sociocultural issues.

5

MEDIA AND CONTESTED CHRISTIAN IDENTITIES

Facebook, Instagram, WhatsApp, Twitter, and Google+ are just a few of the manifestations of social media's infiltration of the Kenyan society as mobilized (mostly) through mobile phones. Consumers are able to pay their utility bills from their mobile phones just as parents are able to pay their children's schools fees via a mobile application, congregations as they sit in some churches tweet short sermon messages to their friends, and television viewers can follow and comment on a live interview via Facebook. This new sociality has many implications for how Christians experience and express their religiosity. This is the twenty-first century, a century that has seen scholarly narratives as well as commercial narratives defining our world in terms of information. A popular phrase at the turn of the century was the information superhighway. This phrase was chosen to represent the high-speed information sharing and access that were going to revolutionize socioeconomic life propelled by the internet. Information was expected, especially in Bill Clinton's presidency of the 1990s, to level the playing field for education regardless of the social status of the learner (Brooks and Boal 1995). This prediction was not to be, despite the expanded access to the internet that has been witnessed in countries like Kenya today. What is undeniable, however, is the important role mass media has played in shaping the lives of many Kenyans, especially their ideas about politics, purchasing, and international affairs, as well as the public definitions of social problems. For the most part, media can and does shape people's sense of reality.

French sociologist and cultural theorist Jean Baudrillard's analyses of modes of mediation and representation of reality through technology mostly conclude that there is a very fine line between reality and its representations. Baudrillard provocatively states that in the world we live in today there is no such thing as reality because people's consciousness cannot really differentiate reality from its simulation. He specifically develops this line of thinking in his work on simulacra and simulation, wherein he argues that human experience is a simulation of reality because humans have replaced reality with symbols and signs (1983). Social media today, including Facebook, Twitter, Instagram, and Tumblr, can be considered the new forms of this kind of representation of reality. Twitter, for instance, has emerged as one form of media that represents the "real" picture or news of what is really going on in a specific place at a specific time. In 2011's Arab Spring, the Egyptian government was determined to censor or block all news coming out of the country. Twitter and YouTube messages or images shared by Egyptians with smartphones became the representation of what reality was like on the ground.

Youth in Kenya particularly are very much part of the "real" world created through Twitter and Facebook. During a widely popularized July 7, 2014, rally, the opposition political parties called at Nairobi's Uhuru Park, Twitter became an important site for seeking out and sharing news of the event following a media blackout that did not cover the live proceedings as had been the tradition for past events. Besides providing such a forum for news and information sharing in Kenya, these social-media outlets also allow youth to create their own personas and identities very much apart from who they are physically. Individuals are able to exist in two "worlds" but are sometimes unable to separate them or at other times able to keep them informing each other. One can, for instance, live in the world of Facebook and Twitter where one can construct an identity of whoever one wants to be while inhabiting a physical world that limits flexibility and resources to construct self into whoever one chooses to be. Despite this apparent tension or disconnect between the real and the constructed worlds of youth, the social-media world does provide an important platform for developing one's identity that can be useful in the physical world. One of the reasons Baudrillard provided to account for this simulation of reality is directly related to television and new media. Both often blur the line between the products needed to live one's everyday life and the "needs" that are created by the commercial images that they carry (Felluga 2011). Distances between people and nations seem to be decreased by media, through its reports and features of the lives and events of people living in faraway places. Such reports and features often create intimate stories that draw in viewers to often relate with the characters or storylines highlighted.

As William Gamson et al. argue regarding the power of media to shape perceptions of reality: "We walk around with media-generated images of the world, using them to construct meaning about political and social issues. The lens through which we receive these images is not neutral but evinces the power and point of view of the political and economic elites who operate and focus it" (1992:373). We cannot, however, assume homogeneity of those who "consume" media but, rather, note that each image, message, or code projected by media is received and decoded based on one's past experience, social identity, and spatial and temporal context. Moreover, within social media, messages and news are received within an active back-and-forth community comprised of other participants. Such interactive and communal reception of media products makes its place and analysis very attractive to me. Following Juliani's social-media presence as well as analyzing constructions of his identity and meanings of his music through media interviews has helped in understanding the implications of social media to ethnography. When a church in Nairobi, for instance, chooses to engage its present and prospective congregants through social media, then the analysis becomes all the more intriguing. Religious experience for the most part is seen as compatible with a physical church because of the element of sociality, providing a community or social life beyond one's immediate family. But social media can also connect individuals to a church virtually through recorded sermons, online Bible studies, podcasts, tweeted prayer requests, and so on. Some churches in Kenya have taken advantage of this media opportunity to reach out to congregants and draw others to the physical church. It is to the place of social media and other contemporary forms of communication and how they relate to Christian identity that I now turn.

Of all life stages that humans go through, youthhood seems to be the one stage in which there is so much desire and even pressure to construct and even reconstruct one's identity. For many Kenyan youth, such construction and reconstruction is predicated on a long history of not only self-definition in reference to external stimulus shaped by Western education and modernity but also heightened by a growing sense of connection to a world outside of their own in the twenty-first century. With growing numbers of youth who possess more formal education than previous generations, partly due to expansion of secondary and tertiary education in Kenya, images of what life is and could be have greatly been amplified. Add to this educational background the availability of mass media that projects the real and imagined local and international lifestyles and there emerges a whole world of images and projections of reality that youth simultaneously consume and construct.

Kenyan youth living in urban areas where access to this new media is prevalent predominantly espouse this sense of self-definition as they often follow trends that have been set by youth in other locations, especially urban African Americans. Sagging pants and braided hair are a few examples of the trends popularized by African American youth that have now come to dominate Kenyan youth and their sense of fashion. Other styles embodied by many Kenyan youth, especially artists, include wearing earrings and wearing hair in braids or dreadlocks. In a country where gender identity is expected to be clearly marked in public, braided hair and earrings for men present major cultural challenges. In 2011 Gidion Mbuvi, member of parliament for Makadara constituency in Nairobi, who is also popularly known as Mike Sonko (Sonko is Sheng for "rich"), was ejected from parliament for wearing earrings and bling bling. Sonko's popularity among his constituents was evident when he went on to win a Nairobi senate seat in 2013, beating popular evangelical leader Bishop Margaret Wanjiru, who had until then been the member of parliament for Starehe constituency in Nairobi.

Kenya's Chief Justice Willy Mutunga's appointment to that prestigious position was also marred by controversy regarding his practice of wearing an earring, which he attributes to his traditional spiritual identity. Those opposed to such grooming argued for clear masculine and feminine identities, suggesting that a man wearing an earring signaled some feminized identity. And, yet, these are the rich cultural expressions that Kenyan youth have generally adopted from different cultural sources, which are not always embraced locally. For the youth, however, such opposition to "foreign" influences does not deter their continued creativity and cultural "boundary crossing."

Anthropologist Jesse W. Shipley notes that many urban African youth's perceptions of life have been greatly shaped by their access to images and commodities often mediated through new media as well as "the intermingling of African and African Diasporic popular aesthetics" (2009:631). Noting the way that youth take this media into their lived experiences, Shipley says: "Popular social styles provide creative ways for youth to imagine themselves as part of a broader Black cosmopolitan world. Local variants of hip hop from Morocco to South Africa, Kenya to Senegal play an unexpectedly central role in how the rising generation—as both artists and audiences—engage national politics, morality, and economics in the language of African Diasporic bodily expression" (209:631). Drawing their images from hip hop and film as well as projecting some kind of urban cultural sophistication helps shape the youth's aspirations for these identities. Mass media helps in availing multiple images of music and sports stars whose public presentations of self are both envied and emulated. Popular music artists are often part of the local celebrity scene, with their dress and personal grooming being subjected to all manner of scrutiny and spotlighting by radio and televisions shows as well as popular magazines.

Given such public attention and scrutiny on their lives, especially the emphasis on glamor and success, many of these artists strive to present an image of success. They get caught up in the life of "swag," doing things so that others can see how successful they are even when such success is often a façade. This "performed" identity is very much prevalent in Kenya and has been noted by artists like Juliani. In his song "Church on Monday" from *Mtaa Mentality*, Juliani captures this performed lifestyle of success even when one cannot afford it:

> *Siagree juu wee unatoka D wee ni mneedy*
> *Hiyo ni excuse, mjinga anadrive Hummer na amerent SQ*
> *So nahustle sikeep talking*
> *Hii race ya mzee kobe na Kipchoge Keino*
> *God shock absorber kwa pothole za shida*
> *Me simind nitashinda*

> I don't agree that because you are from Dandora you are needy (poor).
> That is an excuse, the fool is driving a Hummer and rents a servant's
>   quarter.
> So I am hustling I will not just talk.
> This is a race for the tortoise against Kipchoge Keino.
> God is a shock absorber for potholes brought by problems.
> I don't mind I will be triumphant.

Juliani combines two identities here—one of a person located in a poor neighborhood who uses that residency as a reason to perceive and even project him- or herself as poor and needy and another poor person who perceives or projects him- or herself as rich. Someone who drives a Hummer and rents a servant's quarter for a residence represents the latter. Many homes in Nairobi include what is locally termed a servant quarter (SQ), which ideally is a separate living space from the main house for household help. A remnant from Kenya's colonial past, this practice continues to date, but instead of being used by the household help, this space is often converted into a tenant space for a single person. Such space provides extra income for the homeowner and, for the tenant, an affordable space within an otherwise expensive residential area. In this case, however, Juliani shows that the person living in this kind of space also drives an expensive vehicle, a Hummer, which does not align with the socioeconomic level of the residential space. A person driving such an expensive vehicle is expected to be living in the main house, not in the servant quarter.

Juliani provides his own example, saying that he is hustling instead of talking and as such hinting at the difference between him and that one with misplaced priorities. By saying he is not just talking about his hustling but actually doing it, he is trying to move away from the "swag" mentality of showing off when one does not really "own" the symbols of success that are being flaunted. He then compares success with a race that is between a tortoise and Kenya's renowned long-distance runner Kipchoge Keino, who shows that the race requires perseverance despite the obstacles, even when pitted against some of the best runners. Juliani shares a similar message in "I Do It" from *Exponential Potential*, where he says in the refrain, "*Sio tu kutweet I do it*" (I don't just tweet I do it), and adds "*Vita si ya*" (War is not for) the strongest but the willing, suggesting again not only the value of steadfastness and endurance but also taking action rather than just talking about it.

This approach to success suggested by Juliani here aligns with what is often termed "patient capital," whereby an investor forgoes a quick return on investment for a larger gain much later. In today's fast-paced life, such an approach is not the norm. Many, especially youth, want a life of immediate results. For those in tough socioeconomic conditions, this immediacy of results is all the more important. Another issue that sheds light on the phenomenon Juliani addresses here is that one is unable to tell the difference between those who have and those who have not "made it" by just looking at their physical attributes. Juliani attributes this to technology and fashion, saying in the same song:

> *Fashion na technology Nairobi inafanya watu wakae likewise*
> *Difference ni bank account inasema otherwise*

> Fashion and technology in Nairobi are making people look similar.
> Difference is in bank accounts that says otherwise.

One can see a person on the streets of Nairobi and not really tell his or her social class on the basis of what he or she is wearing, which makes Juliani say they look "likewise." This external (public) identity, represented by the clothes (fashion) and technology one has access to, is different from internal (private) identity, represented by a bank account, which denotes one's true worth.

It is the interactions that occur between, on the one hand, these external identities and ideas created through new media platforms and, on the other, fashion and technology that provide youth with the most creative strategies for cultivating a presence in their physical locations. For most youth living in challenging socioeconomic circumstances and yet able to access communication products, such as cell phones and the internet, this presents a conundrum. How do they inhabit both worlds? Some end up developing practices of visibility and invisibility or display and disguise, driving a Hummer while renting residential space in a servant's quarter to project a larger-than-life image. While some are afraid of what such display of material prosperity could mean to their identities and "survival" in the community, others try to construct images of self that reflect modernity while trying to not to reveal too much and attract envy from their peers who lack such material products (Archambault 2013).

Many Kenyan youth get access to the internet and such social-media platforms as Twitter and Facebook through their cell phones. Some service providers, such as Safaricom (the largest cell-phone company in Kenya), offer Facebook as part of their already installed applications for subscribers. Moreover, since 2010 Safaricom has provided all its subscribers a service that allows them to send and receive email and chat messages without the need to have internet access.[1] Through mobile phone–based access to these kinds of platforms, Kenyan youth are able to virtually enter the wider world beyond their immediate environs, see life or constructions of it in other locations, imagine how it relates or contrasts or both with their own lives, and engage with it either by making meaning of their own lives or constructing it as they choose.

Sometimes when constructing their identities online, these young Kenyans pose as anonymous characters or as celebrities with no particular reference to their actual identities. Such constructed identities allow them to post comments on online newspaper articles without being immediately identifiable. Virtual life can, therefore, offer them a sense of confidence or what John Suler (2004) calls the "online disinhibition effect," which leads some participants to post negative and inflammatory messages. This latter practice, often referred to as "trolling" (Zhou 2010), has become so common in Kenya that it has been deemed dangerous for national cohesion. In July 2014 the Kenya government, using the hashtag #StopHateSpeechKe, launched a social-media campaign through Twitter to stop hate speech. Such a move by the government is best understood within the context of past experiences where the media was (mis)used to fan ethnic chauvinism that stimulated and exacerbated the violence that followed the 2007–8 elections. While the government is well aware of the power of media, one can only wonder how a Twitter message can deter social action.

Media does also offer youth multiple opportunities to construct images of themselves based on aspirations of what they would like to become or to construct larger-than-life images, a kind of imagined self-identity. It is this kind of multiple-identity formation that Julie Archambault's work on cell-phone use among Mozambican youth highlights. Archambault says that the balance of disguise and display that youth create through cell phones occurs "in a context of uncertainty and growing disparity, where everyday life involves seeking a balance between displaying enough without revealing too much, between accessing social status and deflecting envy, and between having a good time and preserving respectability, while embellishing reality, often through concealment" (2013:88). As social-status symbols as well as communication tools, cell phones in the hands of youth often produce numerous uses and meanings. First, a cell phone is a tool for the exchange of information, and, second, it is a tool that produces social meaning. Having it allows others to assume certain qualities about the person. These experiences of youth in Mozambique are very much similar to those of youth in Kenya and in other African countries where cell phones have completely taken over the place of fixed telephone lines.

One the one hand, cell phones have allowed access to a wider world previously unavailable to many youth, especially those from the kind of mitaa in which Juliani grew up. On the other hand, cell phones have greatly improved communication across different parts of Kenya, something that was difficult to achieve during the era of the monopoly of the fixed phone line. My own experiences of telephone access and use in Nairobi between the mid-1980s and early 2000s are full of memories of disappointment and frustration, trying to apply for and getting access to fixed-line telephones from the then Kenya Postal and Telecommunications Company. One would wait up to six months before getting a new line installed and even longer for an existing line to be repaired. The irony was that we often would see employees of the telecommunications company working at the various installation and distribution points in our residential areas but without much change in the operations of the telephone systems. Corruption and inefficiency were rampant.

When cell phones made their entry into the local scene in the 1990s and became relatively affordable thereafter, many people made the shift from no phone to cell phone. In 1979 there were 70,000 direct-exchange lines (land or fixed lines that allow for direct dialing as opposed to operator-assisted dialing) compared to 207,000 in 1992 (Tyler et.al 1999). Those with fixed-line phones held onto them long enough for clients, friends, and family to know the new cell-phone numbers they had acquired and then minimized their use of fixed lines altogether. Cell phones quickly filled in a void that had been created by an inefficient telecommunications company and in turn produced a new kind of social interaction that had previously been slow, rare, or completely absent.

Today, cell-phone access and use are so widespread in the country that it is hard to imagine life without a cell phone. Besides communications between individuals, cell phones are used to pay utility bills, check national-examination results, track prices of products in the market, and send and receive money. In 2014 cell-phone penetration in Kenya was at 82 percent, translating into 31.3 million people in a country of 41.3 million inhabitants (Pew Research Center 2015b). Kenya has also been a leader in cell-phone innovations with the most widely recognized of these innovations being the money-transfer platform known as M-Pesa and the crowd-sourcing platform known as Ushahidi. Started in 2007 by Safaricom, M-Pesa is a cell phone–based money transfer and microfinancing service that allows customers to send money across the network as well as pay bills. Later, the service was expanded to savings that allow customers to save money and get loans in a program known as M-Shwari ("M" for mobile and "Shwari," Swahili for "calm").

Other cell-phone companies in Kenya launched their own money-transfer programs, including Orange Money owned by Orange Kenya, Zap owned by Airtel, and YuCash owned by Yu Mobile. Organizations, various arms of the government, and corporations, as well as individuals also use cell-phone text messaging to promote causes, solicit public opinion on various issues and topics, or advertise new products. In September 2011 Juliani teamed up with Emmanuel Jal (South Sudanese former child soldier, political activist, and musician) and Boniface Mwangi (Kenyan photojournalist and social and political activist) to launch a text line through which Kenyans could pledge their support for peace in preparation for the 2012 general elections. The launch was also symbolic because it took place at Mau Mau Camp in Dandora, where Juliani cut his hip hop teeth. About the choice of the venue to launch the project, Juliani said: "We had to do something in my music home by giving it a reason. The reason we are in the Mau Mau Camp where everything happened, where hip hop was born and where I was nurtured as an artiste is to show Kenya and the world at large the passion that has sparked this campaign. We want to send a message to everyone to be better than they are now by affirming as the Kenyan youth that Kenya ni yetu (Kenya is ours), we are not going anywhere" (Kerongo 2011). Since each text message cost 20.00 Kenyan shillings (about US$.20), participants had to be invested in the project to participate. This widespread use of technology, especially the cell phone and internet, is what contributes to the visibility of youth in Kenya. But it also marks a kind of expansion of the social and even economic space available to youth in the country.

Juliani has also been very active in using social media for various goals, including selling his music, drawing crowds to his concerts, and providing commentary on socioeconomic and political matters. In a January 24, 2013, conversation with him in Nairobi, I asked about his strategies for selling recorded music instead of relying on live shows that many Kenyan musicians use to make money. He said that he would like a strategy that made music available to his fans in the same way they had access to cell-phone airtime. He was thinking of widespread availability and affordability of his music, including certain mechanisms that would make it easy to purchase local music the way many purchase airtime around the country, by just walking to a local shop or kiosk.

True to his thinking when he launched his *Exponential Potential* album in June 2014, he used Orange Money shops countrywide to disseminate it. On June 24, 2014, in Facebook notes, he provided thirty-five physical addresses of all shops that were selling his album. The list includes the following regions that cover thirty-five major towns in Kenya: Central, Central Rift, Coast, Nairobi, North Rift, and Western (see appendix for the full list). By selling the album at 500 Kenyan shillings (about US$5) with the option of purchasing it at 400 Kenyan shillings (about US$4) if one chooses to use an Orange Money account, Juliani is also increasing the chances of many of his fans being able to afford it. Many local music albums sell at an average of US$10 in stores (mostly available through major supermarkets in select towns in the country) and can be out of reach for many music fans, especially youth. Such a partnership with a business like Orange Money to sell music is an important avenue through which artists like Juliani have been able to reach their fans in faraway places. In 2011 Juliani partnered with Safaricom and traveled to many parts of the country, performing his *Mtaa Mentality* album at live concerts. Safaricom also had a website that allowed online purchase of Juliani's music along with music of other artists with whom the company had partnered. These are only a handful of examples of how music intersects with media. Next is a look specifically at social media as a tool in and for ethnographic research carried out for this study.

SOCIAL MEDIA AND ETHNOGRAPHIC RESEARCH

For a long time, I was convinced that "real" ethnographic research happens in the physical field, where I, as the ethnographer, meet and spend time with the people whose lives, words, practices, and experiences comprise the primary focus of the study. I was convinced that a "real" ethnography entails what Clifford Geertz calls a "thick description" (1973), assumed to represent the results of spending many hours immersed in a specific location, observing and participating in the lives of the residents of that locale. After all, many are the "classics" within the genre of ethnographies that highlight long durations in the field as a rite of passage for the ethnographer. When I started carrying out research on popular music, however, that "traditional" construction of "the field" started to be a little more than elusive. Focusing on musicians whose craft was defined by mobility from place to place and their products that are mostly accessible through radio and television made my fieldwork complex and at times unbounded by physicality.

Now as a more experienced ethnographer, I am less intimidated by the thought of not being able to carry out "real" fieldwork or provide a thick description of the work that I do. I have come to understand that ethnographic fieldwork is diverse. Much of this bold stance comes from reading the expansive academic statements and discussions regarding ethnography and the many suggestions and even critiques of the enterprise. Some of the critiques claim that ethnographic fieldwork is an enterprise that represents the mere projections and allegories of the researcher (Clifford 1988; Clifford and Marcus 1986), that others see the writing of ethnography as closely related to writing fiction (Narayan 1991), that ethnographic enterprise and product cannot happen without asymmetry, otherness, and foreignness that a researcher who does not share a language with the study group brings to the enterprise (Tedlock 1987), and that there are major limits placed on ethnography by the researcher's unfamiliarity with local vernaculars (Owusu 1978). That there is no agreement on the identity of the ethnography even in these few references here is a testament to the complexity of the practice of making sense of life as observed and interpreted. I, however, remain committed to tools of ethnographic research, such as seeking nuance on observable or stated realities, triangulating sources of information, verifying sources of data, and seeking holistic and contextualized approaches to understanding such data, even when I study "elusive" fields, such as those where popular music occurs.

The emphasis on thick description as the privileged form of ethnographic research comes out of a cultural context within anthropology where for the most part research was carried out by ethnographers who were not familiar with the locales they studied. As a result, there developed a need to not only study the local language in order to access some of the realities of the everyday being observed but also to live in the same place long enough to make sense of what seems banal to a cultural practitioner or insider. In cases where the researcher is familiar with the culture and the language that shapes the subject of the research, I agree with John Jackson Jr. that "some contemporary investments in thick descriptions might warrant reconsideration" including the "kind of overconfidence and arrogance it grants its adherents" (2013:10). But questions about ethnographic work are not just about physical field sites. We now have virtual ethnographies, whose practices have developed to include "digital ethnography, ethnography on/of/through the Internet, connective ethnography, networked ethnography, and cyber ethnography" (Domínguez et al. 2007:1). Anthropologists agree that a networked sociality that the internet brings can augment the physical, social, economic, and political lives of people (Fish 2011) and that ethnography of virtual worlds "is a flexible, responsive methodology, sensitive to emergent phenomena and emergent research questions" (Boellstorff et al. 2012:6).

Research for this manuscript allowed me to combine both virtual and physical spaces as sources of ethnographic data. The internet with online news, YouTube videos, Facebook, and Twitter; face-to-face conversations; and interactions are key sources of my data. For the most part, these virtual sites or platforms acted as archives where information about Juliani, his life, and music were stored as well as acting as a medium through which to communicate with and solicit information from various people whose knowledge and insights inform the work captured in this book. The internet and its accompanying social media were for me places where I was able to collect data about Juliani, which I then augmented with face-to-face conversations. Most of his music performances are available as video recordings on YouTube as are many interviews and commentaries given over the last several years. Specifically, YouTube was a great source of ethnographic data for me because unlike still pictures, which are only able to capture one dimension of a scene, videos allow for one to hear what is going on and to see movement and interactions, despite being the recorders and producers framing the videos in specific ways. I also benefited a lot from lyrics of Juliani's songs available online. With these resources in hand, my face-to-face interviews and interactions with Juliani were opportunities to fill in the gaps of information that were not accessible through these public sources and to ask his opinion on contemporary issues trending in the Kenyan public space. We together constructed the majority of this project, with me doing most of the curating needed to make it into the product it has become.

CURATING JULIANI'S AUTOETHNOGRAPHY

Given the increased iterations of what ethnography has become in this age of information and social media, one of the interesting challenges I had in gathering information for this volume was the realization that Juliani had been crafting his own identity and experience, his own ethnography, just as much as I was crafting one about him. As Tom Boellstorff et al. comment, "authors of ethnographies typically seek to produce detailed and situated accounts of specific cultures in a manner that reflects the perspective of those whose culture is under discussion" (2012:14).

Juliani's life as a musician, his music, what shapes his message, and the kinds of social projects he is involved in are all very much available on the internet. Through his own YouTube user channel, Juliani Music, where he has almost all his music videos; his projects, such as Mtaa Challenge; and interviews he has given to various media outlets, Juliani has a good collection of his public life that I have tried to capture in this book. Add to this the content of many of his songs in which he talks about his life and experiences and his Twitter messages that sometimes capture who he is and what he has experienced over the years, and one has a well-crafted autoethnography. My role as an ethnographer producing totally new information about him seems minimal, given that much of the data I collected was already available virtually in different locations. My task, therefore, was more of a curator than an ethnographer, packaging, for an academic audience, a story that Juliani had already put together. I have had interviews and conversations with him that are not publicly available and that enrich the content of this book, but I did not generate all the data used to complete the project.

Carolyn Ellis, Tony E. Adams, and Arthur P. Bochner's (2011) definition of autoethnography captures much of what Juliani has done to package his life and identity through social media. They define autoethnography as "an approach to research and writing that seeks to describe and systematically analyze (graphy) personal experience (auto) in order to understand cultural experience (ethno). This approach challenges canonical ways of doing research and representing others and treats research as a political, socially-just and socially-conscious act" (2011:1). When Juliani told Larry Madowo to search for his identity on Google, during the interview discussed in chapter 1, he was not just being playful; he was articulating a reality that exists for him as a musician seeking to construct his own identity, an identity openly constructed through social media and the internet. Like many other youth in Kenya, Juliani's identity construction is informed by imagery derived from popular media that has in turn provided for its users easier and more efficient communication. It is an identity that is also shaped by the questions asked by various people at different points in time, it is an identity shaped by what others say about him, and it is an identity always in formation. Cultural theorist Stuart Hall (1997) insists that identity formation and construction are always in production, never completed. Social media, especially the constantly changing nature it embodies, aligns well with this kind of identity construction for youth. Such construction is part of what builds up into a full story about an individual. For Juliani much of this story has been constructed through media. But social media are not just about identity formation or construction. Social media is a platform for economic activity, an avenue through which to mobilize one's merchandise.

Juliani knows this power of social media in mobilizing people and selling products by improving product visibility and availability. He sees social media's value in mobilizing people through information sharing and call to action. In an interview with Shipley at Nairobi's Pawa254 ("pawa," localized version of "power"), off Procession Way in the Africa Alliance of YMCA's building, Juliani notes the power of social media to mobilize youth: "In Twitter I had a homecoming (event) in my hood in Dandora and I was like, 'Hey, anybody want to go out and have meat and whatever, let's go to my hood.' And it was so fast. I don't need to print posters and whatever for that" (2012a). Mobilizing friends and fans seems to have been made easier for him by social media and so have been his attempts to sell his music. In the run-up to launching his third album, *Exponential Potential*, Juliani orchestrated a number of events that made sure that he had an ongoing presence in the local social-media scene. On February 24, 2014, for instance, he posted on his Facebook page a message seeking to recruit "*fan wasugu* (die-hard fans) from different parts of the country" to assist with promoting the album. He signed off the message with "April 22nd," which happens to be his birthday as well as the scheduled date for launching his new album. On March 7, 2014, he added to his Facebook page a Twitter handle, #ExponentialPotential, and again signed off "April 22nd." In an April 5, 2014, tweet, he shared a poster with his picture and the words "Juliani's 3rd Album Exponential Potential available April 22." This constant messaging, focused on the new album and the date, made sure that fans were always aware of the event. Repetition of the same message on social media is important especially because of the very short shelf life that any issue or message has on such a platform. By April 15, 2014, he had secured the partnership of Orange Kenya to help distribute his album throughout the country and followed it up with a tweet and a picture to announce the partnership.

Juliani's persistent messaging on social media was followed by a few other events. The first, held on his birthday, was dubbed a "listening party," with some friends and fans invited to a private gathering to listen to the new album. Local dignitaries, such as Chief Justice Mutunga, Madowo of Nation Television, and Gilad Millo of Amiran Kenya, a business that works with horticulture and floriculture industries to support and advance their work, were there. On May 22 at Nairobi's IMAX lounge, Juliani hosted a "bash" for media personalities to honor them for their continued support. The event, which Juliani had popularized on his social-media platforms, included presenting awards that fans had voted for. Local media personalities who won awards, which included two iPads, were: Madowo, best TV presenter; Mzazi Willy M Tuva, best radio presenter; Tuva's *Mseto East Africa*, best TV show; Crème de la Crème, best dj; Krowbar, best gospel dj; DJ Moz, best gospel presenter; Kambua, best gospel female radio presenter; Robert Alai, best informative blogger; Mohammed Ali, "Jicho Pevu," best investigative journalist; and *Pulse Magazine*, best magazine.

The next event, a "final" concert for his second album, *Pulpit Kwa Street*, at the Carnivore Restaurant on May 31, 2014, was six days before the *Exponential Potential* launch on June 5, 2014. On June 4, Juliani was in the Hot FM 96 radio station's studio with DJ Moz, talking about the album and playing samples of his new album while fans tweeted comments about their interest in the music. As soon as the album was available for purchase, Juliani again used his Twitter and Facebook to advertise it, and he was in person at specific shops to sign copies. He posted pictures of himself with the fans holding the signed albums, and he encouraged others to visit the shop to get their own. When he visited Berlin, Germany, in July 2014 for a social-activism workshop, he posted pictures of him and his fans with copies of the new album. From Nairobi, where he started his album-signing campaign, Juliani visited the Kenyan cities Thika, Nakuru, and Eldoret. In September and October 2014 he thanked his fans for their support with a compilation of all the pictures he had of him and fans who purchased his new album. Clearly, he is comfortable using the media for a diversity of processes and ends.

NEW MEDIA AND THE URBAN CHURCH

Media outlets are not used just by artists like Juliani to promote their products but also by churches to enhance their ministries and reach multiple segments of the populations they serve. On August 18, 2013, I attended a service at the Nairobi Chapel's Ngong Road branch, the newest location of a church that British Army soldiers started in the 1950s on Mamlaka Road, close to the University of Nairobi's residence halls. The congregation declined, and only a few attendees remained in the 1980s when indigenous leader Oscar Muriu and other Kenyans stepped in and started reaching out to the local community within the University of Nairobi (Logos 2011). It is through this local leadership that the church grew and started other churches: Mavuno Church (in downtown Nairobi and along Mombasa Road), Kileleshwa Covenant Church (in Kileleshwa), Mamlaka Hill Chapel (on Nairobi Chapel's original site), Mashariki Church (in Eastlands), Karura Community Church (near the Village Market in Gigiri), Lifespring Chapel (in Embakasi), and the Nairobi Chapel (off Ngong Road). I was aware that Juliani had performed at Mavuno Dome and that he frequently attends Nairobi Chapel. I wanted to find out more about the church and get a feel of what a typical Sunday service was like.

At the church campus I found a large "homestead." Arrows on the main entrance pointed people to various services in the numerous white tents around the well-manicured compound. Tents were set up for services for children, teens, young adults, and adults. Children and youth services ran concurrently. I arrived a few minutes before the first service, at 9:00 A.M., so I had a chance to look around and get a little more familiar with the adult church-service tent that I was planning to attend. The Nairobi Chapel ministries are many, including focus on social justice and the poor, the *kinara* leadership-development program ("kinara" is Swahili for "leader" or "point person; also "candle holder" in the African American Kwanza celebrations), and K-Krew, a media ministry Pastor Moses Mathenge (DJ Moz) started in 2000 through the radio program *Kubamba*, which later morphed into the Citizen Television Sunday show *Kubamba*, discussed in chapter 1. Today, K-Krew also presents a three-hour show *Inuka* (Swahili for "get up") on Hot FM 96, The networks between churches like Mavuno and FM stations are varied but deeply connected.

At the adult church-service tent, I walked on a concrete floor in a large hall full of green plastic chairs. At the front was a platform with many lights and music videos on a large television screen. Two videographers were stationed close to the platform with a pulpit, music equipment, and enough space to fit a large choir. Tables around the hall held communion elements. At about nine, the sound from the speakers got louder, and the music video faded away, replaced by a video of wildebeest in the famous migration across the Mara River (between the Serengeti and Maasai Mara game parks in Tanzania and Kenya, respectively). The wildebeest video's English subtitles stated: "Life has many challenges, like rushing waters there are lurking dangers. Will you make it through the water of life? Are you ready?" A reverse countdown from 5 to 1 began; the series title, DIVE, came up on the screen. This promotional video was for the August 2014 sermon series that Pastor Nick Korir was teaching. This use of a common imagery of wildebeest crossing the crocodile-filled river as an introduction to a sermon series about dangers in life is quite telling, given that wildlife is what many foreigners tend to associate with Kenya.

A worship team of seven females and four males stepped onto the platform as the instrumentalists started to play music. A male worship leader started to sing as other members of the team joined in, and slowly the congregation did as well. I immediately recognized two songs in English and two distinct African languages, one that sounded Nigerian and Zimbabwean, from the instrumentation. A female worship leader took over the lead during the African song session and encouraged the congregation to wave a handkerchief or bulletin. It seemed like this congregation participation was common because within a short time, bulletins and handkerchiefs were in the air. The music tempo slowed, and the male leader took over the singing again and led a slower song. This was followed by communion, which some young people in school uniform assisted in serving; announcements; and offering. During offertory the music director was asked to share one of his compositions scheduled to launch the following week at the Alliance Française Cultural Center in downtown Nairobi. Everything seemed to work very well.

After prayer, Pastor Korir came up to the platform and started talking about "The Jubilee Ride," a project that was part of the church's fund-raising for the Jubilee Scholars program, to which the students who helped serve communion belonged. For the Jubilee Ride, riders traveled from Nairobi to Cairo, Egypt, on off-road motorbikes to raise 15,000,000 Kenyan shillings (about US$150,000) for four years' tuition for fifty students in secondary school. The church had already supported 260 scholars as of August 2013 with the goal to increase to more than 300. According to Pastor Korir, the church had so far collected 2,100,000 Kenyan shillings (about US$21,000). Several corporate sponsors had made commitments to support the project, including Cooper Motors Corporation (Kenya)—CMC (K)—which offered five new trucks to provide support along the way for the riders; Kenya Methodist University, which would assist the scholars with university education; Nation Television, which provided free advertising on all its media outlets; and Stoic Satellite Tracking, which donated vehicle tracking during the trip. Pastor Korir challenged the congregation to give 195 Kenyan shillings (US$1.95), the equivalent of educating one student for one day. Everyone at the service received a brochure about the project with more information on how to donate and an M-Pesa paybill number to use when contributing the 195 Kenyan shillings.

For "Crocodiles Around," the third sermon of the DIVE series, Pastor Korir started by saying that crocodiles around us intimidate and discourage us because they are very close to us. He read from John 5:1–9, the story of a man who could not get into the pool of Bethesda to be healed. Pastor Korir commented that one of the crocodiles around us was excuses that people give by pointing to others and not taking responsibility, often blaming the location within which they find themselves, thinking that they are not in the right place and then blaming their conditions, saying, "As soon as I . . ." These practices, he said, press the "pause" button on one's life instead of allowing people to move forward. He, however, noted that marriages were being restored, financial problems solved, and broken relationships mended every day. These same issues are the focus of Apostle Paul, Sheikh Ismail, and Dr. Wazanga, discussed in chapter 3.

All the presentations, including sessions before and during the service, were so well polished that they almost felt like performances. Everything worked according to plan, the songs fell smoothly into place, the video and the music were well timed, and the pastor's message was short and to the point. There was almost a sense of artificiality about the entire service that made it feel and look like a staged presentation. Even the sermon might be regarded as yet another "pull yourself up by the bootstraps" presentation that might be associated with some of the popular televangelists on local televisions stations. But then one has to be cognizant of the context. The church caters to a cosmopolitan congregation living in a digital age, an age where their own lives are littered with structured presentations that ought to be seamless. Compared to a church service I attended in Meru the previous Sunday at Mwanika Methodist Church, close to my sister's home, this was night and day. At the Mwanika Church the local primary-school students attempted to provide a musical presentation with a song played on the church computer. They tried three times to get the computer to work, to no avail, and had to abandon the presentation all together. Such malfunctioning

would not be part of the Nairobi Chapel experience. These were two different congregations experiencing media differently but in the same country.
I enjoyed the Nairobi Chapel's service, the message, and the precision with
which things worked, unlike the Mwanika Church that left me frustrated
because I did not get a chance to hear the children.

After the service I texted Juliani to ask if he was attending the second service, so we could meet briefly. He said he was on his way. I told him he would
enjoy the sermon because it aligned with his Kama Si Sisi philosophy. In a
follow-up text later, I asked, "*Ulisikiaje hiyo message ya Nick*" (What did you
think of that message by Nick)? "*Moto kabisa* (Very hot)! Excuses on why
we are not!" I figured Juliani would especially resonate with the critique of
excuses that people give for their circumstances because, as noted in chapter
3, Juliani's message is an attempt to balance one's efforts and drive to change
one's circumstances and the impeding challenges. I thought that he would
connect well with the sermon, having said on many occasions that sometimes
it is not circumstances but work ethic that keeps youth down. The previous
day Juliani and I had been at Art Café at the Junction shopping mall along
Ngong Road. He told me he used to think "the challenge was that people
were poor, from the ghetto, but I am now convinced that it [youth inability
to advance in life] has to do a lot with attitude and morality" (pers. comm.,
January 24, 2013).

A number of sociocultural practices at the Nairobi Chapel challenge earlier practices of the Church (discussed in the first two chapters). Unlike the
other churches that prefer a more subdued pastor when it comes to music
and dance at the pulpit, Pastor Korir is comfortable dancing vigorously before he gives his sermon. Just before delivering "Crocodiles Ahead of Me,"
the first of his DIVE sermon series, Pastor Korir joined nine dancers from
Nairobi Chapel's youth group DICE (Dancing in Christ's Expressions) on
stage, and together they went through a highly rigorous and choreographed
dance routine that got the congregation ululating and cheering.[2] DICE was
before the congregation to say thank-you for their contributions to help buy
uniforms. The group, three females and six males, all dressed in black and
red, were ready to be commissioned for a mission trip to Mombasa to work
with Nairobi Chapel's sister church, Trinity Chapel. The group would then
run a youth camp in Voi, north of Mombasa. Pastor Korir announced that
Oscar Muriu, the church's senior pastor, was one of the key speakers at the
2013 Willow Creek Church's Global Leadership Summit on August 16, 2013.
Pastor Muriu's speech was simulcast to numerous global locations, including
my current city, Grand Rapids, Michigan. These are the realities of media

use for not only individuals but also some Kenyan churches. However, not all church use of media ends up positively.

BLURRED LINES, SOCIAL MEDIA, AND CONTEXTUALIZED GOSPEL

In February 2014 Nairobi's Mavuno Church was at the center of Kenya's social-media discussion because the church provocatively advertised a series of sex-education programs for teenagers at the church on each Sunday in March 2014. Each of the series' four parts had a provocative title: "You Can Gerrit!" from the US television show *Single Ladies*, a comedy drama on sex and relationships; "Shades of Grey," one book title in a series of erotic romance novels that has been a US and UK best-seller; "Blurred Lines," a song by American artists Robin Thicke and Pharrell Williams, which says women are animals and want sex; and "Friends with a Monster," by popular musician Rihanna in collaboration with rapper Eminem. The image with the series' titles is of a young couple holding each other closely and looking into each other's eyes in a provocative and sensual way. The female has on very short shorts, generally termed "hot pants." Within a few hours of the poster appearing on social media, there was an immediate response, with some shocked that a Kenyan church could have such a series and advertise it in such language. Others saw it as an important intervention in a culture that needed to have an honest and blunt conversation on the topic. The term coined for it is "twerkusifu," which sounds like the Swahili "twakusifu," which means "we praise you," but is a blend of "twerk," a sexually provocative dance, and "kusifu," to praise, which loosely translates to "sexually provocative praising."

The hashtag #MavunoPoster, which focused on the poster, was started on Twitter on February 22, 2014, and trended until March 4, 2014 (Mavuno Church 2014a). Media houses were busy seeking out Mavuno Church pastors for comment. One of the pastors, David Kuria, was asked if the church was sorry for posting such a racy image. He told Capital FM news on February 25, 2014: "We don't apologize for the conversations we are having. We do believe that they are important conversations for our generation right now. Did we set out to cause controversy? No, we did not, but we stay on track. If people's reception to anything is what determines how you are going to respond, then you really won't go very far" (Capital FM Kenya 2014). Pastor Murithi Wanjau, senior pastor at Mavuno Church, appeared on almost every television station in Kenya that week and kept repeating the same message when asked why the church put up the poster. He insisted that Mavuno Church always sought to meet people where they were because it wanted to transform individuals to be influencers of the places they inhabit. Pastor Wanjau was invited to KTN's *Checkpoint*, along with Kanjii Mbugua (music director at Mavuno Church) and two other pastors. When asked why the church put up the poster, Pastor Wanjau responded: "We want to reach people where they are. We see that as a biblical model. Jesus always started with where people were, then took them to where God wanted them to go. If you look at society, what is society like? If we look at society today, it is not where it was, and many don't seem to realize this" (KTN News 2014). In the same program, Rev. Dr. Charles Kibicho, former chair of NCCK and current chaplain at Presbyterian University of East Africa, said that he did not see anything wrong with the poster: "I have just seen the picture today, and my first reaction would be this is our real world. This is where we are as opposed to when I was growing up. It was different. But someone somewhere needs to be able to talk to our world now. I think Jesus would leave the 99 and go for 1, that one. And I am saying that picture represents so many today. I think the Church needs to be bold not to shun off from the reality of life" (KTN News 2014). Why did this poster cause so much controversy and derive such interest from social and broadcast media? Was it because it had really crossed the expected boundaries of morality, or did it hit a nerve that many were familiar with and yet chose to avoid talking about? When he appeared on NTV's show *#thetrend*, Pastor Wanjau told Madowo: "The girl in the poster is wearing hot pants. I go to Yaya even today and walk outside. Even the schools out there kids are dressed exactly like that. I don't even know how this whole charge comes up when you say it is pornography. The whole thing about sin, you know, that the church should not be seen around issues like this, this is probably one of the reasons why we are not having an effect on the nation. We must speak about issues as they are" (NTV Kenya 2014). The poster was clearly providing an opportunity for some very spirited conversation not only on what topics or images a church can engage with publicly but also why such a conversation was important in the first place. In the three decades that I have been keenly interested in the practice of Christianity in Kenya, I have not encountered such a bold and even controversial discussion of a cultural topic. For the most part, Christianity in Kenya has tended to take a very conservative approach to matters of culture, and it is not surprising that there was a heated debate following the sexuality series at Mavuno Church. I was surprised, however, that Mavuno Church pastors defended their decision to advertise the series and that they received support from many of their congregants who posted comments on various social-media platforms. On further analysis, I realized that reactions to sexual content are not restricted to Kenya. Controversy and opposition seem to follow sex education in many Christian contexts. In the case of the United States, Janice Irvine states, "Initiatives to protect children from exposure to allegedly corrupting sex talk, whether from sex education programs or the media, are central to conservative cultural politics" (2002:30). As I have shown in my earlier work on responses to sex education in East Africa (2009), it is very difficult to have a consensus on the teaching of sex education in schools. Opposition to such education comes mostly from Christians who see sex education as a gateway to immorality (2009:117).

In her study of Kenyan Christian parents' attitudes toward sex education, Njeri Mbugua notes, "Most Kenyan mothers do not teach their children about sex or sexually transmitted diseases such as HIV/AIDS" (2007:1079). While this statement covers all mothers generally, Mbugua narrows her work down to Christians: "Because most of the churches in Kenya propagate the culture of silence regarding sex, and at the same time they oppose traditional initiation rites, many adolescent girls brought up in Christian homes do not receive sex-education that is given their agemates who participate in traditional initiation rites. Unfortunately, neither do they receive meaningful sex education from their parents" (2007:1082). This silence toward sex education or avoidance of any public mention or discussion of sex and sexuality has links to Victorian-era morality that permeated European missionary discourses and practices shared with Kenyan converts. As Mbugua continues to show, "European missionaries also discouraged the use of 'dirty' language that was used when the extended members of the family gave sex-education to the young. Even today, most Kenyan Christians take offense to the mention of any parts of the genitals or sexual intercourse. Indeed, Christianity plays a significant role in inhibiting most Kenyan parents, teachers and leaders from teaching or discussing most matters related to sex, except when condemning sex outside marriage or contraceptive usage" (2007:1081). Christian opposition to contraceptive use that Mbugua mentions here is an ongoing practice. In 2013 a government-sponsored advertisement was pulled off the air after religious leaders (Christian and Muslim) along with other citizens said it was encouraging adultery instead of curbing HIV/AIDS infections. The ad features two women talking with each other, one complaining about a husband who spends most of his time in a bar but then confiding in her friend about another man that she is seeing. The ad ends with the second woman beseeching her not to forget to use a condom (Niaje TV 2013). In response to the public outcry that led to the ad being taken off the air, Peter Cherutich, deputy director of the National AIDS and STI Control Program (NASCOP), noted that the ad had been promoted because research had shown that up to 30 percent of Kenyan couples had other partners (BBC 2013). As discussed in chapter 3, this practice of *Mpango wa Kando* (side plan) has almost become normalized, and following the Kenyan parliament's passing of a polygamy bill, the practice was further made formal.

As I contemplated the relationship between this television ad and the Mavuno Church poster, I could not help but be puzzled by the fact that one of the churches opposed to this ad was Mavuno Church itself. When interviewed on *Talk360* on Capital FM, Pastor Mugambi Kyama from Mavuno Church is reported to have said, "The advert was trying to resolve the infidelity issue with the use of a condom," and wanted to work with other interested parties, including NASCOP, to create a more effective and efficient message (Kangethe 2013). Mavuno Church is known for raising eyebrows by always going against the grain, and maybe the sexuality series is one of many of its bold approaches to Christianity in Kenya today. In a 2013 edition of Nairobi Chapel's magazine *Chapelites*, Tim Kamuzu Banda says that when Mavuno Church started, "eye-brows were raised when it provided a suitable place to worship for thousands of young people who would otherwise not go to church. It made it possible for you to go and worship the Lord in your sagging jeans, earrings, coloured hairstyles for women among other habits that would raise eye-brows in most churches in Kenya" (2013:13). This willingness to push the boundaries of what was considered acceptable style of dress or personal grooming as well as who could feel welcome in the church service is an important identity for today's Church not just in Kenya. There are a number of churches in Europe and North America where casual wear is the acceptable dress code for not only congregants but pastors and other leaders (Sargeant 2000). Mavuno Church seeks to provide sermons that are as provocative and challenging as the controversy the poster caused. A number of congregants have testified to having been drawn to the church because it was not the "usual" kind of church and that they felt comfortable coming into the church just the way they were both in terms of their spiritual-emotional state and their social identities at the time. Mavuno Church is known in Nairobi as a place where artists feel comfortable and can grow spiritually and socially. Hip hop promoter Moses Mbasu, who is commonly known as Buddha Blaze, shares his own story about finding a home at Mavuno Church after being "lost" and doing all the "wrong" things. Not raised in a Christian home, Mbasu says he went to Mavuno following the urging of his friends and found it refreshing, and it has been a great place for him ever since (Mavuno Church 2014b).

The new emphasis on people attending church just the way they are as compared to earlier restrictions on how one presented oneself before feeling comfortable attending church is laudable. Many challenges are facing the Kenyan Church, and many churches will have to contend with many more issues than sex-education posters or the mode of dress attendees adopt. One such challenge will have to do with regular church attendance. Despite the emphasis on the expanded presence of Christianity in Kenya and other African countries, the number of those who attend church regularly is much smaller than national numbers of those who claim Christian identity. In Kenya, where the official number of Christians is placed at 83 percent (divided into 45 percent Protestant and 33 percent Catholic), less than 20 percent of Protestants attend church on a regular basis. A study the African Center for Mission Finish the Task (ACM FTT) carried out on the number of Protestants attending church on Sunday found that the then Nairobi Province led the country in church attendance at 16 percent. Other provinces reported include Eastern Province with 12 percent, Rift Valley and Central Provinces with 7 percent each, Nyanza with 6 percent, Western and Coast with 5 percent each, and North Eastern with 0.13 percent (ACM FTT 2004).

As Juliani has wondered, how is it that a nation with so many people self-identifying as Christians can support many "unchristian" practices? Why are drivers not obeying traffic rules on public roads in a country of Christians (Juliani 2014a)? Clearly, the link between stated ideals and praxis is much more complex, but Juliani does have a valid point in questioning the role of one's stated Christian faith and the specific actions one takes and practices one engages in. Maybe, it is time for churches to engage their congregations boldly even if it means talking about sex and sexuality in provocative ways. This could be an important expression of the connection between Christianity and the street that Juliani's music seeks to highlight.

6

JULIANI
LYRICAL GENIUS WITH A
SOCIALLY CONSCIOUS MESSAGE

Beyond his ability to make Christianity relevant to the everyday realities youth encounter in Kenya, Juliani is also known for his lyrical prowess. He plays with words, uses current affairs as song titles or part of his verses, and combines multiple messages or issues in the same song in ways that not many artists in Kenya are able to do. This chapter focuses on Juliani's songs that tackle issues of love, sex and sexuality, politics, religiosity, and economics, along with his ability to play with words to make even more intriguing inroads into Kenya's sociocultural planes. I also highlight Juliani's ability to engage with tough social issues through creatively woven lyrics and rhyme. By analyzing Juliani's songs from his three albums (*Mtaa Mentality*, *Pulpit Kwa Street*, and *Exponential Potential*) as well as his mixtape (*Vultures vs. Voters*), I identify certain recurrent themes that appear in almost all of his work. Some of the themes are sexuality, love, and relationships; tensions between perceived and real social practices; masculine and feminine identities; socioeconomic and political challenges; and the everyday experiences of spiritual life. It is these specific themes that I highlight here and show why he is able to reach across a wide array of fans.

LOVE AND SEXUALITY

Many of Juliani's commentaries on sexuality have to do with premarital sex and girls getting pregnant. While it "takes two to tango" and a girl's pregnancy is a result of a relationship with a male partner, studies show that young women in urban areas in Kenya who engage in sex or begin dating early face a number of psychosocial and economic challenges, including being more likely to drop out of secondary school than their male counterparts (Clark and Mathur 2012). Moreover, 46 percent of females in Kenya give birth by the age of twenty (Mumah et al. 2014). High sexual activity among youth is therefore a real issue, and Juliani's songs capture a prevalent social phenomenon. In his song "Morio and Juliet," Juliani talks about different kinds of love that lead to different kinds of outcomes. He, for instance, seems to prefer the kind of love that is patient, one that allows a boy to go out of his way to court and build a relationship with a girl, and one that leads to marriage and childbearing within marriage. As of July 2014 when this song was released, Juliani was still single, and one can only assume that his focus on premarital sex provides a lens through which to see his preferred sexual relationship. He sings in "Morio and Juliet":

> Kubeba maua kwa street kwa G ka me si kitu rahisi
> Lakini nitavumilia, siwezi compare ukininebea nine months my seed
> Hii ni mapenzi ya dhati si mapenzi ya thirsty.

> Carrying flowers across the street for a ghetto man like me is hard
> But I'll be patient, I cannot compare to you carrying my seed for nine months
> This is sincere love not thirsty love.

The song's title is a play on Shakespeare's *Romeo and Juliet*, which emphasizes romance and whose plot focuses on young lovers. "Morio" (a young man) is a street word derived from the Kikuyu language and in a way is a combination of Western-style romance and street social life. Juliani talks about the challenge of a ghetto youth, or G, like him carrying flowers, a sign of romance, on the streets because it is something he is not used to but this is not as difficult as it is for the woman to carry through with a pregnancy. Juliani also qualifies the man's seemingly unusual behavior as one way of displaying sincere love as opposed to lust (thirsty love). Juliani showcases some of his lyrical abilities, selecting the Swahili word "dhati" (sincere) to rhyme with "thirsty" while capturing powerfully the contrast between the two forms of love. He intersperses such rhyming pieces through the song, sometimes with words that share the same syllables as other words, which when pronounced in the local Kenyan dictum sound almost the same. In this excerpt, for instance, I recognize rhyme in the ends of "compare" and "ukinibebea." Juliani differentiates the two types of love:

> Love inajenga home lust inatafuta room
> Agape love imekuwa una ngapi love.

Love builds a home lust looks for a room (to have sex).
Agape love has turned into "how much do you have" love.

Again I see rhyme in "home" and "room" and "agape love" and "una ngapi love." The theme of sincere love versus lust appears in other parts of the song as well. Juliani compares two couples:

Unaprefer couple kwa bus stop mkono pamoja chini ya umbrella
Ama wale looking anywhere else but each other ndani ya Corolla?

Do you prefer a couple at a bus stop holding hands under an umbrella
Or those looking everywhere else but each other in a Corolla?

This comparison introduces the issue of relationships based on material things instead of sincere love that allows the couple to endure hardships together. Juliani seems to suggest a relationship mismatch with the couple depicted by a symbol of "progress" (a Corolla car) shown to have no love for each other as symbolized by their reported action of looking everywhere but each other, compared to a couple that is depicted as having comparatively fewer material resources, symbolized by being at a bus stop waiting to take public transportation together and to care more for each other by sharing an umbrella. In his song "Pendo Kweli" from *Mtaa Mentality*, Juliani again shares this approach to love:

Unamarry manzi sababu ya sura na hips, je uzee izipanguze off?
Una sugardaddy familia kuvunjika divorce
Kitanda yake kaburi ya wanaongozwa na lust
Vidole ilikuvisha pete inakupa black eye, mapenzi inavumilia chai dubia
Urembo inavuta karibu lakini inahifadhiwa na tabia.

You marry a girl for her hips what if age wipes them off?
You have a sugar daddy—broken family and a divorce.
Its bed is a grave for those led by lust fingers that gave you a ring are
Giving you a black eye, love endures tea without sugar.
Beauty brings closer, but it is sustained by character.

Juliani implies that when a man marries a woman for her beauty and hips, what happens when old age takes that beauty away? Sugar daddies come into the picture, and the family ends up in divorce because it is a grave for those led by lust. He then says that the same (man's) fingers that put a ring on (woman's) finger are the ones giving the woman a black eye. Love endures all hardships, which he symbolizes as tea without sugar, and adds that beauty draws people to each other, but good character maintains the relationship.

In January 2015 Brenda Wairimu, Juliani's girlfriend, gave birth to a baby girl. When I had dinner with Juliani in Westlands, a suburb of Nairobi, on January 6, 2015, Juliani mentioned that he was spending most of his time in Mombasa with his daughter and girlfriend.

The absence of true love leads to casual relationships that Juliani characterizes as built on lust. In each case, however, he contrasts bad and good practices—love and lust, premarital sex and abstinence, love for material things and sincere love, and so on. In his first single, "Jesusnosis," for instance, he offers this contrast about the ease and prevalence of premarital sex:

> *Unapenda stra za kuvuana bra mbona ukishado unafeel guilty?*
> *Manzi tubaki mabeste sikuguzi hadi nikuvalishe pete*
> *Nishow boy anareason hivi nikushow nywele kwa kichwa ya TD Jakes*

> You like games of removing bras. Why do you feel guilty after doing it?
> Girl, let us remain best friends. Won't touch you till I give you a ring.
> Show me a boy who thinks this way, and I will show you hair on TD
> Jake's head.

Juliani's claims that there is no boy who thinks of having a relationship with a girl without having sex with her resonate with scholarly evidence of high levels of sexual behavior among adolescents and youth in Kenya. As far back as 1985, a year after Juliani was born, more than 50 percent of Kenyan youth were sexually active, with many debuting their sexual intercourse between ages thirteen and fourteen (Ajayi et al. 1991). In 1998 Kenyan youth were reported to have started having sex much earlier than their peers in other countries in sub-Saharan Africa (National Council for Population and Development 1999).

In a 2003 study, more than 50 percent of Kenyan rural adolescent girls were reported to have had their first pregnancy when they were single (Taffa et al. 2003). This data corresponds also with an opinion shared by Pastor Murithi Wanjau after the Mavuno Church poster controversy, discussed in chapter 5. In a February 22, 2014, interview with Mwanaisha Chidzuga, who hosts *Leo Wikendi*, a KTN news bulletin show, Wanjau gave some of his views on sex and sexuality in Kenya: "Sex has become so commoditized. We have become so sexualized in our generation that you can't even have a normal relationship with a workmate without thinking of how you are going to get her into bed" (KTN 2014b). Juliani tries to offer an alternative approach to this commoditized view of sex and sexual relationships, emphasizing the need to have less of a transactional sexual relationship and more of a relationship based on mutual respect and attraction. For him such a relationship leads to sexual intercourse only after marriage. For those unable to follow this path of abstinence, Juliani suggests that they tend to rush into marriage not because they are ready for it but because they are seeking legal access to sex. In "Hela" from *Mtaa Mentality*, he sings:

> *Anaingia kwa marriage sex iwe legal*
> *We ni mfaithful haumangimangi ama hauna dough za lojo?*

> He/she gets into marriage so as to have access to sex legally.
> You are faithful and don't stray, or is it that you don't have money for
>   lodging?

Nairobi, like many other cities and urban centers in Kenya, has numerous facilities where prostitution takes place, but the most common are premises called "lodgings." Many of these facilities are in the city center or its surrounding areas and comprise single rooms rented out on a short- or long-term basis. Occasionally, police undertake a "swoop" and arrest prostitutes, who are almost always female and who often rent out space in lodgings close to their clientele. It is, however, puzzling why only females tend to be arrested in these police raids even though it is men who keep these facilities operating as patrons.

When Juliani talks about sex being legal in marriage, he is not only making reference to the accepted form of relationships where sex is accepted but the legality of having sex in any one of the many lodgings, which he refers to with a Sheng word "lojo." In many of his songs, Juliani talks against premarital sex and shares many lines in his lyrics that capture what happens when one does not heed such advice, including many negative consequences—unwanted pregnancies, heartbreak, and abuse—that especially befall females. In "Morio and Juliet," Juliani says:

> *Boy and girl wakigo out kitambo tulisema wanapush*
> *Girl akiwa pregnant anabaki peke yake maternity akipush*

> Long ago when a girl and a boy went out, we said they were pushing.
> When a girl gets pregnant, she is left alone in the maternity pushing.

Juliani here highlights not only the consequences of premarital sex or unprotected sex but also the imbalance in the resulting consequences. The female is left on her own after the sexual encounter leads to pregnancy. This imbalance in sexual relations plays out also when it comes to elementary and high school attendance when a girl becomes pregnant while in school. The tendency is to drop out, while the boy carries on with his education. Until the mid-2000s it was the common practice in schools in Kenya for a pregnant girl to be expelled from school. This practice has started to change but is still the default approach to teen pregnancies. In a number of communities and households, girls are stigmatized when they become pregnant while in school and are not yet married. Many of those girls face the challenges of being ostracized from their homes or getting no support for continuing with school. In his song "Church on Monday" from the *Pulpit Kwa Street*, Juliani addresses this challenge:

> *Dada hajafika 18 anashika ball aliachwa offside peke yake na boy*
> *Ana large surface area so anaavoid cafeteria*
> *Hapati lovey-dovey love ina price uliza p.i.m.p.*

A girl younger than eighteen years is pregnant left alone by the boy responsible

Has a large surface area and now avoids the cafeteria.

She is not getting the love because love has a price, ask a pimp.

The issue of avoiding the cafeteria tallies with the challenges girls face not only during their pregnancies but also after the baby is born. As mentioned above, peer, family, and public responses are not at all positive but for the most part comprise ridicule and even outright rejection with many blaming her for the her situation. The girls often avoid going back to school for this reason. Research reports on school attendance in Kenya for elementary- and secondary-level education show that while the numbers of boys and girls are equal in elementary school, the ratio changes in high school where girls' numbers drop to 35 percent compared to 50 percent for boys (Muganda-Onyando and Omondi 2008).

Juliani provides an interesting take on the perceived relationship between a boy and a girl and the harsh realities that befall the girl in cases where she is left to suffer the consequences of an unplanned pregnancy as the boy goes on with his life (in school) uninterrupted. It is quite telling that he asks the girl in the same song, "*Kama yeye ni man of your dreams mbona anakupa sleepless nights?*" (If he is the boy of your dreams, why does he give you sleepless nights?). This ability to combine the actual consequences of life's practices with a play on words is part of Juliani's musical abilities. How is it that a girl who has these dreams about this boy ends up staying awake (depicted by Juliani as sleepless nights) because of the same boy? In this case, the girl may dream of a great relationship with a boy, but when she gets pregnant, she alone suffers the consequences, facing many sleepless nights. Juliani uses the same strategy of playing with words in his song "Biceps" from his *Mtaa Mentality*:

> *Si mbaya msichana na kijana kukeep in touch*
> *Lakini pete ndio inakupa ruhusa ya kukeep na kutouch*

> It's not wrong for a girl and a boy to keep in touch
> But it's a ring that gives you permission to keep and to touch

It is interesting to hear Juliani commenting here that a ring (symbolizing marriage) gives one the permission to "touch" and "keep" (have sexual relations) and yet seems to ridicule one's action of getting married so as to make "sex legal," as in "Hela." This sense of cynicism in a person's ability to sincerely enter into a marriage is what characterizes much of Juliani's assessment of people's social practices and motives. He seems to question their sincerity. Are they genuinely entering into marriage, or is it a way of making sex legal? Are they faithful in their relationships, or are they unable to afford the cost of booking a room in a lodging?

Juliani uses "Biceps" to also talk about masculinity and femininity, saying that men and women cry when in crisis, and in a way redefining the common narrative about what it means to be masculine and feminine. In many African cultures, crying is often associated with women, who are seen as weak, and any man who cries, especially publicly, or admits to doing so is seen as weak or feminized. Aware of these social expectations, Juliani says:

> *Pia me hucry kwa crisis pia mi najua mwanaume sio biceps*
> *Pia me hucry kwa crisis pia me najua urembo sio cutex*

> I also cry in crisis I know manhood is not defined by biceps.
> I also cry in crisis. I know beauty is not defined by nail polish.

The use of the word "biceps" denotes muscle power and physical strength that is often seen as playing a large part in what defines a man. Cutex, a brand name for nail polish widely used in Kenya, again points to the assumption that beauty (external) might be regarded as the most important marker of femininity. Each part of the song representing the different genders is sung by the appropriate gender, Juliani the man's part and a singer named LC the woman's. Juliani ends up arguing that true masculine and feminine identities are not to be found in these physical qualities constructed by culture but in a relationship with Christ. This theme of identity through Christ is also expressed in "Rimz Timz" from *Mtaa Mentality*, in which he confesses:

Sina marimz timz na bling bling
Lakini nina uhusiano na king of kings

I don't have rims tims or bling bling
But have a relationship with the king of kings.

Juliani performed this song in April 2008 at the Nairobi Pentecostal Church, Ngara branch, and the audience recited these two lines with him, and whenever he recited them, there were cheers and ululations from the audience (Njau 2013).

In many of his songs, Juliani also seems to prefer what may be considered "natural beauty," where one avoids using makeup or other forms of products to enhance one's beauty. In "Masterpiece" from *Exponential Potential*, Juliani says:

Kioo ni ya kuconfirm God's awesomeness
Si ya kupaka makeup
Ni kama alikosa akikuumba unamkosoa maker.

The mirror confirms God's awesomeness
Not for putting on makeup.
It's like God made a mistake creating you, and you are correcting the
    maker.

Juliani wears his hair in dreadlocks, a style often associated with artists as well as other Kenyans (and Africans) who seek to challenge received narratives about "good" hair and hairstyles. When he started performing as a Christian, Juliani had on a number of occasions to put on a hat to cover his dreadlocks, including when in 2008 at the Nairobi Pentecostal Church, he wore a white hat that covered all his hair. While wearing dreadlocks is widespread in Kenya, it has not always been a representation of "good" personal grooming. Often associated with rebellion and especially with Kenya's pre-independence freedom fighters, the Mau Mau, or more recently with Rastafarianism, dreadlocks have cultural and philosophical undertones. Sociology of religion scholar Ennis B. Edmonds notes that dreadlocks signify a number of identity markers and philosophies for people of African descent and especially those in the Rasta tradition. He says, for instance, "Aesthetically, dreadlocks indicate a rejection of Babylon's definition of beauty, especially as it relates to European features and hair quality. According to Rastas, hair straightening and skin bleaching by black people reflect a yearning for Whiteness and are therefore symptomatic of alienation from a sense of their African beauty.

Against this background, dreadlocks signify the reconstitution of a sense of pride in one's African physical characteristics" (1998:32). There are many debates about straightened hair for Africans and its connections to definitions of self (Etemesi 2007; Robinson 2011), but by preferring one's natural beauty instead of applying makeup, Juliani is touching on a very important topic. Juliani's association with Ukooflani Mau Mau from his early years as a musician does have similar philosophical connections to the group's use of hair as a sign of African identity. Most of the artists within Mau Mau Camp have at different times had dreadlocks. It is this attention to African natural beauty that I argue leads Juliani to castigate those who try to "correct" the maker's initial molding of their natural identity. Wearing dreadlocks is a deliberate undertaking as Juliani suggests in "Biceps": "*Wazembe waezichana nywele wakaita dredi*" (The lazy are unable to comb their hair, then they call it dreadlocks).

In "Jesusnosis," Juliani talks about his spiritual transformation that might not be apparent when one looks at his physical attributes, including dreaded hair. He comments, "*Bado nina dredi kwa kichwa, bado nasag, bado nabounce / Mabadiliko ni goal*" (I still wear dreadlocks, I sag my pants and walk in a bounce / Difference is in my goals), things he did when he was not a born-again Christian. Now he is changed, and such change is not necessarily manifested physically. What is different about him is his goal.

POLITICS AND GOVERNANCE

Juliani has progressively changed his position and views on politics and governance from the time he released *Mtaa Mentality* in 2008 to his mixtape *Vultures vs. Voters* in 2013. In "Who Is to Blame" (*Mtaa Mentality*), Juliani says this about politics in Kenya:

> *Kura kupiga ni kuchafua tu pinky finger na ink ya blue*
> *Church haina cha kuoffer isipokuwa kikapu offering*
> *Judiciary ni scare crow inatisha lakini haiezi uma*
> *Mwanasiasa drooling for power mwingine full of it crumbs hawaezi*
>   *gawa*

> Voting is just soiling your pinky finger with blue ink.
> Even the church has nothing to offer other than an offering basket.
> The judiciary is a scare crow, threatens but cannot bite.
> One politician drools for power, another so full of it he cannot even
>   share crumbs.

At this time in his life, just after the 2007–8 elections, Juliani seems to be disillusioned about politics and considered the whole electoral process a waste of time and voting as a practice of dirtying a little finger. But before the 2012–13 general elections, he presented a different take on politics, seeing people's participation as critical in changing the direction of the country. What changed? In conversations with him, I learned that he felt youth especially were not getting themselves ready for political change through participating in elections. He noted that in the 2012–13 electoral campaigns, many had a desire to not repeat the 2007–8 postelection violence, and his political songs were a way of sensitizing people to get ready for a different kind of politics in which they made wise decisions at the polls.

In "Voters vs. Vultures" from his 2013 mixtape, Juliani presents a critique of politics and politicians that reflects this changed view of political participation. He starts, "*Tusibleed ndio walead*, people, power, possibilities" (We shouldn't bleed so they can lead, people, power, possibilities), clearly showing the need to see the power of ordinary citizens in changing the course of their political history. Due to rampant corruption and vote rigging that characterize most general elections in Kenya, many eligible voters have often considered their voting inconsequential to changing their political circumstances. Today, Juliani is a changed person and even critiques the apathy the middle class display toward public issues. In "Samaki Baharini" from *Exponential Potential*, he says about the middle class:

Kama k kwa knife wako silent middle class indifference
Huge M-Pesa transfer haitabuy your guilt
Nani atakusaidia ukitembelewa na wageni wale watumiangi gate?
Uko sufle sufle na chef si tuna idle plates

They are silent like "k" in knife due to middle-class indifference.
A large transfer of money through M-Pesa will not buy your guilt.
Who will help you when guests who don't use the gate visit you?
You are all about soufflé with a chef while all we have are idle plates.

The middle class is depicted as mostly concerned with material comfort and relying on finances to solve their problems but quite blind to the precarious nature of such comfort. Juliani asks about what will happen to them when crime comes to their doorstep. It is probably this question of middle-class apathy that led another Christian musician, Pete Odera, to write an open letter to Nairobi's middle class, castigating them for not participating in the electoral process to nominate candidates for various city political offices in

2012. He rhetorically wonders on his blog why, when he went out to nominate a candidate for the city's leadership, he did not see any middle-class participants and responds: "The simple reason is: You are more willing to read this online than to go out and vote. You complain about politics and yet you are not a member of any useful organisation or political party except Facebook & Twitter—how these contribute to the betterment of our nation's critical issues other than to launder diverse opinions is yet to become clear to me" (2013). Odera seems quite disillusioned by the actions of Nairobi's middle class, but Juliani is more positive, seeing a possibility for political change. In "Voters vs. Vultures," Juliani sings about the power of people to change the political process:

> *Kutoka kila corner tunakusanyika*
> *Damu ya ukabila na ink ya blue kwa kidole gani thicker?*
> *Tattoo kwa skin ya nyoka leo iko kesho si hivyo*
> *Same na promises za mjumbe au sio?*

> From all corners we gather.
> Tribal blood and blue ink on a finger, which is thicker?
> Tattoo on a snake's skin is there today and gone tomorrow
> Just like the politician's promises.

People are gathered from every corner, and Juliani wonders what is thicker, blood of tribalism or blue ink? He challenges people to critically evaluate the promises made by politicians, likening them to a tattoo on a snake's skin, which is there today, and tomorrow is shed off. He makes reference to some political scandals reported at the time, especially a major scandal in which senior government politicians in 2009 were implicated in misappropriating money meant to buy maize for starving Kenyans. The common practice had been that the National Cereals and Produce Board (NCPB) would buy maize on behalf of the government during a season of surplus and sell it when supplies were low to provide a cushion for farmers. However, in this case that led to the scandal, the NCPB sold the maize to a broker who sold the maize to the government at double the market price (Aron 2009; Mathangani 2011).

In a story *Standard Media* posted almost two years later, the reporter claims that information from Wikileaks attributed to former US ambassador to Kenya Michael Ranneberger shows that former Prime Minister Raila Odinga's family and that of former President Mwai Kibaki were involved in the scandal (Aron 2009; Mathangani 2011). This is the scandal that leads Juliani to say:

Mahindi ilitoka kwa shamba lakini haikufika tumbo ya starving Kenyan
Walahi tena hawataki kumake change wanataka kumake headlines

Maize from the garden did not make it to a starving Kenyan's stomach.
I swear they do not want to make changes, they want to make
  headlines.

These direct critiques of people in power can be dangerous in a country where despite strides made in allowing for freedom of expression, political censorship and repression still occur. When asked if he is afraid of "them" coming for him due to his hard-hitting lyrics, Juliani comments: "Well, even if you fly away by airplane, they will come after you. You can never be safe enough. People just need to know whatever I sing about comes from listening to people and documenting it with lyrics and poetry" (2014a). Juliani does not just blame politicians for the socioeconomic challenges that Kenyans deal with daily, however, but sees the voters as culpable as well. That is why he continues to say in "Voters vs. Vultures":

Maji inatake shape ya glass
Expectation ya mwananchi inadetermine leadership
ukitaka kakitu utapata kakitu
Ukitaka kaT-shirt utapata kaT-shirt.
Ukitaka maisha mazuri vote wisely.

Water takes the shape of a glass.
It's the expectations of the citizens that determine leadership.
If you want something small, you get something small.
If you want a T-shirt, you get a T-shirt.
If you want a good life, vote wisely.

As chapter 4 argues, Kenyan politics have a strong patronage culture where voters act as clients and politicians as their patrons who occasionally distribute resources based on demonstrated support and loyalty. During political campaigns, especially before general elections in Kenya, it is very common to see politicians giving out goodies, such as T-shirts, leso, sugar, cash, alcohol, and blankets to prospective voters to persuade them to vote for them. These are the T-shirts Juliani mentions and lead him to say that the "gift" that voters receive during campaigns is what they will get in return for voting the politicians in and not the real socioeconomic changes that they and their communities need.

Juliani's interest in the political process led him to collaborate with Kenyan photojournalist and social activist Boniface Mwangi for this song's video version (Juliani 2013). The video is shot in a low-income residential area, and Juliani is singing "Voters vs. Vultures" from the top of a tall building overlooking the city center. Five males walk through the area, wearing black hooded sweatshirts whose backs have a large vulture crossed off in red. The group comes up to a wall full of simulated political campaign posters: "Vote for Rapists," "Vote for a Murderer," "Vote for Scavengers Democratic Alliance," and "Vote for Warlord," among others. These posters show male torsos in gray-and-black suits with various neckties, but the head of the males are those of black vultures. The group stops momentarily and tears down those posters, only to immediately replace them with their own posters of a white vulture against a black background and an X across all of it. Their sweatshirts and the campaign posters they put up bear the same image. In another shot, one person in the group goes up a tall building and drops smaller versions of the campaign poster between buildings, and some people pick them up.

The theme of politicians as scavengers the vultures represent dominated public graffiti painted on Nairobi city's Muindi Mbingu Street in February 2012. A very well-painted mural depicting a politician with a vulture's head, wearing a suit and tie, sitting on a chair chained to a suitcase of money attracted a number of city residents. The politician says, "Am a tribal leader, they loot, rape, kill, and burn in my defense, I steal their taxes, grab land, but the idiots will still vote for me" (NTV Kenya 2012). It almost seems irrational that a people would elect leaders who have mostly misused their positions to advance their self-interest. However, scholars show that in countries like Kenya where ethnicity plays an important role in voting patterns, "ethnicity may act as an informational shortcut, helping voters predict how candidates will direct flows of patronage, choose policy, or protect the security of different groups" (Ferree, Gibson, and Long 2014:3). The graffiti was part of a series of graffiti art that dotted walls of public buildings, including public toilets and pavements, to sensitize Nairobi city residents to the opportunity they had to vote out the politicians running for political office who had many unscrupulous histories. It is these images of vultures that dominate the video version of Juliani's song. Another shot in the video shows Juliani with his two hands raised and fists clenched, his back facing the camera to reveal his own sweatshirt with the vulture with a red X on it. The refrain for the song says:

> Wakati umefika sauti yako kusikika
> Tutasimama na wala hatutatishika
> Watoe fake leaders, mavulture tunawamulika
> Ink ya blue kwa pinky finger ya informed voter ni sumu kwa vulture

Time has come for your voice to be heard.
We will stand firm and not be scared.
Remove fake leaders, we are spotlighting the vultures.
Blue ink on the finger of an informed voter is poison to a vulture.

The outcome of the elections did not match these aspirations, as a coalition of two major ethnic blocs—the Kikuyu and Kalenjin—represented by Uhuru Kenyatta and William Ruto, respectively, prevailed.

Despite these electoral outcomes, Juliani's perspectives on politics and the electoral process did show a marked change from his earlier ones, where he preferred to play down their importance. In 2008 voting (symbolized by blue ink) was seen as a waste of time, but in 2013 voting is regarded as an important tool for social change. Showing these changes that took place in his own thinking and that of other youth voters, Juliani continues in "Voters vs. Vultures":

Kama time is money mbona idler mtaani wako broke?
Umati kwa rally si popularity ya party
Ni increased number of the unemployed
Sitakurudisha track record yako haijang'aa kaa viatu vyangu

If time is money, why are idlers broke?
A large crowd at a rally is not the popularity of the party.
It's the increased number of the unemployed.
I will not reelect you because your track record is not shiny like my
      shoe.

Starting with the phrase about time being money and idlers still being poor, yet they have so much of time, Juliani seeks to highlight the state of unemployment rampant in Kenya. He provides evidence of this when he mentions the large crowds at political rallies as signs of the growing numbers of the unemployed. With youth in Kenya comprising the largest percentage of the unemployed, this song is clearly about their lives and their specific needs. Juliani continues:

Wana raha ila tuko huru Kenya
Hata na Jirongo zenu tunawapa wiper
Mmesalia na muda tunawaroot out
Five years ago nilikupa chance
This time around hutapata hata vote of thanks

They have fun, but we are not free in Kenya.
Even with your Jirongo we give you wiper.

You have some time left, we will root you out.

Five years ago I gave you a chance.

This time around you won't get even a vote of thanks.

He gets into a play with words that seem to work well in Swahili, where personal names can sound like nouns or verbs in the language. The names of politicians running for office in 2012, including Raila Odinga, Uhuru Kenyatta, Musalia Mudavadi, and Cyrus Jirongo, are all mentioned but in ways disguised as Swahili words and phrases. "Raila" becomes condensed into "*wana raha ila*" (they have fun but), "Uhuru" is "*hatuko huru Kenya*" (we are not free in Kenya), and "Mudavadi" is "*mmesalia na muda*" (you only have time remaining). The commonly used short form of "Mudavadi," "Muda," corresponds with the Swahili word for "time." The word "Jirongo" has long been used in Kenya to denote a 500 shilling note that came out in the 1990s with the repeal of Section 2A of the Kenyan constitution, which allowed for multiparty politics. The then government of Daniel Arap Moi printed money that young politicians, especially Jirongo and Ruto, used in what was called "Youth for Kanu" to bribe the masses to support Moi's presidential campaigns.

Another candidate, Kalonzo Musyoka, had a political party named Wiper, which Juliani mentions. This thinly veiled references to the main politicians vying for high political offices in Kenya and who are then told that their track records do not shine like his shoes are in a way protecting the musician from being accused of directly castigating specific individuals. Juliani is able to do that while remaining relevant and pointed in his critique. In his interview with Maskani ya Taifa, an organization of citizens defending their rights, Juliani says that even though it is true Kenya has bad leaders, it is the people who voted them in who should take the blame because leadership reflects the electorate. Leaders, he argues, do not necessarily share the same daily challenges with the electorate because "when there are potholes on the road, they have 4x4 vehicles, and when there is a problem with the education system and teachers go on strike, their children are at Braeburn [a private K–12 school]" (2014a). The electorate should, therefore, consider these realities when they vote for "their" people.

This marked difference between the lives of the political elite and the electorate is not only fueled by social class but by mismanagement and misappropriation of public funds through corruption. As Mongoljingoo Damdinjav et al. argue, "Kenyan political elites have resorted to corrupt methods to exploit their influence over public resources for self-interested purposes" (2013:5), a practice that has penetrated the lives of many Kenyans (Hope 2012). These sociopolitical realities are the ones that Juliani, especially in "Voters vs Vultures," hopes to highlight so as to ultimately shape minds to make the right decisions at the ballot box. He brings similar contrasts in his other songs as he focuses on socioeconomic challenges facing youth in Kenya.

SOCIOECONOMIC ISSUES

Given his target audience and his own experience growing up—youth mostly living in low socioeconomic contexts—Juliani has crafted his music to address these and other related social realities that youth in Kenya face. In "Mtaa Mentality" from his album of the same title, Juliani says:

> *Politician kuja base tuna njaa anabelch*
> *Kuget through tosti inado angle theta sole ya kiatu*
> *Wengine ikizidi greencard vuka border*
> *Mi noma kuafford hata bodaboda*

> A politician comes to our residence; we are hungry and he/she burps.
> Toast is good enough to get by; soles of my shoes are like angle theta.
> When it gets too much for some, they get a green card and cross the border.
> For me it is very hard to afford even a local motorbike taxi.

Juliani contrasts the life of those who have socioeconomic means and those without just as he does in his comments above in Maskani ya Taifa. On the one hand, he talks about a politician burping when visiting them in their neighborhood, while, on the other, he tells of some local residents getting a green card to migrate to the United States. Not all people have similar options, especially those so poor that they can only walk, as evidenced by their worn-out soles that resemble an angle theta. The word "bodaboda" is a local corruption of "border border," which bicycle and motorbike taxi drivers along the Kenya-Uganda border would shout to get their clients. Motorbike and bicycle taxis have come to be known as bodaboda and are found in almost all cities in Kenya. Again Juliani plays with words to bring out his message, focusing on the opportunities for running away from poverty or lack of opportunities, signified by inability to "cross" the poverty "border."

Juliani clearly shows the difference between two categories of people—the politician who has access to a lot of food that makes him or her burp and those he or she is meeting, who have not had any food and are hungry. For the poor, the ability to even get through their day is so difficult they have to rely on toast for sustenance. Their shoes are so worn out that the sole is tilted, taking the shape of angle theta. Overwhelmed by the lack of opportunities in Kenya, some leave Kenya, but for others like Juliani cannot even pay for a bodaboda. These economic challenges are partly a result of misappropriation of national resources, as Juliani shows in "Bahasha ya Ocampo" from *Pulpit Kwa Street*: "*Funds za elimu free inalipia mtoto wa minister private school fees*" (Money for free education is paying private school fees for the minister's child). With high levels of corruption and a highly paid political class in parliament, it is not unusual for public funds to find their way into private pockets.

In 2010 Kenyan members of parliament were earning about $120,000 per year, a salary at par with that of the US Congress (Hughes 2010). In May 2013, following public outcry, including a protest Boniface Mwangi led outside parliament, members of parliament agreed to a $75,000 annual salary. The members, however, receive a one-time grant of $59,000 to put toward the purchase of a vehicle of their choice for which they can claim mileage; the MPs receive allowances for attending parliamentary committee sessions that could amount to $230 a day. With no cap to the number of such sessions one can attend, this allowance can rise greatly each month. The socioeconomic disparity alluded to here is what makes Juliani say in "Kitanda Yangu 4 by 6" from *Pulpit Kwa Street*:

> *Ghetto kuna njaa na sewage zimejaa haimake sense*
> *Patience pays no wonder wazazi walitaka niwe daktari*
> *Toto vumilia ugali hii salary*
> *Ingenunua nyama but nalipa taxes*
> *MPs wapate entertainment allowances*

> There is hunger in the ghetto but sewer system is full; this doesn't make any sense.
> Patience pays, no wonder parents wanted us to be doctors.
> Be patient with Ugali, my child, my salary
> Would've bought meat but I am paying taxes
> So that MPs could get entertainment allowances.

Juliani again contrasts the lives of the rich and poor, the powerful and weak. He wonders how sewer systems in the ghetto can be full, and yet the people who live there are hungry. One explanation is that those sewers could be connected to others from places from where a lot of refuse is channeled through them, or it could be that the sewers are not well maintained and tend to fill up quickly due to poor services by the city government. But the point here is that Juliani is contrasting what happens in the life of a poor person and that of the political elite who live in the same country but have two different socioeconomic and political experiences. The poor person's child is asked to endure eating *ugali* (corn meal) instead of eating the preferred meat because the father is paying taxes so members of parliament can take money meant to support social services for the people. These contrasts, often coming out as binary oppositions, are very common in most of Juliani's songs. He also plays with words when he says that parents used to encourage them to become doctors because "patience pays." The word "patience" (payshyens) is here pronounced to sound like "patients" (pashyentz). Taking the existing practice of cost sharing in Kenyan health centers, it is not surprising that Juliani says patience, or patients, pay. Later in the song, his plan is:

> *Si kutoshea nguo za fat Joe*
> *Chapo dondo nifukuze njaa first*
> *Then for njaro naorder Mocha Java*

> Did not fit into fat Joe's clothes.
> I eat chapatti and beans to chase away hunger first.
> Then for show I order mocha at Java.

Representing both the realities of poverty and the aspirations of a "modern" life, Juliani contrasts eating street food (chapatti and beans) with buying an expensive coffee at an upmarket cafeteria called Java (Nairobi Java House). This street mentality of living one kind of life and imagining another is a major theme running through "Mtaa Mentality." It is the lived reality of many youth, who, as argued above, have access to a better education but not corresponding material opportunities to live the life that such education symbolizes. In the song "Mtaa Mentality," Juliani offers:

> *Ndoto za kula sahani moja na Bill Gates*
> *Kutoa Sukuma Ugali kwa menu niweke pizza, burger*

> Dreams of sharing a plate with Bill Gates.
> Remove kale and Ugali from the menu; put pizza and burger.

Juliani represents the social realities of many youth in Kenya as well as their aspirations. The character in this song is depicted as having dreams of getting to Bill Gates's level and sharing a plate of food with him. As a result, he or she wants not sukuma (kale or spinach) and ugali but those of his or her aspirations and that mark a higher socioeconomic and cultural status (pizza and burger). It is one thing to know one's socioeconomic limits and yet another to do something about it. In the case of Juliani, who takes up the role of the protagonist in this song, he realized he had limits and did not have power. He, therefore, turned to the one with power and got saved:

Ninahitaji base kugundua sina uwezo
Kendea mwenye uwezo nikaokoka

I need a base to know my limits.
Approached the powerful one and got saved.

This expressed sense of helplessness is articulated in Juliani's sentiments, captured in chapter 1, when he talks about feeling powerless as a rapper until he followed God's story.

FAITH AND RELIGIOSITY

These contrasts regarding lived and aspired lives also cross to the area of faith and religiosity. The refrain in "Mtaa Mentality" is that people on the streets ask, "What is going on, and where is the solution to all the challenges we face, and how can one make a difference?" The answer Juliani provides is located in his Christian faith. Trying to make a difference, realizing that he does not have power of his own, and deciding to get saved might seem like Juliani is falling into fatalism. However, in his numerous interviews, he has argued that becoming a born-again Christian was a moment of clarity for him, allowing him to realize his purpose and approach to life's issues that he faced each day. He does not just give his problems to God but understands his own specific mandate and approach to those problems. Far from being fatalistic, Juliani uses his faith to challenge fellow Christians on how to associate with all facets of life, including how they relate to God. It is by shifting the center of power from the individual to God that allows Juliani to admit that he, as a man, does cry when he is in crises and that a man's strength is not in his biceps, as explored in his song "Biceps." Juliani also uses his songs to paint an image of God that is relevant to the youth that he targets.

In "Friend Request" from *Pulpit Kwa Street*, Juliani gives an interesting analysis of God's identity framed within a canvas of social media. The title itself is in reference to Facebook's common practice of becoming friends where a person sends a potential friend a "friend request." He starts:

Tots za dry gin zinafanya nilose my way
Nisimame online na niko computer illiterate
Dunia ikicrash utalost kama hujasave

Tots of dry gin are causing me to lose my way,
To stand online and I am computer illiterate.
When the world crashes, you will lose [data] if you have not saved.

This song, directed at "*wasee wako kwa web*," those youth who are on the web, uses the language and symbolisms of Facebook to construct the song texts. Juliani starts by admitting that being drunk on dry gin has made him disoriented, and now he's lost but trying to go online even though he knows nothing about computers. Juliani combines a number of interesting lyrical creativity practices in this song. First, getting drunk usually makes one lose balance and unable really to even stand. He uses stand "online" instead of "in" line. People stand "in line" but go "online" when using the internet. By highlighting the effects of dry gin on the individual, Juliani is highlighting the abilities and the skills needed to make effective interactions with social media. He finally talks about the Earth crashing as a hard drive would and the consequences of losing (data) if not saved. The suggestion of losing one's life if not saved (born again) is present here.

Talking about his own experience as a Christian but in the language of new media, Juliani continues:

> Maisha ya Christ nilicopy-paste; daily nitakugoogle prayer nitamail
> Freedom ni one of the packages address yako Gmail ama Yahoo?
> Nikushikilie kaa suspender ya Larry King
> Prayer yangu iko kwa desktop yako

I copied and pasted Christ's life; I will daily Google you and send my
    prayer.
Freedom is one of the packages, is your address Gmail or Yahoo?
I will hold onto you like Larry King's suspenders.
My prayer is an icon on your desktop.

Then Juliani asks:

> God awe na page Facebook
> Angeaccept friends requests za Saints ama prostitutes
> Wall yake ingejaa repentance ama shukrani tu?

If God had a Facebook page
Would he accept friend requests from saints or prostitutes?
Would his wall be full of repentance or only gratitude?

Because of his critique of the social and cultural role of Christians in Kenya's public arena today, it is not surprising that he wants to challenge any assumptions that Christians might have about their own goodness. The cynicism and critiques of the sincerity of Christians in living out their faith daily lead him to caution against assuming that God will only accept certain people as "friends." He suggests that God's wall will reflect friendship with sinners and saints, the bad and the good. These are the tensions that Juliani sees in the life of humans and especially Christians. Evil and good can coexist, and it is not easy to tell who has what until one carefully considers praxis.

For Juliani, these tensions that coexist in the same Christian body, both individual and corporate, allow for the complication of Christian practice, making it more blurred and gray than black and white. Dualism, whether in terms of life here on Earth and the anticipated afterlife or be it secular and gospel music, is insufficient as a philosophy or praxis for Christianity. Instead, for him life is murky, complex, intertwined, and always in the process of being reconfigured, renewed, and reshaped by its practitioners. Christians might be well served by seeing their faith in this way articulated by Juliani. He, much like we do in anthropological analysis, favors reflexivity, allowing practitioners to recognize what they do in terms of living out their faith and what informs those practices. Christians, in Juliani's expressions, are implored to continually ask themselves why they believe and behave in the specific ways they do. This self-critical analysis of Christian faith allows the practitioners to be aware of how their faith is shaped by their subject-position as Kenyans belonging to a specific ethnic group, gender, socioeconomic class, and political persuasion. As my analysis in the preceding chapters shows, Juliani is very much aware of his own subject-position and has used it to inform his music style and choice of content. Generally, the acceptable moral subject in Kenyan Christian imagination is one who avoids sex or talking about it and stays clear of politics because it is a "dirty game." Juliani simultaneously challenges and embraces these sentiments by talking candidly about sex and sexuality and encouraging youth to engage in political processes to make a difference in their country but in a revolutionary tone that is reminiscent of the work of Ukooflani Mau Mau. The next chapter concludes this book with my own reflexive analysis, showing how my own ethnographic nurturing started in contexts very similar to Juliani's youth. I also show how my own subject-position as a Christian and professional anthropologist intersect well with Juliani's aspirations as an artist keen on making a difference in his community.

CONCLUSION
PARALLEL BUT INTERSECTING PATHS

A March 16, 2015, tweet from Juliani captures the main argument sustained throughout this book—that hip hop has been an important platform through which Christianity in Kenya has been reimagined and articulated in order to align with youth aspirations and sensibilities: "Prize is to later meet our maker, even better is to live and experience the promises, accomplish the plan in every single day of our lives." It acknowledges that popular culture is a platform through which Christian ideas, experiences, and expectations are formed, debated, articulated, weighed, and even challenged. I have argued that contemporary expressions and expectations of what it is to be Christian in Kenya present competing ideologies and practices. In this tweet is a different narrative: Juliani acknowledges the value of keeping the ultimate prize in sight (by meeting one's Maker) but also shows that it is equally important to live and experience God's promises right here on Earth by accomplishing God's "plan in every single day of our lives." This integrated "and," rather than either/or approach to Christian living, is what I see as unique in the way hip hop presents Christianity compared to the way many churches and churchgoers in Kenya conceive of and present Christianity.

To develop this argument further, I have emphasized the preponderant focus on the afterlife in much of Christianity in Kenya. Such otherworldly focus has generated less emphasis on individual agency and has contributed to a disconnected relationship between faith and everyday lived realities of many Kenyan Christians, especially the youth. I have made a case for Juliani's ability to transcend certain boundaries of what constitutes Christianity, at least in public, by moving its core message from the Church to the street, challenging the focus on a God who is removed from the everyday and emphasizing a God with whom Christians can have candid conversations. I also use Juliani's music as a springboard from which to dive into ways of reconfiguring music texts and the meanings they carry in order to provide a fresh interpretation of lived realities and aspirations of youth as well as an understanding of what constitutes gospel music.

In this way I see Juliani's music extending the realm and definition of gospel music to include content that highlights anxiety, frustrations, and complexities of life without neglecting biblical stories and themes that dominate gospel music today and the kind that he grew up with in the 1990s. Juliani's work simultaneously challenges and affirms Christianity, gospel music, and the role of the Church in society. Instead of just making gospel music about biblical themes and words, he injects into it what I term the "messiness" of life. His work provides parallel trajectories for music and religious sensibilities that often proceed independently and yet also intersect at various points that allow for a more complex rendering of experiences and expressions. He challenges conservative Christianity but also affirms some of its principles. He highlights the need to change what constitutes the content of gospel music but also affirms the genre's focus on personal religiosity. These are not the only examples of parallels and intersections in this work, though.

As I delved deeper into Juliani's life and work, I was intrigued by the intersections that he and I share about the place of faith in everyday life. This is best captured in the emphasis we both put on demonstrating our faith commitments, rather than just speaking them. In retrospect I now realize that one of the attractions I have to Juliani's music is his focus on challenging Christian practices, rather than its theology or ideology. His work presents an artist who is interested more in how Christians live out their everyday lives of faith than what they say about their faith. In the examples I share about his own public pronouncements and actions, Juliani is much more at home with his faith commitments being judged through his practices and "products" than through any statements he may make of that faith. This approach resonates with my own religious and faith sensibilities, which prefer what some see as lifestyle evangelism, rather than what some see as confrontational evangelism. Rather than say who I am, I prefer to let my actions and relations demonstrate such identity.

Another area of life where our interests or commitments intersect is in the realm of social justice. I am older than Juliani or his peers, but my own youth was lined up with a deep passion for social justice, a commitment that has endured over the years. Growing up, I was exposed to the practices and sensibilities of popular culture that created a foundation from which I learned the ways youth could challenge authority for the good of society. In the early 1980s, when I had just turned twenty and was going through my own identity issues and was in that physiosocial period of transition, I and other university-bound high school graduates waited our turn to join the National Youth Service pre-university training program. This was a national program initiated for students before entering the university as a way to instill in them some sense of patriotism and an ethic of community service. Regular graduates from the National Youth Service would usually be assigned specific tasks that support community development, such as grading roads or dam construction. Our participating was a way of introducing us to some of these qualities of service to our country. For me, however, it was popular culture that gave me a tangible and broad sense of social justice.

Prior to joining the National Youth Service, I had briefly lived with family in Nairobi, where I had an opportunity to expand my social life through popular culture. For the first time I had access to television and movies at the major theaters, which introduced me to movies featuring youth interested in music just like we were. At the time the few movies that had a major impact on me were about break dancing—*Breakin'*, *Breakin' 2*, and *Electric Boogaloo*. The break-dancing craze was all over the major Kenyan cities, and there were moments to come face-to-face with its manifestations. I was awed with my cousins' break-dancing hairstyles, long, curly hair that was uncommon in Kenya at the time but quite prevalent among the African American youth that we saw in US entertainment magazines and some of the main characters in the break-dancing movies we were watching.

Another dimension to the fascination I had with US youth in popular culture, especially break dancing, was the young Americans who represented youth defying authority. In *Breakin'*, for instance, the dance group is denied an opportunity to participate in a competition because they "do not fit into the genre." Not convinced by the verdict, they defy the judge and persist on participating in the competition and end up winning him over. The judge and the initial opposition to the dance group represented authority figures in our own lives, including parents, teachers, government officials, and others, whom we saw as hindrances to our idea of having fun. That the break-dancing group was able to convince the judge to reverse his decision was very attractive to us.

Similarly, in *Breakin' 2*, when a developer tries to bulldoze a community recreation center, local break-dancers mobilize support to try and stop it. That dancers would resist the push-back they encounter from a destructive bulldozer also sparked a certain level of connection with many of us growing up in a country where political repression was the order of the day. The sociocultural context within which this youth cultural expression emerged coincided with high levels of political insecurities and uncertainties that we were witnessing in Kenya. A failed coup attempt in 1982 resulted in political repression, media censorship, and expanded use of spies to limit freedom of expression. Many of our peers in the university disappeared or got locked up for suspicion of being critical of the government. Fear and anxiety were very common experiences for us in Kenya.

These cultural influences that we experienced in the 1980s have retained important elements discernible in the larger social ecology of youth in Kenya today and have shaped the content and even style of Juliani's music. Having experienced those initial stages of intense cultural influences by US popular culture actually led me to scrutinize whether similar influences may have shaped hip hop in Kenya, in general, and Juliani's own growing up and music making, specifically. I was surprised to see reference made to memories of that time, in the 1980s and 1990s, when more popular cultural artifacts were available to Kenyan youth following the weakening of state control over socioeconomic structures. Kama of Kalamashaka relates that rap music from the United States was instrumental in shaping his own journey into hip hop in Kenya. I, too, found US cultural artifacts, such as break dancing, important parts of how I was constructing my own sense of self. I slowly became a convert to break-dancing culture in order to become hip. I learned how to break-dance and gave myself a hip hop name. I became Jam Master G, following Grandmaster Flash (Joseph Saddler) and The Furious Five, whose song "The Message" was very popular at the time.

Christianity and its relationship to hip hop provides yet another intersection to the parallels I see in this book. Hip hop is a genre that is very much about the first person singular and represents the life and aspirations of many youth. I have also argued that hip hop is quite relatable to Christianity that itself focuses on the individual as the agent of transformation. These two come together through Juliani's work and identity. Juliani's identity as a Christian and his performance of a style of hip hop that captures the realities of a disenfranchised population create a great intersection with Christianity. Christians are often associated with a focus on the marginalized and the suffering.

Hip hop emerged in spaces with many socioeconomic challenges and then was embraced by members of populations that felt disenfranchised. It only seems logical, therefore, that hip hop and Christianity connect and collaborate more. If Christians seek to reach out to the marginalized, and hip hop is an expression of some of the experiences and aspirations of the marginalized, then hip hop becomes an ally for Christianity and a medium through which to articulate and express it. This connection between hip hop and Christianity is what I have sought to capture by analyzing Juliani's music. Relying on his song texts and how they correspond to social reality, I found an important window into the way hip hop interacts and shapes perceptions of Christianity in Kenya and why the two are more compatriots than antagonists. Rather than hip hop being seen as an antithesis to Christianity, it provides Christianity an important canvas to explore and express social reality outside of the confines of the church. When looked at from the lens of hip hop, Christianity then begins to speak to many other facets of life that illuminate concrete social realities Christians and others alike face. In hip hop is found a language and emotion that try to capture those areas of life Christianity seeks to engage. It engages the intangibles, the raw, and the ever-changing.

All these intersections I see between, on the one hand, Juliani, his music, and public presentations and, on the other, Christianity and gospel music could well be influenced by my own identity and preferences. To mitigate against such bias (to the extent that it is possible), I asked a few others on July 1, 2014, as I was finishing up this book, about their own reflections on what they considered to be Juliani's importance and success as a Christian hip hop artist. These people, who include Peter Mudamba, Larry Madowo, and Dorothy Ooko, have a high regard for Juliani's music and had individually interacted regularly with him as representatives of organizations or companies that he has worked with in some form. I sent them a text message: "Would you send me a paragraph of who/why/what you consider Juliani to be such an important figure in Kenyan Christian and music scene for my book on him. Will include your words in the first pages of the book."

I sent the same message to Juliani to share with his social networks, especially social media. He responded, "Send me kwa tweeter I retweet" (Send to me via Twitter, and I will retweet). I obliged with a modified message, for space limits and to make it more general, to @Julianikenya: "Why do you consider Juliani to be such an important figure in Kenyan Christian and music scene today?" Juliani retweeted and followed it with his own Tweet: "What's yo thought on Christianity, Juliani & Hip hop? US prophesor @ mwendantarangwi asking yo honest opinion might b featured in the book." I was excited by the thought of my question reaching thousands of Juliani's followers on Twitter and was imagining the number of responses it might get. I did get a few and have shared them below.

JULIANI AND HIS MUSIC: WHAT OTHERS SAY

Larry Madowo, anchor, Nation Television (NTV), Kenya:

> I first met Juliani in 2007 when he was just starting out in Christian music. His style was compelling and arresting, and he was obviously quite hungry to make a name for himself. In the years since then, Juliani has gone on to be one of the most successful people in all of Kenyan music. The most fascinating aspect of Juliani's career is that he's become even more influential in the gospel music scene by dropping the "gospel" tag. He maintains that he is born again, and his new music still features an overriding Christian theme. But symbolically walking out of the limiting—and often viscerally judgmental—Christian music bracket has allowed him to impact a larger audience, and remain relevant to his core constituency. That is the best form of fearless influence. (pers. comm., July 14, 2014)

Peter Mudamba, project director, Docubox, Kenya:

> Juliani is an astute and passionate musician who rose from most humble beginnings in the rugged slums of Dandora, where most of his peers must have ended up dampened, with a contrite spirit, full of anger and vengeance. Where death dominates through opportunistic diseases, muggings, mob justice, etc. If you live, you are dead to your dreams, with little or no hope of raising your head above the mucky and sludgy byproducts of that dump sites situation. From this hopeless state rises an ever-smiling, smart and astute musician, who relegates all anger and possible rage to the dustbins and instead becomes a voice of reason. Not a savage but salvage to the youth around and beyond Dandora, an envy of multitudes of university students, who cannot help but marvel at the lyrical prowess of this poetic musician who is unashamed of his humble beginnings. He is tiny in stature but walks tall, with a rare ever so caring spirit, willing to serve to society more and more from his well of life. He is willing to sacrifice his time, talent, ideas, and resources, if only to see the neighborhoods gain hope. Even his sweet but stinging music is all about liberation, and a great sense of purpose. Youth love him, but those who know what he stands for, love him even more. A strong believer of change that starts with self he believes in self-empowerment and actualization as well as the realization that it is possible if only one tries. He is a great mobilizer who likes to lead from the sides just to disguise himself from the great limelight he attracts.
>
> Juliani's music is laden with Christian messages in a style that appeals to the youth and may be the only person who is really careful about what he says and how he communicates, being quite aware of his great influence. A great defender of the Eastlands and Eastlanders and more so Dandora where

he grew up, he often visits with his friends, taking his CEO friends to those spaces and having them take matatu rides with him without fear because he just loves the simple things in life. (pers. comm., July 16, 2014)

Ambani Nelson

Huyu msee ni God's mail. Huyu msee huongea ukweli mpaka amefanya niache utapeli, ulevi, ulazy na nitrust Mwenyezi Mungu (This guy is God's mail. This guy speaks the truth and has made me stop con artistry, drunkenness, laziness and to start trusting in Almighty God) (Twitter, July 1, 2014)

Dorothy Ooko, communications and public affairs manager, East and Francophone Africa, Google Kenya:

Juliani is a top Kenyan music artist—gospel rapper—and social activist and the one Kenyan artist whose music cuts across all ages and classes in the society. I first met Juliani in 2010, when he was releasing "Bahasha ya Ocampo" as a music app and I wanted him to sign the CD for me. He was gracious as I tried to engage him in my rehearsed Swahili while he responded in Sheng that I tried to comprehend. We have kept in touch ever since. He understood the importance of the digital platform before any other artist in Kenya did and has been active on all social media platforms. He engages with his powerful lyrics and messages and is the voice of the people. His performances are electrifying and Juliani will pull up a crowd for any event. The second time I worked with Juliani was when he was releasing his song "Exponential Potential" exclusively on his YouTube channel. We had talked to a number of musicians about such a deal; but only Juliani understood the power of an online promotion of his channel and music video. He is a visionary and this sets him apart from many artists who just want to make quick bucks. He is endearing and keeps it real. (pers. comm., July 14, 2014)

Othole Fruityloops:

He sets trends. Has a huge following. He is God's mouthpiece. To me the top Christian artist. (Twitter, July 1, 2014)

This is only a slice of the different perspectives many people have of Juliani, but they all affirm what I have said about him and his music. As a genre, hip hop combines the creativity of individual artists with the global relevance of its message. The same can be said of Christianity, where individual convictions resonate with the sensibilities of many. Popular culture is an important platform through which to articulate, gauge, and even reconfigure the lives of youth. Specifically, social media has allowed for communication, sharing of information, and constructions of self to be sped up and to easily cross spatial and temporal boundaries. Hip hop's ability to express the raw truth of society has a prophetic role to play in Christianity. In a 2013 article featuring, among others, US Christian hip hop artist Lecrae, Owen Strachan discusses something about Lecrae's lyrical and social role that can be applied to Juliani's work: "Lecrae has developed a hard-hitting, straight-talking style that speaks to the everyday realities of fallen sinners and unfolds the cosmic solution to the problem of evil: Jesus Christ" (Strachan 2013). It is hip hop's ability to use a hard-hitting style to deliver its Christian message that makes it such a tool for youth to make sense of their beliefs and aspirations that simultaneously challenge and affirm traditional religious ideologies. It is no wonder that Lecrae's work is very much similar to that of Juliani, despite being separated by many miles of geography and having grown up in different sociocultural contexts. At "Hip Hop and Social Change," a lecture at Calvin College in Michigan, Lecrae talked about his own youth and remembered his mother tuning her car radio to gospel music and on the way back after church R&B and soul music. Lecrae often wondered why there was such a dichotomy between church and all the other spaces he and his mother occupied. He gave an example of times when he and a friend named Chris would be driving around their neighborhood with music blaring from their car speakers, and as soon as they approached a church, Chris would turn down the music, again leading Lecrae to wonder if God did not have presence in all the other spaces through which they were driving. I see these sentiments by Lecrae as very similar to Juliani's, especially Juliani's question about gospel music for the six days beyond Sunday.

I argue that these similarities between Lecrae and Juliani are not coincidental but, rather, a reflection of the power of hip hop to reconfigure any received sociocultural norms about youth experiences and expressions of their identities, be they economic, political, social, or religious. Following KRS One's assertion "Hip hop is a way of life," it does make sense that these two artists as well as many others do see their work as Christians beyond any dichotomies that other music genres or social categories may have created. Many times there have been attempts to restrict some musical genres to certain topics or spheres of life. There have also been times when Christians and the Church have been restricted to what would be considered "spiritual" realms. When the Church comments on or challenges the work and words of politicians in Kenya, for instance, Christians are often advised to stay away from politics and focus on the spiritual realm. Such assumptions that dichotomize the lives of people are what the very existence of Christian hip hop artists, such as Juliani, have challenged. Hip hop is not just a genre of music but a lived experience of life in its fullness, and to restrict it to certain areas is to deny its very nature to be part of everything. As a Christian hip hop artist, Juliani cannot help but be about every aspect of life that Christians engage and encounter daily. This is what makes him such a powerful artist and Christian.

APPENDIX

NAIROBI

- Extelecomm's Orange Shop, Extelcom House, Haile-Selassie Avenue
- Galleria Orange Shop, Karen, Galleria Shopping Mall
- Green Span Orange Shop, Savannah Road
- Industrial Area Orange Shop, Dar-es-Salaam Road
- Mega Orange Shop Telephone House, opposite Holy Family Basilica
- Naivas Machakos Shop, first floor of Naivas, Mbaitu Super Center, Syoki-mau Road
- Ngara Orange Shop, Ngara Shopping Complex, Ngara Road
- Prestige Orange Shop, Prestige Mall, junction of Ngong Road and Mugo Kabiru Road
- Sarit Centre, ground floor
- Taj Mall Orange Shop, Embakasi, junction of Outering Road and New Eastern bypass
- Telkom Plaza Orange Shop, Telkom Plaza, Ralph Bunche Road
- T-Mall Orange Shop, ground floor, T-Mall, off Langata Road and Mbaga-thi Way roundabout

CENTRAL

- Embu Orange Shop, Telephone House, near Kenya National Library, Embu
- Garissa Orange Shop, Maendeleo Plaza, Harambee Avenue
- Meru Orange Shop, Telephone House, Nanyuki Highway
- Nanyuki Orange Shop, first floor, Nanyuki Nakumatt Building

- Nyeri Orange Shop, Karson House, Kimathi Highway
- Thika Orange Shop, Telephone House, Commercial Street
- Wajir Orange Shop, Wajir Telkom Yard

CENTRAL RIFT

- Kericho Orange Shop, Telekom House, Temple Road
- Naivasha Orange Shop, next to Telephone House
- Naivas Narok Orange Shop, ground floor, Naivas Building, Njoro Road
- Nakuru Orange Shop, Telephone House, Moi Road

COAST

- Diani Mall Orange Shop, Centre Point Complex, Beach Road
- Diani Orange Shop, Arusha building, Ramisi–Lunga Lunga Road
- Kilifi Orange Shop, Telephone House, opposite Star Petrol station
- Malindi Orange Shop, Telephone House, Kenyatta Road
- Mombasa Orange Shop, Telephone House, Moi Avenue
- Nyali Orange Shop, shop 1, Nakumatt Nyali Mall

NORTH RIFT

- Eldoret Orange Shop, Telephone House, Kenyatta Street
- Kitale Orange Shop, Telephone House, Kitale Posta Road

WESTERN

- Kakamega Orange Shop, Telkom Building, Kisumu Road
- Kisii Orange Shop, ground floor, Zonic Hotel
- Kisumu Orange Shop, Telkom Plaza, Oginga Odinga Street
- Mega City Orange Shop, ground floor, Mega City Nakumatt Mall, off Nairobi Road

NOTES

1. INTERSECTIONS, OVERLAPS, AND COLLABORATIONS

1. In a study of Christian colleges in the United States, for instance, anthropologist Todd Vandenberg (2009) found the majority of the colleges did not offer majors in anthropology, unlike their non-Christian private peers.

2. See my book *Reversed Gaze*.

3. Because the artist has not given me permission to use his name, I am leaving his identity anonymous.

4. Juliani repeated this in a May 29, 2013, Twitter post. In 2011 when he, Emmanuel Jal, and Boniface Mwangi created an SMS line for promoting peace before the 2012 general elections in Kenya, they launched it at the Mau Mau Camp in Dandora where Ukooflani Mau Mau met and where Juliani learned to become a better rapper.

5. CHAT stands for Chaguo La Teeniez (Choice of teens) Awards and is a project of the *Insyder Magazine*, which recognizes Kenyan youth who have made notable contributions in sports, arts, and academics. Started in 2002, the CHAT Awards are held annually in April, when many youth in Kenya are on their school break. The Kisima Music Awards started in 1994 to acknowledge and reward excellence in music in the country and came with a hefty cash prize of one million Kenyan shillings (US$10,000) in 2011. Groove Awards, started in 2004, is the Kenyan and East Africa region's premier gospel music awards showcase. It promotes and gives recognition to artists, writers, and others for their contributions to the industry; and opens doors for upcoming aspiring singers, songwriters, and musicians. Talanta Awards was started in 1998 by Kenyans in the United States to bring restoration and realization of lost dreams and healing to wounded souls whose form of worship and expression have often been met with condemnation and judgment instead of love and guidance. For more information about Kisima and Groove, see their Kenyan websites; for the Talanta awards, see its US website.

6. On June 22, 2014, Juliani was asked the same question about the categorization of his music as gospel at an interview on *Tukuza Plus*, a Kenya Television Network show, and again talked about his faith and how it shapes all the work he does (2014b).

2. CULTURAL PREFERENCES, CHRISTIANITY, AND THE STREET

1. One case in point is the churches' response to HIV and AIDS in much of Africa, as discussed in Patterson (2006; 2010), who shows the two major responses the Church provided—completely ignoring the issue or outright condemnation. The position of the Church on HIV and AIDS has subsequently changed, but there still remain clear elements of blaming and condemning the victim. As I show in chapter 4, however, some churches are willing to engage racy and culturally controversial issues.

2. Gifford also notes that the AIC left the National Council of Churches in Kenya (NCCK) primarily because of NCCK's opposition to Moi's regime (1998:51).

3. During the Kibaki regime, for instance, the church was unable to offer an alternative voice and instead was quite often being drawn into specific political camps aligned with ethnic identities, so much so that the NCCK issued an apology to Kenyans in August 2008 for failing to maintain its "Christian identity" and instead "elevated ethnic identities" (Mue 2011:182).

4. For a critique of "prosperity Gospel" or "wealth and health Gospel," see Fee (2006); Fortner (2012); and Bowens (2012), among many others. Not all popular churches pursue this line of theology, though. Pentecostal Church leader Mensah Otabil from Ghana, whose church services are often watched on Kenyan television, challenges Christians to deal with socioeconomic issues not with prayer but with structural changes: "We can get everyone in Africa saved but that won't solve our problem. The poverty in Africa is not spiritual. Poverty is physical. Poverty is a social condition. You can bind, it won't be bound. If you are in a poor nation, you will be poor. Your personal individual prosperity is tied up with the prosperity of the nation" (Gifford 1998:240).

5. Between 1990 and 2010, for instance, there has been a steady rise in the number of hip hop artists in different parts of the continent as often reflected in the growing list at Africanhiphop's website and scholarly work by Charry (2012); Ntarangwi (2009); Osumare (2012); Saucier (2011); Shipley (2013); and Weiss (2005), among others.

6. In the 2013 general elections, there was relative peace even as the Supreme Court was deciding the presidential election results.

7. When Juliani's song "Utawala" was released in early 2013, there was quite a following, and comments on Twitter and Facebook praised Juliani for the content of the song. On October 10, 2013, Juliani retweeted an entry by Miraj Mohamud, who through his twitter handle @mirajmiskiz said: "Am Muslim I don't listen to Gospel but big up to @julianikenya, #Utawala is just a good story not a song."

8. Kiswahili does not have gender marking; the prefix used in reference to God could be either male or female.

9. For the poster and a short story, see "S£XY Mavuno Church Poster Irks Kenyans."

10. Leso is a piece of cloth commonly used women in East Africa as a wraparound. According to text on the song's YouTube site (Juliani 2013), the song is about the state of Kenya's politics and of the failure of Kenya's citizens to take responsibility for their contribution to the corrupt status quo. The song is a call on Kenyans to be introspective and judge not just the political leaders but themselves as well and to "fuata sheria," to respect the rule of law. The song was written after Boniface Mwangi, a photojournalist and activist in Kenya, shared a list of the scandals in Kenya's politics from the last five years with George Nderitu, the Sarabi band manager. They discovered that one consistent thing on that list of scandals was a government-appointed commission of inquiry.

3. HIP HOP'S RECASTING OF CHRISTIANITY AND GOSPEL MUSIC IN KENYA

1. See also Kidula (2013) for a similar example from Western Kenya.

2. These songs were very popular in the 1980s and 1990s and were played on radio and on a television show called *Joy Bringers* that aired every Sunday on Voice of Kenya (VOK) hosted by the late David Nthiwa. The Kassangas' song "Mjaribu Yesu" is on their album *Vol. 3*, and "Maisha ya Mwanandamu" is on *Vol. 1*. Kassangas Gospel Music Production (2015) gives a list of their music.

3. This is not limited to African Christians but is a phenomenon found among Christians across the globe. Stanley Hauerwas (2013), for instance, shows how American Protestantism developed along with America's capitalist identity in ways that soon conflated the two.

4. These universities include Africa Nazarene University, Catholic University of Eastern Africa, Daystar University, and Kabarak University.

5. In Ben Heron's 2007 feature documentary, *Democracy in Dakar: Hip Hop and Politics in Senegal*, Normadic Wax shows how in Senegalese national elections, two thousand hip hop artists played a major role in the eventual win of Abdoulaye Wade. Later in 2011 as Alcinda Honwana (2012) shows, hip hop artists again mobilized for a successful rejection of Wade's attempt to change the constitution to allow him to run for a third term. Joyce Nyairo and James Ogude (2005) show how "Unbwogable," a song of the hip hop duo GidiGidi MajiMaji, was appropriated by the Rainbow Coalition in Kenya as a way of mobilizing votes to seek to oust the Daniel Moi regime. In Mozambique, hip hop artist Edson d Luz, commonly known as Azagaia, was accused in 2008 of instigating the masses leading to riots in the city of Maputo through his song "Povo no Poder" (People in power). The prosecutor grilled Azagaia for an hour and a half, wanting to know, "Had he written the song? What was the purpose of the song? And did he not think that the lyrics would incite people to violence?" ("City" 2008).

6. See Condry (2007) for a close analysis of how hip hop emerged through these processes even in places far away from New York.

7. For more information, see the documentary "+Juliani—The Road Trip: *Connections*" (Juliani Music 2012).

4. KAMA SI SISI NANI? JULIANI'S GOSPEL OF SELF-EMPOWERMENT

1. Orange Kenya, a telecommunications company that offers mobile and fixed phone and internet services in Kenya, is one of the business partners working with Juliani and partly sponsored the Mtaa Challenge program for 2014. In June 2014 when Juliani released his third album, *Exponential Potential*, Orange Kenya shops around the country sold it at 20 percent off the retail price.

2. For the video of the song, see Princecam Media (2013).

3. In September 2013 reporter Vincent Achuka claimed that tour companies were charging tourists between $100 and $250 for a tour of Kibera.

4. A demonstration of the game is available on an Unbound blog ("Games" 2013).

5. MEDIA AND CONTESTED CHRISTIAN IDENTITIES

1. Safaricom's service *Kipokezi* (Swahili for "receiver") allows subscribers to send and receive e-mail and chat messages and is made available to those with phones able to use the short message service (SMS) feature. For more information on this service launch, see Njihia 2010.

2. The four-part sermon series can be heard on Nairobi Chapel's website.

GLOSSARY

bodaboda   a bicycle or motorcycle taxi

Dandora   residential area in Nairobi's eastern region where many early hip hop artists, including Juliani, grew up

Gilgil   town in the great Rift Valley with many military posts and training facilities

inuka   Swahili for "get up"; in this volume refers to a gospel radio program on the 96 FM station in Nairobi

kama si sisi   "if not us"; Juliani's program for youth empowerment

K24   television station established in 2007, broadcasting from Nairobi and the first to offer twenty-four-hour programming

Kalenjin   ethnic community inhabiting much of the Rift Valley region

Kamba   ethnic community in eastern Kenya

KBC   Kenya Broadcasting Corporation

Kikuyu   largest ethnic group in Kenya, mostly located in central Kenya

Kiswahili   "Ki-" is a prefix for a language spoken throughout east and central Africa as a lingua franca; the official and national language in Kenya and Tanzania; many times there the word "Swahili" is used but more suitable to mean the people and culture

KTN   Kenya Television Network

Kubamba   gospel television show on Citizen Television; slang for "to catch or capture"

leso   cotton wraparound, worn mostly by women; comes in multiple colors and has sayings or metaphors

mandazi   fried buns

maskani ya taifa   literally, "a nation's dwelling place"; an online conversation platform through Facebook, Google+, Twitter, and even print media to discuss national issues and citizen's rights

Meru	geographic region on the eastern slopes of Mt. Kenya; a language; an ethnic group
M-Pesa	mobile-phone money-transfer service by Kenya's Safaricom, a mobile-phone service provider
matatu	commuter omni bus
mpango wa kando	literally, "a side plan"; commonly used to refer to a mistress
msee (pl. wasee)	slang for young man
mtaa (pl. mitaa)	residential area
NTV	Nation Television
Sheng	urban slang that mixes mostly Swahili (sh) and English (eng)
sukuma	Swahili word meaning "push"; in Kenya a short form for sukuma wiki, literally "push the week," in reference to kale or spinach, which often accompanies ugali, which is preferred with meat but kale or spinach used to push the week until enough money to buy meat
tukuza	Kiswahili word for "praise" but here denotes a gospel television show on KTN
ugali	starchy meal of maize or corn flour made with water to a dough-like consistency; stiff porridge and served with cooked vegetables, stew, or beans
Ukooflani Mau Mau	group of hip hop artists based in Dandora

DISCOGRAPHY

This discography lists songs used in the analyses in this text.

"Bahasha ya Ocampo," Juliani, *Pulpit Kwa Street* (2011)
"Biceps," Juliani, *Mtaa Mentality* (2009)
"Church on Monday," Juliani, *Pulpit Kwa Street* (2011)
"Exponential Potential," Juliani, *Mtaa Mentality* (2009)
"Friend Request," Juliani, *Pulpit Kwa Street* (2011)
"Hela," Juliani, *Mtaa Mentality* (2009)
"I Do It," Juliani, *Exponential Potential* (2014)
"Jesusnosis," Ukooflani Mau Mau, *Dandora Burning* (2006)
"Kama Si Sisi," Juliani, *Mtaa Mentality* (2009)
"Kitanda Yangu 4 by 6," Juliani, *Pulpit Kwa Street* (2011)
"Masterpiece," Juliani, *Exponential Potential* (2014)
"MH370," Juliani, *Exponential Potential* (2014)
"Morio na Juliet," Juliani, *Exponential Potential* (2014)
"One Day," Juliani, *Exponential Potential* (2014)
"Pendo Kweli," Juliani, *Mtaa Mentality* (2009)
"Rimz na Timz," Juliani, *Mtaa Mentality* (2009)
"Samaki Baharini," Juliani, *Exponential Potential* (2014)
"Voters vs. Vultures," Juliani, *Voters vs. Vultures* (2013)
"Who Is to Blame," Juliani, *Mtaa Mentality* (2009)

BIBLIOGRAPHY

Abbink, Jon, and Ineke van Kessel, eds. 2005. *Vanguard or Vandals: Youth Politics and Conflict in Africa*. Leiden: Brill.

"About Uwezo Fund." 2015. *Uwezo Fund*. Accessed February 12, 2015. www.uwezo.go.ke.

"About Youth Enterprise Development Fund." 2015. *Youth Enterprise Development Fund*. Accessed October 1, 2015. http://www.youthfund.go.ke/.

Achuka, Vincent. 2013. "Slum Tourism: The New Fad for Foreigners Visiting Kenya." *Nairobi Daily Nation*, September 7. Accessed July 5, 2014. http://mobile.nation .co.ke/lifestyle/Slum+tourism+The+new+fad+for+foreigners+visiting+Kenya +/-/1950774/1983218/-/format/xhtml/-/11vfcfc/-/index.html.

ACM FTT (Africa Centre for Missions Finish the Task). 2004. *The Unfinished Task, a National Survey of Churches in Kenya*. Nairobi, Kenya: Africa Centre for Missions Finish the Task.

Ajayi, Ayo A., Leah T. Marangu, Janice Miller, and John M. Paximan. 1991. "Adolescent Sexuality and Fertility in Kenya: A Survey of Knowledge, Perceptions, and Practices." *Studies in Family Planning* 22 (4): 205–16.

Allen, Curtis "Voice." 2013. *Does God Listen to Rap? Christians and the World's Most Controversial Music*. Hudson, OH: Curciform Press.

Amutabi, Maurice. 2006. *The NGO Factor in Africa: The Case of Arrested Development in Kenya*. New York: Routledge.

Archambault, Julie. 2013. "Cruising through Uncertainty: Cell Phones and the Politics of Display and Disguise in Inhambane, Mozambique." *America Ethnologist* 40 (1): 88–101.

Arnold, Dean. 2006. "Why Are There So Few Christian Anthropologists? Reflections on the Tensions between Christianity and Anthropology." *Perspectives on Science and Christian Faith* 58 (4): 266–82.

Aron, Morris. 2009. "Kenya Lost Ksh23b in Maize Scandal." *Nairobi Standard Media*, December 19. Accessed July 26, 2014. http://www.standardmedia.co.ke/business/article/1144030785/kenya-lost-sh23b-in-maize-scandal.

Arriola, Leonard. 2009. "Patronage and Political Stability in Africa." *Comparative Political Studies* 42 (10): 1339–62.

Asamoah-Gyadu, J. Kwabena. 2005. ""Christ Is the Answer": What Is the Question?' A Ghana Airways Prayer Vigil and Its Implications for Religion, Evil, and Public Space." *Journal of Religion in Africa* 35 (1): 93–117

Atieno, Mary. 2015[1989]. "Adamu na Eva" (Adam and Eve). *Society of Kenya*. Accessed February 14, 2014. https://www.youtube.com/watch?v=2faZEj4C5Uc.

Banda, Collium. 2005. "The Sufficiency of Christ in Africa: A Christological Challenge from African Traditional Religions." Master's thesis, University of South Africa. Accessed January 2, 2011. http://uir.unisa.ac.za/bitstream/handle/10500/1434/dissertation.pdf.

Banda, Tim Kamuzu. 2013. "Mavuno Church." *Chapelites. Nairobi Chapel*, February 13. Accessed July 26, 2014. http://nairobichapel.org/NC/downloads/Chapelites FebEdition-2013.pdf.

Ban Ki-Moon. 2014. "Realizing the Future They Want." Address, United Nations Economic and Social Council Youth Forum, New York, July 2. Accessed July 5, 2014. http://webtv.un.org/watch/ban-ki-moon-ecosoc-youth-forum-2014/3601541870001/.

Baudrillard, Jean. 1983. *Simulations*. Cambridge, MA: MIT Press.

BBC. 2013. "Kenya Condom Advert Pulled after Religious Complaints." *BBC*, March 20. Accessed July 21, 2014. http://www.bbc.com/news/world-africa-21859665.

———. 2014. "Kenya's Nairobi Hit by Twin Bomb Blasts in Gikomba Market." *BBC*, May 16. Accessed May 20, 2014. www.bbc.com/news/world-africa-27443474.

Bediako, Kwame. 2000. "Africa and Christianity on the Threshold of the Third Millennium: The Religious Dimension." *African Affairs* 99:303–23.

Bell, Elizabeth. 2008. *Theories of Performance*. Thousand Oaks, CA: Sage.

Bodewes, Christine. 2011. "The Catholic Church and Civic Education in the Slums of Nairobi." In *Jesus and Ubuntu: Exploring the Social Impact of Christianity in Africa*, edited by Mwenda Ntarangwi, 147–74. Trenton, NJ: Africa World Press.

Boellstorff, Tom, Bonnie Nardi, Celia Pearce, and T. L. Taylor. 2012. *Ethnography and Virtual Worlds: A Handbook of Method*. Princeton: Princeton University Press.

Bowens, Jeffrey B. 2012. *Prosperity Gospel and Its Effect on the 21st Century Church: A Historical and Theological Perspective*. Bloomington, IN: Xlibris.

Boyo, Bernard. 2009. *Theology and Politics: The Role of the Church*. Saarbrücken, Germany: Lambert Academic.

Bratt, James D. 1998. *Abraham Kuyper: A Centennial Reader*. Grand Rapids, MI: Eerdmans.

Bratton, Michael. 1994. "Civil Society and Political Transitions in Africa." In *Civil Society and the State in Africa*, edited by John W. Haberson, Donald Rothchild, and Naomi Chazan, 51–81. Boulder, CO: Rienner.

Brooks, James, and Ian Boal, eds. 1995. *Resisting the Virtual Life: The Culture and Politics of Information*. San Francisco: City Lights.

Bruner, Edward M. 1991. "The Transformation of Self in Tourism." *Annals of Tourism Research* 18 (2): 238–50.

Bruyns, Clint Le. 2012. "The Rebirth of Kairos Theology? A Public Theological Perspective." *Academia.edu*, 2012. Accessed October 19, 2013. http://www.academia.edu/1484082/The_Rebirth_of_Kairos_Theology_A_Public_Theological_Perspective.

Buckley, Thomas. 1987. "Dialogue and Shared Authority: Informants as Critics." *Central Issues in Anthropology* 7 (1): 13–23.

Burgess, G. Thomas, and Andrew Burton. 2010. Introduction to *Generations Past: Youth in East African History*, edited by Andrew Burton and Helen Charton-Bigot, 1–24. Athens: Ohio University Press.

Capital FM Kenya. 2014. "Mavuno Church: Apologise for What?" *Capitol FM Kenya*, February 25. Accessed July 21, 2014. www.youtube.com/watch?v=7ym5g WALHic.

Carpenter, Joel. 2006. "The Christian Scholar in an Age of World Christianity." In *Christianity and the Soul of the University*, edited by Douglas Henry and Michael Beaty, 65–84. Grand Rapids, MI: Baker.

Charry, Eric. 2012. "A Capsule History of African Rap." In *Hip Hop Africa: New African Music in a Globalizing World*, edited by Charry, 1–28. Bloomington: Indiana University Press.

Chepkwony, Adam. 2005. "Religion and Science: Living 'Double' Lives in Africa." Paper presented at the Metanexus Institute program "Science and Religion: Global Perspectives," Philadelphia, PA, June 4–8. Accessed June 19, 2014. http://www.metanexus.net/archive/conference2005/pdf/arap_chepkwony.pdf.

Citizen TV. 2015. "TV Schedule." Accessed October 2, 2105. http://citizentv.co.ke/tv/tv-schedule/.

"City Authorities Called Rapper In for Questioning." 2008. *Freemuse*, 2000–14. Accessed July 3, 2011. http://freemuse.org/archives/1223.

Clark, Msia K. 2012. "Hip Hop as Social Commentary in Accra and Dar es Salaam." *African Studies Quarterly* 13 (3): 23–46. Accessed June 2, 2014. http://www.africa.ufl.edu/asq/v13/v13i3a2.pdf.

Clark, Shelley, and Rohini Mathur. 2012. "Dating, Sex, and Schooling in Urban Kenya." *Studies in Family Planning* 43 (3): 161–74.

Clifford, James. 1988. *The Predicament of Culture: Twentieth-Century Ethnography, Literature, and Art*. Cambridge, MA: Harvard University Press.

Clifford, James, and George Marcus, eds. 1986. *Writing Culture: The Poetics and Politics of Ethnography*. Berkeley: University of California Press.

Codrington, Raymond. 2007. "Hip Hop beyond Appropriation: An Introduction to the Series." *Transforming Anthropology* 15 (2): 138–40.

Cohen, David William, and E. S. Atieno Odhiambo. 1992. *Burying SM: The Politics of Knowledge and the Sociology of Power in Africa*. London: James Currey.

Cole, Jennifer. 2004. "Fresh Contact in Tamatave, Madagascar: Sex, Money, and Intergenerational Transformation." *American Ethnologist* 31 (4): 573–88.

Comaroff, Jean, and John Comaroff. 1993. Introduction to *Modernity and Its Malcontents: Ritual and Power in Postcolonial Africa*, edited by Comaroff and Comaroff, xi–xxxvii. Chicago: University of Chicago Press.

Condry, Ian. 2001. "Japanese Hip-Hop and the Globalization of Popular Culture." In *Urban Life: Readings in the Anthropology of the City*, edited by George Gmelch and Walter Zenner, 357–87. Prospect Heights, IL: Waveland.

———. 2007. *Hip-Hop Japan: Rap and the Paths of Cultural Globalization.* Durham: Duke University Press.

Cooper, Barbara. 2006. *Evangelical Christians in the Muslim Sahel.* Bloomington: Indiana University Press.

Corbett, Steve, and Brian Fikkert. 2009. *When Helping Hurts: How to Alleviate Poverty without Hurting the Poor.* Chicago: Moody.

Damdinjav, Mongoljingoo, Isabel Garcia, Emily Lawson, David Margolis, and Ben Nemeth. 2013. "Institutional Failure in Kenya and a Way Forward." *Journal of Political Inquiry* (Spring): 1–25. Accessed July 30, 2014. http://www.jpinyu.com/wp-content/uploads/2015/01/institutional_failure_in_kenya_and_a_way_forward1.pdf.

Delaney, Ryan. 2013. "Using Tech to Make Kenya's Problems Harder to Ignore." *Innovation Trail*, October 1. Accessed June 1, 2014. http://innovationtrail.org/post/using-tech-make-kenyas-problems-harder-ignore.

Dewey, Susan, and Karen Brison, eds. 2012. *Super Girls, Gangstas, Freeters, and Xenomaniacs: Gender and Modernity in Global Youth Cultures.* Syracuse: Syracuse University Press.

Dijk, Rijk van. 1999. *Pentecostalism, Gerontocratic Rule, and Democratization in Malawi: The Changing Position of the Young in Political Culture.* New York: St. Martin's.

Dijk, Rijk van, Mirjam de Bruijn, Carlos Cardoso, and Inge Butter. 2011. "Introduction: Ideologies of Youth." *Africa Development* 36 (3–4): 1–17.

Domínguez, Daniel, Anne Beaulieu, Adolfo Estalella, Edgar Gómez, Bernt Schnettler, and Rosie Read. 2007. "Virtual Ethnography." *Forum: Qualitative Sozialforschung / Forum: Qualitative Social Research* 8 (3): 1–3. Accessed July 16, 2014. http://www.qualitative-research.net/index.php/fqs/article/view/274/601.

Durham, Deborah. 2000. "Youth and the Social Imagination in Africa: Introduction to Parts 1 and 2." *Anthropological Quarterly* 73 (3): 113–20.

Edelman, Marc, and Angelique Haugerud. 2005. "Introduction: The Anthropology of Development and Globalization." In *The Anthropology of Development and Globalization*, edited by Edelman and Haugerud, 1–74. Malden, MA: Blackwell.

Edmonds, Ennis B. 1998. "Dread 'I' In-a-Babylon: Ideological Resistance and Cultural Revitalization." In *Chanting Down Babylon: The Rastafari Reader*, edited by Nathaniel Samuel Murrell, William David Spencer, and Adrian Anthony McFarlane, 23–35. Philadelphia: Temple University Press.

Ellis, Carolyn, Tony E. Adams, and Arthur P. Bochner. 2010. "Autoethnography: An Overview." *Forum Qualitative Sozialforschung / Forum: Qualitative Social Research* 12 (1). Accessed July 23, 2014. 8.

Etemesi, Beatrice A. 2007. "Impact of Hair Relaxers in Women in Nakuru, Kenya." *International Journal of Dermatology* 46 (1): 23–25.

Eze, Michael Onyebuchi. 2010. *Intellectual History in Contemporary South Africa.* London: Palgrave.

Fasholé-Luke, Edward. 1978. Introduction to *Christianity in Independent Africa,* edited by Fasholé-Luke, Richard Gray, Adrian Hastings, and Godwin Tasie, 355–67. London: Rex Collings.

Fee, Gordon D. 2006. *The Disease of the Health and Wealth Gospels.* Vancouver: Regent College.

Felluga, Dino. 2002. "Modules on Baudrillard: On Postmodernity." In *Introductory Guide to Critical Theory. Purdue U.* Accessed July 7, 2014. http://www.purdue.edu/guidetotheory/postmodernism/modules/baudrillardpostmodernity.html.

Ferree, Karen, Clark Gibson, and James Long. 2014. "Voting Behavior and Electoral Irregularities in Kenya's 2013 Election." *Journal of Eastern Africa Studies* 10 (48): 1–20.

Fish, Adam. 2011. "Indigenous Digital Media and the History of the Internet on the Columbia Plateau." *Journal of Northwest Anthropology* 45 (1): 91–114.

Forster, Dion. 2006. "Self-Validating Consciousness in Strong Artificial Intelligence: An African Theological Contribution." PhD dissertation, University of South Africa Pretoria.

Fortner, Michael D. 2012. *The Prosperity Gospel Exposed: And Other False Doctrines.* Seattle, WA: CreateSpace.

"Games Children Play in Africa: Bano (Swahili for Marbles)." 2013. *Unbound,* July 30. Accessed July 13, 2014. http://blog.unbound.org/2013/07/30/games-children-play-in-africa-bano-swahili-for-marbles/.

Gamson, William, David Croteau, William Hoynes, and Theodore Sasson. 1992. "Media Images and the Social Construction of Reality." *Annual Review of Sociology* 18:373–93.

Gathu, Jimmy. 1991. "Stay Alive." Accessed September 21, 2015. https://www.youtube.com/watch?v=EwWZsdmYd1E.

Geertz, Clifford. 1973. *Interpretation of Cultures: Selected Essays.* New York: Basic Books.

Gifford, Paul. 1992. Introduction to *New Dimensions in African Christianity,* edited by Gifford, 1–23. Nairobi: All Africa Conference of Churches.

———. 1998. *African Christianity: Its Public Role.* Bloomington: Indiana University Press.

———. 2004. *Ghana's New Christianity: Pentecostalism in a Globalising African Economy.* Bloomington: Indiana University Press.

———, ed. 2009. *Christianity, Politics, and Public Life in Kenya.* New York: Columbia University Press.

Gitari, David. 1996. *In Season and Out of Season: Sermons to a Nation*. Eugene, OR: Wipf and Stock.

Gitau, Elly. 2015. "Bob Collymore Gives Personal Gym to Juliani." *Nairobi Star*. Accessed February 24, 2015. http://www.the-star.co.ke/article/bob-collymore-gives -personal-gym-juliani.

Google. 2013. "Zeitgeist 2012: Kenya Search Trends." Accessed June 2014. http://www .google.co.in/zeitgeist/2012/#kenya/searches.

Gottlieb, Alma, and Philip Graham. 1993. *Parallel Worlds: An Anthropologist and a Writer Encounter Africa*. Chicago: University of Chicago Press.

Gueye, Marame. 2013. "Urban Guerrilla Poetry: The Movement Y'en a Marre and the Socio-Political Influences of Hip Hop in Senegal." *Journal of Pan-African Studies* 6 (3): 22–42.

Hall, Stuart. 1997. *Representation: Cultural Representations and Signifying Practices*. London: Sage.

Hansen, Karen T. 2005. "Getting Stuck in the Compound: Some Odds against Social Adulthood in Lusaka, Zambia." *Africa Today* 51 (4): 3–16.

Hauerwas, Stanley. 2013. "The End of American Protestantism." *ABC Religion and Ethics*, July 2. Accessed October 8, 2013. http://www.abc.net.au/religion/articles/ 2013/07/02/3794561.htm.

Haugerud, Angelique. 1997. *The Culture of Politics in Modern Kenya*. Cambridge: Cambridge University Press.

Henderson, Patti. 2003. *Annotated Bibliography on Childhood with Emphasis on Africa: Outline, General Findings, and Research Recommendations*. Dakar, Senegal: CODESRIA Books.

Hodge, Daniel White. 2010. *The Soul of Hip Hop: Rims, Tims, and a Cultural Theology*. Downers Grove, IL: InterVarsity.

Hodgson, Geoffrey M. 2007. "Meanings of Methodological Individualism." *Journal of Economic Methodology* 14 (2): 211–26.

Hoekema, David. 2010. "Religious Rights: Christians and Muslims in Kenya." *Christian Century*, June 15. Accessed August 23, 2011. http://www.christiancentury.org/ article/2010-06/religious-rights.

Holy Bible New International Version (NIV). 2011. Grand Rapids, MI: Zondervan.

Honwana, Alcinda. 2012. *The Time of Youth: Work, Social Change, and Politics in Africa*. Sterling, VA: Kumarian.

Honwana, Alcinda Manuel, and Filip de Boeck, eds. 2005. *Makers and Breakers: Children and Youth in Postcolonial Africa*. Oxford: James Currey.

Hope, Kempe Ronald, Sr. 2012. *The Political Economy of Development in Kenya*. New York: Continuum International.

Howell, Brian. 2007. "The Repugnant Other Speaks Back: Christian Identity as an Ethnographic 'Standpoint.'" *Anthropological Theory* 7 (4): 371–91.

———. 2015. "Anthropology and the Making of Bill Graham: Evangelicalism and Anthropology in the 20th-Century United States." *American Anthropologist* 117 (1): 59–70.

Howell, Brian, and Jenell Paris. 2010. *Introducing Cultural Anthropology: A Christian Perspective*. Grand Rapids, MI: Baker Academic.

Hughes, Dana. 2010. "Some of the Best Paid Politicians in the World Are in . . . Kenya???" *ABC News*, July 1. Accessed July 30, 2014. blogs/abcnews.com/the worldnewser/2010/07/some-of-the-best-paid-politicians-in-the-world-are-in -kenya/html.

Hunter, James Davison. 2010. *To Change the World: The Irony, Tragedy, and Possibility of Christianity in the Late Modern World*. New York: Oxford University Press.

Inda, Jonathan Xavier, and Renato Rosaldo. 2007. *The Anthropology of Globalization: A Reader*, Malden, MA: Wiley.

International Labour Organization. 2012. "Africa's Response to Youth Employment Crisis." *ILO*, March–May. Accessed July 5, 2014. http://www.ilo.org/wcmsp5/ groups/public/---africa/documents/publication/wcms_184325.pdf.

Irvine, Janice. 2002. *Talk about Sex: The Battle over Sex Education in the United States*. Berkeley: University of California Press.

Jackson, John L., Jr. 2013. *Thin Description: Ethnography and the African Hebrew Israelites of Jerusalem*. Cambridge, MA: Harvard University Press.

Jeffrey, Craig. 2010. "Timepass: Youth, Class, and Time among Unemployed Young Men in India." *American Ethnologist* 37 (3): 465–81.

Jenkins, Philip. 2002. *The Next Christendom: The Coming of Global Christianity*. New York: Oxford University Press.

———. 2006. *The New Faces of Christianity: Believing the Bible in the Global South*. New York: Oxford University Press.

Jones, E. Stanley. 1925. *Christ of the Indian Road*. Cincinnati, OH: Abingdon.

Juliani (Julius Owino). 2004. "Jesusnosis." https://www.youtube.com/watch?v =reJH7Dt8vxs.

———. 2011a. Interview with Jeff Koinange. "*Capital Talk* Julius Owino: Juliani Part 1." *K24TV*, April 4, 2011. Accessed July 21, 2012. http://www.youtube.com/watch?v =eHCMDL5z3A8.

———. 2011b. Interview with Jeff Koinange. "*Capital Talk* Julius Owino: Juliani Part 2." *K24TV*, April 6, 2011. Accessed June 11, 2014. www.youtube.com/watch?v =84hpMo5aTyc&list=PLE7AA29F6D7DC262B&index=2.

———. 2011c. Interview with Jeff Koinange. "*Capital Talk* Julius Owino: Juliani Part 4." *K24TV*, April 6, 2011. Accessed June 9, 2014. https://www.youtube.com/ watch?v=21FI02v9qio.

———. 2012a. Interview with Jesse Shipley. *Kenya 2*, March 9. Accessed April 12, 2014. https://www.youtube.com/watch?v=5-0wZ-8Kzas.

———. 2012b. "Unmasking Juliani." Interview with Larry Madowo. *#theTrend*, *NTV*, December 11. Accessed May 23, 2013. http://www.ntv.co.ke/news2/topheadlines/ thetrend-unmasking-juliani/.

———. 2013. "Fuata Sheria (Follow the law) by Sarabi Band ft. Juliani." http://www .youtube.com/watch?v=8QGx_6lMjGI.

———. 2013–15. Twitter account. https://www.twitter.com/julianikenya.

———. 2014a. Interview with Maskani ya Taifa. *Google+ Hangout*, March 20. Accessed March 22, 2014. https://www.youtube.com/watch?v=73M1Vyt3fN4.

———. 2014b. "Title vs Function: Juliani Explains His Style of Music." *Tukuza Plus*. *KTN News*, June 22. Accessed July 5, 2014. https://www.youtube.com/watch?v=mx6fRKnvLs8.

Juliani Music. 2012. "+Juliani—The Road Trip: *Connections.*" Accessed April 29, 2014. https://www.youtube.com/watch?v=zV5FT_jhmsU.

———. 2013a. "Chocolate City: Kibera Ad Mtaa Challenge." June 2. Accessed July 5, 2014. https://www.youtube.com/watch?v=9BDgnKFsDJs.

———. 2013b. "Juliani: Voters vs Vultures ft. Dela." Julianimusic, February 13. Accessed July 30, 2014. https://www.youtube.com/watch?v=7DMMlpIrIIw.

———. 2014–15. *Facebook*. https://www.facebook.com/julianimusic.

"Juliani: The Voice of Reason with a Mic." 2013. *Smart Life (a Lifestyle Magazine for Nakumatt Shoppers)*, July–September, 58–59.

Kaberia, Isaac Kubai. 2013. "Just Reconciliation: The Church's Response to Ethnopolitical Violence in Kenya." PhD dissertation, MF Norwegian School of Theology, Oslo, Norway. Accessed September 27, 2015. http://brage.bibsys.no/xmlui/bitstream/handle/11250/161409/AVH5010-kand-nr-3020-masteravhandling-Matinavn.pdf.

Kalu, Ogbu. 1998. "The Third Response: Pentecostalism and the Reconstruction of Christian Experience in Africa, 1970–1995." *Journal of African Christian Thought* 1 (2): 3–16.

———. 2007. "Pentecostalism and Mission in Africa, 1970–2000." *Mission Studies* 24:9–45.

Kama Si Sisi. 2014. "About Kama Si Sisi." *Facebook*, 2014. Accessed June 6, 2014. https://www.facebook.com/KAMASISISI/info.

Kangethe, Kennedy. 2013. "Call for Consensus over Condom Advert." *Bizcommunity.com*, March 25. Accessed July 21, 2014. http://www.bizcommunity.co.ke/Print.aspx?l=111&c=66&ct=1&ci=91130.

Karanja, Beatrice. 2012. "How Africa Tweets." *Portland Communications*. Accessed December 3, 2013. http://www.portland-communications.com/publications/the-quarterly-issue-6/how-africa-tweets/.

Kariuki, John. 1990. "Gospel Music in Vogue." *Nairobi Sunday Nation*, April 8, 1990, 2.

Kasali, David. 1998. "Kenya: Plagued by Superficiality." *Christianity Today* 42 (13): 56–58.

Kassanga, Japheth, and Ann Kassanga. "Maisha ya Mwanadamu" (Human life). *Praise Him: KMC Collection Vol. 2*. Accessed October 18, 2015. https://itunes.apple.com/us/album/kmc-collection-vol.-3-mjaribu/id983347034.

———. "Mjaribu Yesu/Yesu Ni Dawa ya Pekee" (Try Jesus/Jesus is the only medicine/answer). 2015. *Mjaribu Yesu: KMC Collection Vol. 3*. Accessed October 18, 2015. https://itunes.apple.com/us/album/kmc-collection-2-praise-him/id983469772.

Kassangas Gospel Music Production. 2015. "Gospel Music Database." Accessed October 2, 2015. www.ssmk.net/kassangas.htm.

Katongole, Emmanuel. 2010. *The Sacrifice of Africa: A Political Theology.* Grand Rapids, MI: Eerdmans.

Kenya National Bureau of Statistics (KNBS). 2010. *Kenya Demographic and Health Survey 2008–2009.* Nairobi, Kenya: KNBS.

———. 2014. "Kenya Facts and Figures 2014." *KNBS.* Accessed July 7, 2014. http://www.knbs.or.ke/.

———. 2015. "Religious Affiliation." *KNBS,* 2015. Accessed January 23, 2015. http://www.knbs.or.ke/.

Kenya Open Data. 2010. "2009 Census Volume 2 Table 12 Population by Religious Affiliation." Accessed October 2, 2015. https://www.opendata.go.ke/Religion/2009-Census-Volume-2-Table-12-Population-by-Religi/jrmn-krnf.

"Kenya Television Network." 2015. *Wikipedia.* http://en.wikipedia.org/wiki/Kenya_Television_Network.

Kerongo, Grace. 2011. "Juliani and Jal Launch SMS Peace Line." *Nairobi Star,* September 8. Accessed June 1, 2013. http://www.the-star.co.ke/news/article-50302/juliani-and-jal-launch-sms-peace-line#sthash.q7y2QoUq.dpuf.

Kidula, Jean. 2000. "Polishing the Luster of the Stars: Music Professionalism Made Workable in Kenya." *Ethnomusicology* 44 (3): 408–28.

———. 2012. "The Local and Global in Kenyan Rap and Hip Hop Culture." In *Hip Hop Africa: New African Music in a Globalizing World,* edited by Eric Charry, 171–86. Bloomington: Indiana University Press.

———. 2013. *Music in Kenyan Christianity: Logooli Religious Song.* Bloomington: Indiana University Press.

Kisaka, Oliver. 2008. "Religion's Role in Kenya." *PBS,* June 18. Accessed November 22, 2013. http://www.pbs.org/wnet/religionandethics/2008/06/13/june-13-2008-religions-role-in-kenya/51/.

Kretzmann, Jody, and John McKnight. 1993. *Building Communities from the Inside Out.* Chicago: ACTA.

KTN News Kenya. 2014a. "Checkpoint: Interview—Mavuno Church Leaders." *KTN,* February 24. Accessed July 21, 2014. https://www.youtube.com/watch?v=7D_aOlj5QAw.

———. 2014b. "Viongozi wa kanisa la Mavuno wajitokeza wazi na kujitetea" (Mavuno Church leaders come out to defend themselves). *KTN,* February 23. Accessed July 25, 2014. https://www.youtube.com/watch?v=ScD2z2swuwQ.

Kuyper, Abraham. 1998. *Abraham Kuyper: A Centennial Reader.* Edited by James D. Bratt. Grand Rapids, MI: Eerdmans.

Lamont, Mark. 2010. "Lip-Synch Gospel: Christian Music and the Ethnopoetics of Identity in Kenya, Africa." *Journal of the International Africa Institute* 80 (3): 473–96.

Light, Vernon Ellis. 2010. "The Evangelical Church in Africa: Towards a Model for Christian Discipleship." Masters thesis, Fort Hare University, Alice, South Africa.

Lindhardt, Martin. 2009. "More Than Just Money: The Faith Gospel and Occult Economies in Contemporary Tanzania." *Nova Religio: The Journal of Alternative and Emergent Religions* 13 (1): 41–67.

Livermore, David. 2006. *Serving with Eyes Wide Open: Doing Short-Term Missions with Cultural Intelligence.* Grand Rapids, MI: Baker.

Logos Christian School. 2011. "About Nairobi Chapel." Accessed July 20, 2014. http://www.logos.ac.ke/nairobi_chapel.html.

Louw, Daniel. 2001. "Ubuntu and the Challenges of Multiculturalism in Post-Apartheid South Africa." *Quest: An African Journal of Philosophy* 15 (1–2): 15–36.

Maimela, Simon. 1991. "Traditional African Anthropology and Christian Theology." *Journal of Theology for Southern Africa* 76:4–14.

Makers Trading Co. 2014. "Nairobi: Juliani." *Makers Trading Co.* Accessed April 4, 2014. https://www.youtube.com/watch?v=dE3ERHlfDzQ.

Marsh, Charles. 2001. *The Last Days: A Son's Story of Sin and Segregation at the Dawn of the New South.* New York: Basic Books.

Mathangani, Patrick. 2011. "Raila's Family Was Involved in Maize Scandal, Claims US Cable." *Nairobi Standard Media,* March 1. Accessed July 26, 2014. http://www.standardmedia.co.ke/business/article/2000030197/raila-s-family-was-involved-in-maize-scandal-claim-us-cables.

Mathewes, Charles. 2007. *A Theology of Public Life.* Cambridge: Cambridge University Press.

Mavuno Church. 2014a. Twitter account. https://twitter.com/mavunochurchorg.

———. 2014b. "We the Fearless—Moses Mbasu." *Mavuno Church,* January 29. Accessed July 26, 2014. https://www.youtube.com/watch?v=vmOu6whc2HQ.

May, Ann. 1996. "Handshops and Hope: Young Street Vendors in Dar es Salaam, Tanzania." *Anthropology of Work Review* 17 (1–2): 25–34.

Mbiti, John S. 1969. *African Religions and Philosophy.* London: Heinemann.

———. 1980. "The Encounter of Christian Faith and African Religion." *Christianity Century* 97, 817–20.

Mbugua, Njeri. 2007. "Factors Inhibiting Educated Mothers in Kenya from Giving Meaningful Sex-Education to their Daughters." *Social Science and Medicine* 64:1079–89.

Meyer, Birgit. 1999. *Translating the Devil: Religion and Modernity among the Ewe in Ghana,* Edinburgh: Edinburgh University Press.

Ministry of State for Youth Affairs. 2009. "Strategic Plan 2007–2012." *Youthpolicy.org.* Accessed October 2, 2015. http://www.youthpolicy.org/national/Kenya_2007_Strategic_Youth_Plan.pdf.

Moore, Lecrae. 2015. "Hip Hop and Social Change." Lecture presented at Calvin College Covenant Fine Arts Center Auditorium, Grand Rapids, MI, March 28.

Moreno-Black, Geraldine, and Pissamal Homchampa. 2008. "Collaboration, Cooperation, and Working Together: Anthropologists Creating a Space for Research and Academic Partnerships." *Annals of Anthropological Practice* 29 (1): 87–93.

Mose, Caroline. 2011. "Jua Cali-Justice: Navigating the 'Mainstream-Underground' Dichotomy in Kenyan Hip-Hop Culture." In *Native Tongues: The African Hip-Hop Reader,* edited by P. K Saucier, 69–104. New York: African World Press.

———. 2013. "'Swag' and 'Cred': Representing Hip Hop in an African City." *Journal of Pan African Studies* 6 (3): 106–32.

"Msanii na Sanaa: Juliani" (Art and artist: Juliani). 2009. *NTV*, July 10. Accessed March 7, 2015. https://www.youtube.com/watch?v=SCd_HuR6WIs.

The Mtaa Challenge. [2014]. *Better, Safer Nairobi: Solutions from the Grassroots.* Nairobi: Storify.

Mue, Njonjo. 2011. "Reflecting on Church-State Relationship in Kenya." In *Jesus and Ubuntu: Exploring the Social Impact of Christianity in Africa*, edited by Mwenda Ntarangwi, 175–90. Trenton, NJ: Africa World Press.

Mueller, Susanne. 2008. "The Political Economy of Kenya's Crisis." *Journal of Eastern African Studies* 2 (2): 185–210.

Mugambi, Jesse K. 1996. "African Churches in Social Transformation." *Journal of International Affairs* 50 (1): 194–220.

Muganda-Onyando, Rosemarie, and Martin Omondi. 2008. *Down the Drain: Counting the Cost of Teenage Pregnancy and School Dropout in Kenya.* Nairobi: Centre for the Study of Adolescence.

Muhula, Raymond. 2007. "Youth and Politics in Kenya: Promise of Peril?" *Africa Insight* 37 (3): 362–75.

Mumah, Joyce, Caroline Kabiru, Carol Mukiira, Jessica Brinton, Michael Mutua, Chimaraoke Izugbara, Harriet Birungi, and Ian Askew. 2014. "Unintended Pregnancies in Kenya: A Country Profile." STEP UP Research Report. Nairobi: African Population and Health Research Center. Accessed January 15, 2016. http://www.popcouncil.org/uploads/pdfs/2014STEPUP_KenyaCountryProfile.pdf

Munishi, Faustin. 1995. "Injili na Siasa" (The gospel and politics). *Malebo Vol. 6*, Nairobi, Kenya. Accessed October 18, 2015. https://www.youtube.com/watch?v=EjAiRsDURVE.

Mwende, Judy. 2015."Kenya Has 26.1 m Internet Users." *Business Review*, April 7. Accessed September 21, 2015. http://www.kenyanbusinessreview.com/701/internet-users-in-kenya/.

Narayan, Kirin. 1991. "Ethnography and Fiction: Where Is the Border?" *Anthropology and Humanism* 24 (2): 134–47.

National Council for Population and Development (NCPD). 1999. "Kenya Demographic and Health Survey 1998." Calverton, MD: NDPD. Accessed July 25, 2014. http://dhsprogram.com/pubs/pdf/FR102/FR102.pdf.

Nduto, Steven. 2014. "The Concept of Death among Pastors in Ukambani." Paper presented at the seminar "Conversation between Church and Academy in Kenya," International Association for the Promotion of Christian Higher Education (IAPCHE), Methodist Guesthouse, Nairobi, Kenya, May 10.

Nelson, Tom. 2011. *Work Matters: Connecting Sunday Worship to Monday Work.* Wheaton, IL: Crossway.

The New Calvinists. 2014. "Piper and Hip Hop." *New Calvinist.* Accessed October 1, 2015. http://www.newcalvinist.com/john-piper-2/piper-and-hip-hop/.

Ngirachu, John. 2014. "New Law Allowing Polygamy Passed." *Nairobi Daily Nation*, March 20. Accessed July 6, 2014. http://mobile.nation.co.ke/news/Marriage-Bill -Amendments-Polygamy-MPs-National-Assembly/-/1950946/2252204/-/format/ xhtml/-/15g7fat/-/index.html.

Niaje TV. 2013. "Banned Kenyan Condom Advert." *Niaje TV*, March 26. Accessed July 21, 2014. https://www.youtube.com/watch?v=lTfpWrG51ms.

Niehous, Isak, Eliazaar Mohlala, and Kally Shokaneo. 2001. *Witchcraft, Power, and Politics: Exploring the Occult in the South African Lowveld*. London: Pluto.

Njau, Richard. 2008. "Hip Hope Presents 'Juliani.'" *YouTube*, 2008. Accessed June 12, 2013. https://www.youtube.com/watch?v=qx2PoKwcPyE.

———. 2011. "Juliani Live on 99 Degrees." *YouTube*, 2011. Accessed December 2, 2013. http://www.youtube.com/watch?v=03Hpx9wE5Og.

Njenga, Moses. 2014. "Bad Work Ethics Are to Blame for High Youth Unemployment." *Nairobi Business Daily*, June 25. Accessed June 29, 2014. http://www.businessdailyafrica .com/Bad-work-ethics-are-to-blame-for-high-youth-unemployment-/-/539444/ 2361512/-/4kfuirz/-/index.html.

Njihia, Mbugua. 2010. "Kipokezi, Another Safaricom Service in Partnership with ForgetMeNot." *The Mind of Mbugua Njia*. Accessed October 2, 2015. http://www .mbuguanjihia.com/business/kipokezi-another-safaricom-service-in-partnership -with-forgetmenot.html.

Njonjo, Katindi Sivi. 2010. *Youth Fact Book: Infinite Possibility or Definite Disaster?* Institute of Economic Affairs, Nairobi. *Foresight for Development*. http://www .foresightfordevelopment.org/sobipro/55/580-youth-factbook-infinite-possibility -or-definite-disaster.

Njoya, Timothy. 2010. Interview with Jeff Koinange. "*Capital Talk*: Rev. Dr. Timothy Njoya: Part 1 of 4." *K24TV*, May 27. Accessed January 8, 2014. http://www.youtube .com/watch?v=MuQwb3roQSw.

Ntarangwi, Mwenda. 2003. *Gender Identity and Performance: Understanding Swahili Cultural Practices through Song*. Trenton, NJ: Africa World.

———. 2009. *East African Hip Hop: Youth Culture and Globalization*. Urbana: University of Illinois Press.

———. 2010a. "African Hip Hop and the Politics of Change in an Era of Rapid Globalization." *History Compass* 8 (12): 1316–27.

———. 2010b. *Reversed Gaze: An African Ethnography of American Anthropology*. Urbana: University of Illinois Press.

———, ed. 2011. *Jesus and Ubuntu: Exploring the Social Impact of Christianity in Africa*. Trenton, NJ: Africa World.

———, 2015. "Hip Hop, Globalisation and the Politics of Youth Identity in Kenya." In *The Youth and Identity Question in Africa*, edited by Nicodemus Fru Awasom and Almon Shumba, 91–111. Dakar, Senegal: CODESRIA.

Nthamburi, Zablon, ed. 1991. *From Mission to Church: A Handbook of Christianity in East Africa*. Nairobi: Uzima.

NTV Kenya. 2012. "Wall Graffiti in Nairobi Street Awes Many." *NTV Kenya*, February 29. Accessed July 26, 2014. https://www.youtube.com/watch?v=iw2DVDENyOA.

———. 2014. "*#theTrend*: Mavuno Senior Pastor Defends Controversial Poster." *NTV Kenya*, March 1. Accessed July 21, 2014. https://www.youtube.com/watch?v=anSIT1rUIcU.

Nyairo, Joyce. 2004. "'Reading the Referents': The Ghost of America in Contemporary Kenyan Popular Music." *Scrutiny* 29 (1): 39–45.

Nyairo, Joyce, and James Ogude. 2005. "Popular Music, Popular Politics: Unbwogable and the Idioms of Freedom in Kenyan Popular Music." *African Affairs* 104 (415): 225–49.

Nyanga, Caroline. 2010. "Mary Atieno: I Am Comfortable with Myself." *Nairobi Standard*, September 19, 2010. Accessed December 3, 2013. http://www.standardmedia.co.ke/?articleID=2000018645&story_title=Mary-Atieno:-I-am-comfortable-with-myself-.

Odera, Adhyambo. 2004. "Other Singers Cry Foul over Hip-Hop Airplay." *Nairobi Daily Nation*, June 6. Accessed October 2, 2015. http://allafrica.com/stories/200406140149.html.

Odera, Pete. 2013. "Dear Nairobi's Middle Class." *Wordpress.com*, January 21. Accessed July 29, 2014. http://peteodera.wordpress.com/2013/01/21/dear-nairobis-middle-class/.

Oginde, David. 2014. "Clarity on Integration, Society and Church." Plenary presentation, Integration of Faith Conference, Daystar University at Maanzoni Lodge, Athi River, Kenya, February 6.

Ondego, Ogova. 2004. "Kisima Music Awards Haunt Organisers." *Art Matters*, June 16. Accessed October 2, 2015. http://artmatters.info/music/2004/06/kisima-music-awards-haunt-organisers/.

Onyango-Ouma, Washington. 2006. "Practising Anthropology at Home: Challenges of Ethical Dilemmas." In *African Anthropologies: History, Practice, and Critique*, edited by Mwenda Ntarangwi, David Mills, and Mustafa Babiker, 250–66. Dakar, Senegal: CODESRIA.

Osumare, Halifu. 2012. *The Hiplife in Ghana: West African Indigenization of Hip Hop*. London: Palgrave.

Owino, Julius. *See* Juliani.

Owusu, Maxwell. 1978. "Ethnography of Africa: The Usefulness of the Useless." *American Anthropologist* 80 (2): 310–34.

Parsitau, Damaris. 2012. "From Prophetic Voices to Lack of Voice: Christian Churches in Kenya and the Dynamics of Voice and Voicelessness in a Multi-religious Space." *Studia Historiae Ecclesiasticae* 38:243–68.

Parsons, Timothy. 1997. "'Kibra Is Our Blood': The Sudanese Military Legacy in Nairobi's Kibera Location, 1902–1968." *International Journal of African Historical Studies* 30 (1): 87–112.

"'Pastor' Curses, Threatens NTV Journalists." 2012. *NTV*, July 22. Accessed November 7, 2013. https://www.youtube.com/watch?v=Pd2nuKDkEBY.

Patterson, Amy. 2006. *The Politics of AIDS in Africa*. Boulder, CO: Rienner.

———. 2010. *The Church and AIDS in Africa: The Politics of Ambiguity*. Boulder, CO: Rienner.

P'Bitek, Okot, 2013 [1966]. *Song of Lawino and Song of Ocol*. Long Grove, IL: Waveland.

Perullo, Alex. 2005. "Hooligans and Heroes: Youth Identity and Hip-Hop in Dar es Salaam, Tanzania." *Africa Today* 51 (4): 75–101.

———. 2011. *Live in Dar es Salaam: Popular Music and Tanzania's Music Economy*. Bloomington: Indiana University Press.

———. 2014. "Piper and Hip Hop." *New Calvinists*. Accessed February 13, 2015. http://www.newcalvinist.com/john-piper-2/piper-and-hip-hop/.

Pew Research Center. 2015a. "Religious Composition by Country, 2010–2050." *Pew Research* Center, 2015. Accessed October 1, 2015. http://www.pewforum.org/2015/04/02/religious-projection-table/2010/number/all/.

———. 2015b. "Cell Phones in Africa: Communication Lifeline." *Pew Research Center*, 2015. Accessed October 2, 2015. http://www.pewglobal.org/2015/04/15/cell-phones-in-africa-communication-lifeline/.

Pope Francis. 2013. "Evangelii Gaudium" (The joy of the Gospel). *Trinity Communications*, November 26. Accessed November 29, 2013. http://www.catholicculture.org/culture/library/view.cfm?recnum=10390#a_joy_ever_new,_a_joy_which_is_shared.

Population Reference Bureau. 2013. *Kenya Adolescent Reproductive Health and Development: Implementation Assessment Report*. Population Reference Bureau, May. Accessed April 4, 2014. www.prb.orgpdf13/kenya-policy-assessment-report.pdf.

Priest, Robert J. 2001. "Missionary Positions: Christian, Modernist, Postmodernist." *Current Anthropology* 42 (1): 29–68.

Princecam Media. 2012. "Kuna Dawa: Esther Wahome (Official Video)." *YouTube.com*. Accessed September 2, 2013. https://www.youtube.com/watch?v=cvbPfEqrPCw#t=131.

———. 2013. "Igwe—Alphy Feat Jacky B and Imani Odero (Official Video)." Accessed October 2, 2015. https://www.youtube.com/watch?v=pqR_t4y9kFU.

Ramose, Mogobe B. 1999. *African Philosophy through Ubuntu*. Harare, Zimbabwe: Mond.

Robinson, Cynthia. 2011. "Hair as Race: Why 'Good Hair' May Be Bad for Black Females." *Howard Journal of Communications* 22 (4): 358–76.

Rose, Tricia. 1994. *Black Noise: Rap Music and Black Culture in Contemporary America*. Hanover, NH: Wesleyan University Press.

Saleebey, Dennis. 2005. *The Strengths Perspective in Social Work Practice*. 4th ed. Boston: Allyn and Bacon.

Samper, David. 2004. "'Africa Is Still Our Mama': Kenyan Rappers, Youth Identity, and the Revitalization of Traditional Values." *African Identities* 2 (1): 37–51.

Sanneh, Lamin. 1989. *Translating the Message: The Missionary Impact on Culture*. Maryknoll, NY: Orbis.

———. 2003. *Whose Religion Is Christianity? The Gospel beyond the West*. Grand Rapids, MI: Eerdmans.

———. 2005. "Introduction: The Changing Face of Christianity: The Cultural Impetus of a World Religion." In *The Changing Face of Christianity: Africa, the West, and the World*, edited by Lamin Saneh and Joel Carpenter, 3–18. New York: Oxford University Press.

———. 2008. *Translating the Message: The Missionary Impact on Culture*. Maryknoll, NY: Orbis.

Sargeant, Kimon H. 2000. *Seeker Churches: Promoting Traditional Religion in a Nontraditional Way*. New Brunswick: Rutgers University Press.

Saucier, Khalil, ed. 2011. *Native Tongues: African Hip Hop Reader*. Trenton, NJ: Africa World.

Scheim, Louisa. 1999. "Performing Modernity." *Cultural Anthropology* 14 (3): 361–95.

Sen, Amatya. 1985. *Commodities and Capabilities*. New York: Elsevier Science.

"S£XY Mavuno Church Poster Irks Kenyans." *Nairobi Wire Media*, 2014. Accessed February 27, 2014. https://nairobiwire.com/2014/02/sxy-mavuno-church-poster -angers-kenyans.html.

Sharma, Nitasha. 2010. *Hip Hop Desis: South Asian Americans, Blackness, and a Global Race Consciousness*. Durham: Duke University Press.

Shipley, Jesse W. 2009. "Aesthetic of the Entrepreneur: Afro-Cosmopolitan Rap and Moral Circulation in Accra, Ghana." *Anthropological Quarterly* 82 (3): 631–68.

———. 2013a. "The Hip Hop Generation: Ghana's Hip Life and Ivory Coast's Coupé-Decalé." With Siddhartha Mitter. *World Music Productions*. Accessed February 13, 2015. http://www.afropop.org/9369/the-hip-hop-generation-ghanas-hip-life-and -ivory-coasts-coupe-decale/.

———. 2013b. *Living the Hiplife: Celebrity and Entrepreneurship in Ghanaian Popular Music*. Durham: Duke University Press.

Shutte, Augustine. 1993. *Philosophy for Africa*. Rondebosch, South Africa: University of Cape Town Press.

Sindima, Harvey J. 1994. *Drums of Redemption: An Introduction to African Christianity*. Westport, CT: Greenwood.

Smith, Effrem, and Phil Jackson. 2005. *The Hip-Hop Church: Connecting with the Movement Shaping Our Culture*. Downers Grove, IL: Intervarsity.

Sommers, Marc. 2006. "In the Shadow of Genocide: Rwanda's Youth Challenge." In *Troublemakers or Peacemakers? Youth and Post-Accord Peacebuilding*, edited by Siobhán McEvoy-Levy, 81–97. South Bend: University of Notre Dame Press.

Stambach, Amy. 2000. "Evangelism and Consumer Culture in Northern Tanzania." *Anthropological Quarterly* 73 (4): 171–79.

Strachan, Owen. 2013. "Hip-Hop Theologians and Preachers: The Artists Most Shaping the Movement." *Christianity Today*, May 3. Accessed May 12, 2014. http://www .christianitytoday.com/ct/2013/may/hip-hop-theologians-and-preachers.html.

Strydom, T. J. 2015. "Facebook Rakes in Nigeria and Kenya, Eyes Rest of Africa." *Reuters*, September 10. Accessed September 28, 2015. http://www.reuters.com/ article/2015/09/10/us-facebook-africa-idUSKCN0RA17L20150910.

Suler, John. 2004. "The Online Disinhibition Effect." *CyberPsychology and Behavior* 7 (3): 321–26.

Taffa, Negussie, David Omollo, and Zoe Matthews. 2003. "Teenage Pregnancy Experiences in Rural Kenya." *International Journal of Adolescent Medical Health* 15 (4): 331–40.

Taylor, John. 1963. *Primal Vision*. Norwich, UK: SCM Press.

Tedlock, Dennis. 1987. "Questions Concerning Dialogical Anthropology." *Journal of Anthropological Research* 43 (4): 325–37.

Tutu, Desmond. 2000. *No Future without Forgiveness*. New York: Image.

Tyler, Michael, Janice Hughes, and Helena Renfrew. 1999. "Kenya: Facing the Challenges of an Open Economy." In *Telecommunications in Africa*, edited by Eli Noam, 79–112. New York: Oxford University Press.

United Nations Development Programme. 2013. "Discussion Paper: Kenya's Youth Employment Challenge." *UNDP*, January 2013. Accessed November 28, 2013. http://www.undp.org/content/dam/undp/library/Poverty%20Reduction/Inclusive %20development/Kenya_YEC_web(jan13).pdf.

"Utapeli kwa jina la Mungu" (Trickery in the name of God). 2012. *NTV Kenya*, July 20. Accessed March 23, 2013. http://www.youtube.com/watch?v=Hh28r2VjL1k.

Vandenberg, Todd. 2009. "More than You Think, but Still Not Enough: Christian Anthropologists." *Perspectives on Science and Christian Faith* 61 (4): 211–19.

Walls, Andrew. 1996. *The Missionary Movement in Christian History*. Maryknoll, NY: Orbis.

Watkins, Ralph Basui. 2011. *Hip-Hop Redemption: Finding God in the Rhythm and the Rhyme*. Grand Rapids, MI: Baker.

Weiss, Brad. 2005. "The Barber in Pain: Consciousness, Affliction and Alterity in East Africa." In *Makers and Breakers: Children and Youth in Postcolonial Africa*, edited by Alcinda Manuel Honwana and Filip de Boeck, 102–20. Oxford: James Currey.

———. 2009. *Street Dreams and Hip Hop Barbershops: Global Fantasy in Urban Tanzania*. Bloomington: Indiana University Press.

Wernerfelt, Burger. 1984. "A Resource Based View of the Firm." *Strategic Management Journal* 5 (2): 171–80.

Yates, Reggie. 2011. "In Pictures: Comic Relief in Kibera." *BBC*, March 10. Accessed July 5, 2014. http://www.bbc.co.uk/news/world-africa-12674543.

Youth and the African Union Commission. 2012. "Welcome to the Youth Division: . . . a Youthful Continent! Africa's Position on Youth." *African Union Commission*. Accessed September 5, 2015. http://africa-youth.org/.

Youth Enterprise Development Fund. 2014. "About the Youth Enterprise Development Fund." *Youth Enterprise Development Fund*. Accessed February 12, 2015. www .youthfund.go.ke/about/.

Zhuo, Julie. 2010. "Where Anonymity Breeds Contempt." *New York Times*, November 29. Accessed June 1, 2014. http://www.nytimes.com/2010/11/30/opinion/30zhuo.html ?_r=0.

INDEX

MWENDA NTARANGWI is an associate professor of anthropology at Calvin College. He is the author of *East African Hip Hop: Youth Culture and Globalization.*

INTERPRETATIONS OF CULTURE IN THE NEW MILLENNIUM

The University of Illinois Press
is a founding member of the
Association of American University Presses.

University of Illinois Press
1325 South Oak Street
Champaign, IL 61820-6903
www.press.uillinois.edu